Melbourne Anglicans

The Diocese of Melbourne
1847 - 1997

Edited by Brian Porter

Mitre Books
Melbourne

Published by

The Joint Board of Christian Education
65 Oxford Street, Collingwood, 3066

Melbourne Anglicans 1847-1997

© Anglican Diocese of Melbourne, 1997

National Library of Australia
Cataloguing-in-Publication entry.

Brian Porter (ed)
Melbourne Anglicans 1847-1997

Bibliography
ISBN: 1 86407 181 1

1. Anglican church of Australia. Diocese of
Melbourne - History. 1. Brian Porter, 1939-. II.
Joint Board of Christian Education.

283.9451

First printed 1997.

Design & Typeset by Kelvin
Printed by Bookworks Pty Ltd

Cover photograph reproduced by permission of
Scancolor Pty Ltd.

JB97/3846

Contents

Foreword

A perceptive observer soon becomes aware of certain characteristics of the Anglican Church of Australia. It is, for example, strongly diocesan in structure, with the national church marked by a corresponding degree of decentralisation. Each of the metropolitan dioceses has its own distinctive flavour, paralleling the distinctive characters of the capital cities. And - corresponding to the high and increasing urbanisation of Australia - the metropolitan dioceses exercise a dominant influence in the national church.

This makes a study of the metropolitan dioceses essential to anyone who would understand Australian Anglicanism. In the case of the Diocese of Melbourne, the completion of one hundred and fifty years of its life makes this an opportune time to reflect on the elements that have shaped the Diocese. This book of essays is a notable contribution to this task.

Anglicanism is characterised by the co-existence of a diversity of perspectives on Christian faith and practice. These are held together in one communion in varying degrees of tension. At its best, this enables a creative interaction of the polarities which have their place in a faith in which there is a strong paradoxical element. At its worst, it can degenerate into negative party spirit which saps energy and destroys unity of purpose and action.

The Diocese of Melbourne has the reputation of embracing the whole spectrum of Anglicanism. To the predominant evangelicalism which was assiduously fostered by its first bishop was added the more liberal attitude of its second. From the late nineteenth century the influence of the catholic revival was increasingly felt. But in both the evangelical and catholic wings of the church a strong concern for social welfare, and increasingly for social justice, tempered the more doctrinaire elements of the traditional parties. In the later decades of the twentieth century, the charismatic movement added its influence.

In various ways, these different emphases fostered the crossing of denominational boundaries. Catholics, evangelicals and charismatics alike discovered much more in common with like-minded members of other churches. At the formal institutional level, Melbourne provided perhaps the most fertile environment in Australia for ecumenical initiatives, and the Anglican Church was an active participant in ecumenical activity. The place of the

Australian intellectual and cultural activity naturally made its mark upon the church. The questions raised by modern science, educational philosophy, the women's movement and changing patterns of theological education all impacted on the church in Melbourne.

In a sense, the Diocese of Melbourne may be seen as the Anglican Communion in microcosm. This gives particular interest to these essays written to commemorate the 150th birthday of the diocese. They do not purport to be a history of the diocese, but they throw piercing light on significant aspects of that history. There are judgements with which not everyone will agree; but I am sure that these essays will stimulate their readers to a better informed and more critical assessment of this great diocese.

Here are pictures of achievement and failure, of determination and wavering, of solid faith and exploratory questioning. For though the Church of God is grounded on divine promise and fortified by God's Spirit, it is yet composed of fallible human beings who only imperfectly grasp and fulfil the will of God.

My hope and prayer is that these studies may increase the self-understanding of all of us who belong to the Diocese of Melbourne, and may encourage us to deeper repentance for past failures, clearer vision of future possibilities, and renewed determination to become a church more ready to respond to the grace of God by which alone we can fulfil the divine purpose.

+ Keith, Melbourne

Bishops and Archbishops of Melbourne

i

ii

iv

v

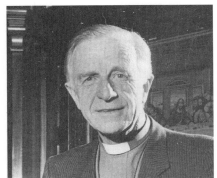

viii

ix

iii

vi

vii

x

xi

i	1847-76	**Charles Perry** Bishop
ii	1876-86	**James Moorhouse** Bishop
iii	1887-1901	**Field Flowers Goe** Bishop
iv	1903-05	**Henry Lowther Clarke** Bishop
	1905-20	Archbishop
v	1921-29	**Harrington Clare Lees** Archbishop
vi	1929-41	**Frederick Waldgrave Head** Archbishop
vii	1942-56	**Joseph John Booth** Archbishop
viii	1957-77	**Frank Woods** Archbishop
ix	1977-83	**Robert William Dann** Archbishop
x	1984-89	**David John Penman** Archbishop
xi	1990-	**Keith Rayner** Archbishop

Preface

This commemorative volume is offered as a tray of hors d'oeuvres before the more substantial menu of a full-scale single-authored history of the Diocese of Melbourne which may be produced before the end of the twentieth century. There are appetisers here as well as samplings. Some chapters will have more appeal than others and some judgements will be viewed as partial or partisan. Nevertheless the essayists have tried to honour the vision of the History of the Diocese Committee which first met in 1989 at the behest of the late Archbishop David Penman. This committee resolved to support both projects: a full-scale history and this collection of essays.

This vision was then embodied in approaches made by the Editor to ten representative historians and social commentators whose specialist insights would together form a composite impression of 150 years in the life of the Diocese. To the History of the Diocese Committee is offered editorial gratitude for its nomination of subject areas, and likewise to the essayists themselves for so willingly accepting their briefs. Special thanks are due also to the two key editorial advisors: Professor A.G.L. Shaw AO and Mr Henry Speagle OAM, the former a distinguished historian of Australia, and the latter a well-remembered Editor of the Victorian Year Book.

The book editing and publishing expertise of Mr Hugh McGinlay, Miss Anna Ridgway and Mr Kelvin Young and the Joint Board of Christian Education is exemplary, and the Diocese of Melbourne expresses its indebtedness to this agency of the Uniting Church for accepting this commission in an ecumenical spirit. To Mrs Judy Savage, secretary to the Archbishop of Melbourne, is also due an expression of thanks for handling so professionally the extensive correspondence and liaison entailed in such a collaborative volume.

Soon after his arrival in Melbourne in 1848, Charles Perry, the first Bishop, whose appointment gave Melbourne its status in colonial Australia, wrote to his supporters in London:

> All is on a small scale. But there
> has been and promises to be a
> rapid growth in everything: in
> population, in wealth, and I trust
> in sound religious principle.

In one hundred and fifty years of growth 'the place for a village' grew to become 'Marvellous Melbourne' and in current estimation, 'one of the world's most liveable cities'. The Anglican Diocese of Melbourne has had a role in all of this which is as unignorable as is St Paul's Cathedral at the main approach to the city from its river. It is to be hoped that this commemorative offering will evoke gratitude, admiration, confidence and hope in 'sound religious principle'. There have been failures, but then a Diocesan motto for much of its life was that sturdy crusader exhortation: 'No Cross, No Crown'.

May those who will be part of the Diocese of Melbourne and its leadership over the next fifty years as it moves towards its bicentenary take fresh heart as they 'taste and see how gracious the Lord is.'

Brian Porter
Editor

On 25 June 1847 by Royal Letters Patent, Queen Victoria established the Diocese of Melbourne, appointed Charles Perry, Vicar of St Paul's Church Cambridge as its first Bishop and designated the town of Melbourne a city. Bishop Perry in turn designated St James' Church Melbourne as his cathedral. This episcopal chair still at St James' Old Cathedral was used by Bishops Perry, Moorhouse and Goe.

Notes on Contributors

The Most Reverend Keith Rayner

AO BA PhD ThD

is Archbishop of Melbourne and Primate of the Anglican Church of Australia.

The Reverend Brian Porter

MA MLitt, Executive Editor

is Chaplain of Ivanhoe Grammar School, Research Fellow and Frank Woods Archivist, Trinity College, University of Melbourne.

The Rt Reverend James Grant

AM BA BD ThL

is Dean and Assistant Bishop of Melbourne, a member of the Standing Committee of General Synod and formerly Bishop Coadjutor of the Diocese of Melbourne 1970-85.

Dr David Hilliard

MA PhD

is Reader in History, The Flinders University of South Australia.

The Reverend Albert McPherson

MA STM ThL

is Chaplain for the Arts, Diocese of Melbourne and formerly Canon Precentor of St Paul's Cathedral, 1971-93.

The Reverend Dr Colin Holden

MA BD PhD

is Associate Priest of St Peter's, Eastern Hill and Associate, History Department, University of Melbourne.

The Very Reverend Stuart Blackler

BA MEd PhD

is Dean of Hobart, formerly Chaplain of Melbourne Girls' Grammar 1971-92.

Dr Shurlee Swain

BA PhD D SocStud

is Lecturer in History, University of Melbourne and the Australian Catholic University.

Dr Muriel Porter

BA BLitt PhD

is Senior Lecturer in Journalism, Royal Melbourne Institute of Technology and a member of the Standing Committee of General Synod.

Canon Peter Adam

BD ThSchol MTh PhD

is Vicar of St Jude's, Carlton and Anglican Chaplain at the University of Melbourne.

The Reverend Douglas Dargaville

BSc ThL MAdmin

was Secretary of the Victorian Council of Churches, 1966-1982.

The Reverend James Minchin

MA ThL

is Vicar of Holy Advent. Armadale and a member of the Standing Committee of General Synod.

To that great cloud of witnesses,
the whole people of God
in the Diocese of Melbourne,
who have been part of its life
1847-1997.

'Bishopscourt' – the official residence of the Anglican Bishops and Archbishops of Melbourne since 1853.

Overview of the history
of the Diocese of Melbourne

Despite its early reputation as Australia's foremost evangelical diocese, Melbourne in the later decades of the twentieth century was viewed by most observers within it and beyond as the most comprehensive in the Australian Church. It accepted and encouraged diverse theologies, spiritualities and pastoral models and strategies, and it was open and innovative in its ecumenical and community relations.

These characteristics, however, were not necessarily approved by all Australian dioceses, particularly monochrome ones, which tended to be less enamoured with the virtues of comprehensiveness, and found a bland, ineffective, *laissez faire* approach characterising many areas of diocesan life.[1] This was in marked contrast to the diocese which Bishop Charles Perry handed over to James Moorhouse in 1876. What is the explanation of this difference?

In 1835 John Batman, agent for a syndicate of Hobart business and

C of E. CENTENARY MELB
NOV. 1947

ADAMSON

The centenary Church Congress, November 1947. Bishop Edward Woods of Lichfield, father of Archbishop Frank Woods, (sixth from right in front row), was the principal diocesan guest.

professional men, reconnoitred the western shore of Port Phillip Bay. On 8 June a cutter from his ship visited the site of Melbourne, and on hearing the report of its crew he pronounced that 'This will be the place for a village'. But hearing of his visit, John Pascoe Fawkner of Launceston organised his own expedition which actually landed and began to build at

the site of Melbourne on 30 August of the same year.

A *Prayer Book* service is recorded as having been read for the first time at this settlement on 18 October 1835, by Fawkner, and the first service by an ordained clergyman of the Church of England, the Reverend J.B. Naylor of Hobart, was held on 30 April 1837. Next year at Easter –

one year after Melbourne's official naming by Sir Richard Bourke - William Grant Broughton, first and only Bishop of Australia, visited the new community. The first resident minister, the Reverend J.C. Grylls, was appointed in September 1838 and the foundation stone of Melbourne's first church, St. James', was laid on 9 November 1839.

However, this rate of progress was not maintained and the following decade saw only slow progress. This should not surprise us: merely to survive in a new, raw settlement afflicted by a sustained business depression following hard upon a burst of rampant speculation was a considerable achievement.

In 1843, Broughton visited both Melbourne and Geelong. He was convinced of the urgent need for more and effective clergy and a bishop to encourage and direct them. His positive recommendation and his willingness to surrender five hundred pounds per annum of his own stipend helped remove official hesitations. By 1846 all that was needed was for the Colonial Secretary to nominate a bishop for Port Phillip.

The appointment of Charles Perry, an able and cultured Cambridge evangelical, as first bishop of Melbourne came as no surprise. There was a need to balance the known Tractarian sympathies of Augustus Short appointed to Adelaide and of William Tyrrell at Newcastle. A high view of episcopacy was unlikely to be welcomed in Port Phillip, where there was a vociferous nonconformist minority headed by the Congregationalist, Fawkner, and the Free Presbyterian, William Kerr. The large contingent of Irish amongst the more influential Anglican laity could be expected to view with suspicion any 'Romish' tendencies in their new bishop. As a bonus, Perry possessed the private means required to supplement the relatively meagre episcopal stipend provided by the Government.

On St. Peter's Day, 29 June 1847, Perry was consecrated bishop in Westminster Abbey along with three others for the colonial dioceses of Adelaide, Newcastle and Capetown. Perry's new diocese comprised the Port Phillip District of New South Wales, with Melbourne as the See city. After three months spent in interviewing potential clergy and ordinands, and collecting money to pay them, Perry sailed in October with his wife, Fanny, his future Dean, Hussey Burgh Macartney and family and other recruits.

On arrival in Melbourne in January 1848, Perry found only three clergy at work - A.C. Thomson at Melbourne, Ebenezer Collins at Geelong, and J.Y. Wilson at Portland, none of whom was making much impact. His coming saw vigorous efforts to extend ministrations both in Melbourne and Geelong, and in the pastoral districts. By July 1851, when the Port Phillip District became the new colony of Victoria, foundations for diocesan and parochial life were being well and truly laid.

The Royal Letters Patent of 25 June 1847, which created the See of Melbourne, gave to its Bishop both responsibility and authority in all matters appertaining to the clergy and to the temporal affairs of the diocese. From his arrival, Perry was unhappy with this situation, but in his anxiety to divest himself of what he saw as autocratic powers he fell foul, for different reasons, of both Anglican laity in Geelong and nonconformists in Melbourne. Bills on clergy discipline and parish patronage which he had begun to promote in the Legislative Council in Sydney had to be withdrawn.

The lesson was well learnt and in all his later efforts to devise a workable legal basis for the Church of England as a voluntary church in an increasingly liberal society, Perry always consulted widely with both clergy and laity. Thus, following the first conference of the Australasian bishops in Sydney in 1850, Perry convened a conference of clergy and lay representatives from parishes to consider the future organisation and government of his diocese. For this unilateral initiative

The Very Reverend Hussey Burgh Macartney, Dean of Melbourne 1851-94, Dean of St Paul's 1879-94. Born in 1799, he died in office in 1894.

he incurred the displeasure of his Metropolitan, Bishop Broughton of Sydney. However, despite evidence of a temperamental incapacity for co-operative action, in his readiness to involve the laity in the government of his diocese, he stood in marked contrast to Broughton and his fellow bishops, Augustus Short of Adelaide and F.R. Nixon of Tasmania. Significantly, the meeting of the Conference from 24 June to 1 July 1851, coincided with the inauguration of the new Colony of Victoria created by the separation of the Port Phillip District from New South Wales.

Attempts were made at Westminster by W.E. Gladstone in 1852 and by the Archbishop of Canterbury, J.B. Summer, in 1853 to secure general legislation for all colonial churches. When these failed, a second conference of clergy and lay representatives held at Melbourne in June 1854 approved the submission of a bill, drafted by W.F. Stawell, the Attorney-General and based on the bill prepared by Sumner, to the Victorian Legislative Council, to provide for the creation of a representative Church Assembly for the Church in Victoria.

In November the bill was passed by the Legislative Council but, despite Perry's personal representations in London, so novel was the legislation that he had to await the appointment of a sympathetic Colonial Secretary, Henry Labouchere, before the Royal Assent was given. Appropriately the first meeting of the Church Assembly in November 1856, coincided with the first meeting of the Victorian Parliament. This simultaneous inauguration of representative government in colony and diocese was facilitated by the substantial common membership of Legislative Council and Church Assembly.

Meanwhile, the discovery of gold in July 1851, brought, first, enormous disruption and then growth to the colony and diocese. Melbourne's population rose from 23 000 in 1851 to 141 00 in 1861, and the rest of Victoria grew in almost the same proportion. This meant an acute shortage of clergy and church buildings, and only generous State aid enabled basic pastoral ministrations to be maintained. The amount available increased in total from 6 000 pounds in 1851 to 30 000 pounds in 1854 and 50 000 pounds in 1856, and of this the Church of England received just over fifty per cent. The improvement in clerical strength which had been achieved by 1851 was not maintained and it took several years to establish anything approaching a regular Anglican ministry on the major goldfields.

Late nineteenth century 'Bush Church', Gippsland, then within the Diocese of Melbourne.

PHOTO: COURTESY OF THE ROYAL HISTORICAL SOCIETY OF VICTORIA.

It was confidently expected that the securing of a firm constitutional basis for the diocese would lead to increased effectiveness at all levels of diocesan life, but this was not so, at least in the short term. On the one hand, the Church of England still commanded the allegiance of a high proportion of professional men and civil servants: it boasted lay leadership of the calibre of W.F. Stawell, W.C. Haines, Charles Sladen, T.T. A'Beckett, J.F. Palmer, H.C.E. Childers, all members of the Legislature; and it was led by Perry, a bishop whom Professor Cable has described as 'certainly the ablest and most intelligent of the bishops in Australia of his generation.'[2] On the other hand in Victoria the Anglican proportion of the population was 40 per cent lower than in the other Australian colonies, South Australia alone excepted; the wealth of the colony was largely in Presbyterian hands; and the greater flexibility of Methodist organisation had attracted many Anglicans, particularly on the goldfields, from the Church of their baptism. Perry in fact was plagued in one of the wealthiest of British communities with the familiar problem of an acute shortage of men and money.

In the absence of any supply of local candidates for ordination, Perry had to look to the Church of England and Ireland. And, despite continued attempts at screening by his English commissaries, there were disappointments. It was a shock, as he himself discovered, to be called 'to disheartening labour far from the seat of the Muses amongst a mammon-seeking and Jacobinical population'.[3] Many of his clergy proved too cultured for bush appointments, but many were not cultured enough for town parishes. In addition, a number of men were excluded as holding unsound theological views, especially on Holy Communion.[4]

Along with this shortage of suitable men went an unexpected shortage of funds to pay them. Perry attributed this to two main causes. First, the parochialism, even congregationalism, of local trustees who preferred to expend large sums on the erection of over-large buildings rather than on supporting church extension either in the 'pampered' goldfields parishes or the remote pastoral districts. Second, a disinclination of men of wealth – Richard Grice excepted – to invest in the future of the Victorian church. Many preferred to amass wealth in Victoria with a view to returning 'home' and it was the mid-1860s before diocesan finances stabilised.

Parochial schools funded by the state through the Denominational Schools Board were established from the 1840s, while the 1850s saw the foundation of the Geelong and Melbourne Grammar Schools. However, lay support for denominational schools weakened progressively through the 1860s. In part, this arose from dissatisfaction with the ineffectiveness of the dual system of denominational and national schools; but in part it arose from the apparently inexorable movement towards a liberal secular society which brought with it the claim that education was the province of the state and not the church. In 1872 the Act which established the Victorian system of free, compulsory and secular (meaning non-sectarian) schools was introduced into parliament by Perry's chancellor, James Wilberforce Stephen. It seems likely that he was not alone in supporting this approach, as many Anglicans supported the Bill.

The Church Assembly provided a useful forum for debate, but Perry soon found that it was almost impossible in such a mixed community as the Victorian one easily to achieve consensus on any issue. Educational issues were the prime example, with no uniform Church of England view emerging from the debates. Though possessed of strong and carefully considered views on most issues, Perry was too much of a constitutional bishop to override or ignore the views of the Church Assembly, and on such matters

Bishop Perry's first Bishopscourt in Jolimont. The house was demolished in 1937.

as re-opening Geelong Grammar School as a joint Anglican-Presbyterian foundation, forbidding choral services, and sending ordination candidates to Moore College, he bowed to the Assembly's decision. In his efforts to liberalise church government through a Church Assembly, he had, not unexpectedly, undermined his own position and encouraged a diversity of opinion.

As part of the same process of secularisation, State aid to religion, after many attempts, was finally withdrawn in 1870. Resistance to its abolition had been led in the Legislative Council by T.T. A'Beckett, Perry's registrar. There, he and other church representatives were able to secure two major concessions for the churches: a five-year phasing-out period and an unfettered right to dispose of the original Crown grants. Some of the final payments were capitalised to form the nucleus of a Bishopric Endowment Fund, and advantage was taken of the last provision to lease much of St James' land, especially the site of 'Parson Thomson's cabbage-patch' – the corner of William and Bourke Streets – for commercial development.

But notwithstanding Perry's original objections to the 'equal endowment of truth and error', State aid had been essential to the establishment of the Church of England within the Victorian community. Paradoxically, its abolition spurred the diocese to contemplate three major projects: the division of the diocese; the building of a cathedral and the establishment of a university college.

In the early 1850s Perry had consciously preferred to strengthen his registry rather than divide his diocese. By 1869 he was prepared to allow the process of creating a second diocese to begin. Archdeacon T.C.B. Stretch began to gather funds for the endowment for a new western diocese, and in 1873 the Church Assembly authorised the establishment of a diocese based on Ballarat. The appointment of the first bishop, Samuel Thornton, was remitted to Perry, Stawell, and the Archbishops of Canterbury and York. In 1869, plans were prepared for a cathedral and a chapter, but further action foundered on the rock of its considerable expense. In 1870 the foundation stone of Trinity College, the first church college to be affiliated with the University of Melbourne, was laid and the first student, J. F. Stretch, later Bishop of Newcastle, was enrolled in 1872.

Perry's reputation as a narrow-minded bigot in matters of churchmanship was established early in his episcopate, and he made no secret of his own theological position. But whatever the rigour of his theological views, he displayed unfailing personal courtesy, even affection, towards his leading 'delinquents', H.H.P. Handfield of St Peter's, Melbourne, and J.H. Gregory of All Saints', St Kilda. If he incurred criticism within the community and increasingly failed to evoke the loyalty and support of 'new' and 'self-made' men within the diocese, he continued to command widespread respect and confidence, particularly from the older 'church laity'. Apart from a few sectarian intransigents, he was widely accepted as the spokesman not only for the Church of England but also the whole Protestant community. He or his wife, Fanny, presided over a wide range of welfare activities that drew support from the whole community. Likewise, his Aboriginal Mission and Missions to the Chinese relied on more than Church of England personnel and finance.

As an assessment of his episcopate, the words of Sir Charles Sladen, a longstanding but not uncritical friend, spoken on the occasion of his departure from Melbourne in 1874, cannot be bettered:

And now we find each of [your]

once-dreaded innovations either adopted by the Church in the colonies, and even in England, or urged upon her by her best friends as essential to her progress, if not to her stability. No-one has acknowledged you as his guide or pointed to you as a leader, but almost all are quietly following in the paths which you have dared to open.[5]

Almost three years were to elapse before his successor, Prebendary James Moorhouse, Vicar of St James' Paddington, London, was enthroned in St James' Pro-Cathedral on 11 January 1877. Born in Sheffield, Moorhouse was an urban creature, a broad churchman, concerned to combat unbelief and to commend Jesus Christ as Lord. The impact of his attractive and vigorous personality was immediate and widespread. Within weeks of his coming, major decisions had been taken to establish a theological faculty at Trinity College and to commence the building of a cathedral.

The first of Moorhouse's legacies to Melbourne was the group of candidates whom he attracted to the new Trinity faculty. These included A.V. Green, Reginald Stephen and G.M. Long, eventually bishops, Archdeacon William Hancock and Canon E.S. Hughes. Within a very short time such ordinands were to provide Australian-born leadership of a very high order.

The second was St Paul's Cathedral. Moorhouse was immediately involved in the choice of its site, contending strongly for a position at the cross-roads of the city. His was also the choice of William Butterfield as architect, a decision which resulted in Melbourne possessing what is, arguably, the finest example of that architect's distinctive style. Fired by the bishop's enthusiasm and aided by his popularity and the beginning of the Land Boom, sufficient funds were at hand for the foundation stone of the new cathedral to be laid on 13 April 1880.

Division of the Diocese allowed church extension efforts to focus on 'selectors' in Gippsland and the Goulburn Valley. The Bishop of Melbourne's Fund for church extension was established and good support enlisted from fashionable suburban parishes. Fledgling clergy, such as (Archdeacon) William Hancock, (Canon) H. F. Tucker and W.G. Hindley, later Archdeacon of Melbourne and Vicar-General, planted new churches in a spirit of high adventure. Melbourne itself was not neglected, with help being made available for new areas and teeming inner suburbs.

Towards the end of his episcopate, Moorhouse became very conscious of the emergence of social problems within the City of Melbourne and the inner suburbs. At his prompting, the Diocesan Mission to the Streets and Lanes was established under Canon Handfield's leadership, even though in the absence of suitable workers no work was actually undertaken during his episcopate. At Christ Church, South Yarra, H.F. Tucker received encouragement for his sometimes unconventional outreach to the sick, the destitute, the unemployed and, not least, Melbourne's 'cabbies'.

On the educational front Moorhouse worked hard but unsuccessfully to introduce non-sectarian Bible teaching to the new state schools. The government would do nothing without the support of all churches and the ecumenical climate was such that the Protestant churches were not prepared to concede any of the Roman Catholic claims for separate instruction. However, within the diocese, the organisation and effectiveness of Sunday Schools were transformed.

Moorhouse commended himself to the community generally by his frank, open and 'manly' approach to the issues of the day. Most years, he offered a series of

Town Hall Lectures which drew thousands to hear him expound the Gospel in popular terms. A measure of his standing in the community came with his election as Chancellor of the University in succession to Sir William Stawell.

His translation to the See of Manchester was not unexpected, but it was universally regretted. Moorhouse is usually accorded the accolade as the greatest of Melbourne's bishops. Nowhere was this more apparent than in his encouragement of a true catholicity within the diocese. He himself claimed his dimensions to be the height and breadth of the Church of England:

with his encouragement this began to be true of his Diocese also.

Moorhouse left Melbourne in January 1886, leaving Dean Macartney at the age of 87 with the responsibility of administering the diocese for the fourth time.[6] In September the committee of English Bishops, including Perry and Moorhouse, to which the Church Assembly had remitted responsibility, offered the See of Melbourne to the Reverend Field Flowers Goe, Rector of St George's, Bloomsbury. Though not the first to be offered the appointment, Goe saw the offer as a call of duty, accepted, and was

enthroned in St James' Pro-Cathedral on 14 April 1887.

Goe was a staunch and decided evangelical, but with a reputation for being 'a fair and a kindly man, of broad sympathies and generous temper, conciliatory in spirit and averse to party'.[7] He was contrasted, unfavourably, with his

Bishops attending the All Australian Anglican Assembly, celebrating the centenary of the City of Melbourne, 1934.

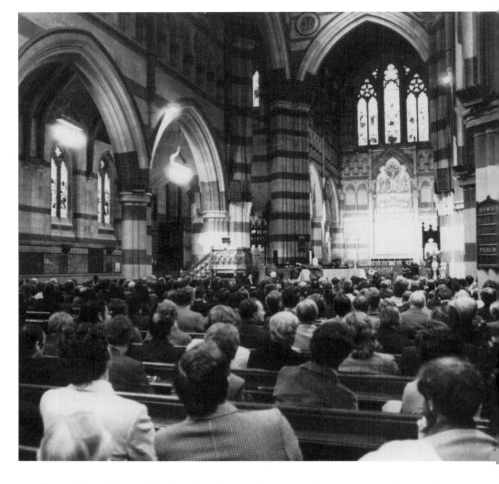

'eloquent, forceful and masterful predecessor', but he consolidated and extended Moorhouse's initiatives. He succeeded at the height of the Land Boom to an unfinished cathedral and an unwieldy Diocese.

The 1880s was a time of great optimism and boundless enthusiasm for Victoria and particularly Melbourne. It seems likely that Goe decided, quite deliberately, to make completion of the cathedral his top priority, and it was opened and consecrated on 22 January 1891. He was responsible for deciding the style of its services, for approving its choral foundation, and for the decision that the cathedral would not have a parish of its own. As it happened, the successful completion of the cathedral project was just in time.

The 1893 Bank Crash meant drastic reductions in diocesan and parochial income. Plans to divide the Diocese had to be shelved until 1901, when Archdeacon Hindley piloted through the Church Assembly the Act that created out of the Archdeaconries of Sandhurst, Beechworth and Gippsland three new dioceses of Bendigo, Wangaratta and Gippsland. In contrast to the somewhat niggardly provision made for Ballarat in 1873, Melbourne, on this occasion, shared its resources generously with the new dioceses, allowing each a one-sixth share of its patrimony.

Goe's evangelicalism showed itself more in his support for evangelical causes than in his proscription of those holding other theological positions. Thus, while he actively promoted the Irish evangelist George Grubb's Mission to the Diocese in 1891, and the formation of the Church

Missionary Association in 1892, he also encouraged Sister Esther and her 'community' which staffed the Mission to the Streets and Lanes, and did nothing to restrict the spread of Tractarian ideas and practices by younger clergy such as Ernest Hughes and Frank Anderson of St Peter's, Melbourne.

He maintained what Moorhouse had established, namely, the character of Melbourne as a tolerant diocese. While still predominantly evangelical, Melbourne was a relatively peaceful diocese which reflected Goe's own eirenic spirit. His wife, Emma Rodgers Goe, was a tower of strength. She was responsible for the establishment of the Mothers' Union in 1895 and the consolidation of the Girls' Friendly Society in Melbourne, and she was very active in the wider community. He was devoted to her and his resignation in 1901 followed closely upon her death.

To fill the vacancy, the Bishopric Election Board decided, for the first time, not to delegate the appointment to an English committee but to send two of their number, the Honourable F.S. Grimwade MLC, and W.E. Morris, the registrar, to England. On the basis of their report, Canon Henry Lowther Clarke, Vicar of Huddersfield, was eventually nominated. He accepted the offer and, after consecration by Archbishop Frederick Temple in London, was enthroned in St Paul's Cathedral on 3 March 1903.

The diocese to which Clarke came, though much reduced in size, still contained more than half of Victoria's population. He quickly saw that the urgent priority was to improve the training and conditions of the clergy. St John's College was opened in 1904 but his plan to establish it as the diocesan college was frustrated by the foundation of the evangelically oriented Ridley College in 1910 and the continuation of theological teaching at Trinity. More successful was his work in establishing the Melbourne College of Divinity, a consortium of non-Roman churches empowered by the Victorian Parliament to grant degrees in theology to graduates of recognised universities. He was also instrumental in establishing the Australian Clergy Provident Fund to make retirement easier for the older clergy.

Clarke had been much involved in educational matters in Yorkshire and worked to evolve a diocesan policy for Melbourne. This involved on the one hand supporting voluntary religious instruction in state schools and on the other increasing Anglican involvement in secondary education. As a result, the enrolment in Anglican schools increased fivefold during his episcopate. New schools were founded, including Melbourne and Geelong Church of England Girls' Grammar Schools, while existing private schools such as Tintern were brought under diocesan aegis.

Under Clarke's leadership, systematic church extension was encouraged through new parishes and societies. In 1906 a Synod Social Questions Committee was established under the leadership of L.V. Biggs, later editor of the *Age*, and E.C. Rigby, later Advocate of the Diocese, to focus Anglican concern on community issues. In 1905 Clarke was designated Archbishop following the organisation of an ecclesiastical province comprising the five Victorian dioceses.

Clarke's tenure of office saw two major disputes over churchmanship. In 1906 he resisted calls for action against E.S. Hughes' services and teaching at St Peter's, Eastern Hill. In 1907 his proceedings against the evangelical Canon Nash of St Columb's, Hawthorn, then Christ Church, Geelong, were opposed by most Evangelicals who queried Clarke's motives. Clarke disclaimed any party allegiance himself, and on the basis of his historical and constitutional scholarship, sought to find a middle way.

Chapel of All Saints', Geelong Grammmar School, opened 1915. Architects: North and Williams.

PHOTO: GEELONG GRAMMAR SCHOOL ARCHIVES.

In the short term such controversy was damaging to both Clarke and the Church of England, but his whole-hearted support – in contrast to the Roman Catholic Archbishop, Daniel Mannix – for recruiting and the 'Yes' vote in the Conscription referenda were widely approved within the Diocese and its Synod. Anglican support for conscription would have enhanced its standing in the community even though no doubt there was minority Anglican opposition. On this issue, for once, Clarke had the total support of Dr Alexander Leeper, the mercurial and erudite Warden of Trinity College from 1876 to 1918.

Apart from sporadic activity in Synod elections, particularly in 1917 when

An early impression of St James' Old Cathedral.

PHOTO: FROM THE ORIGINAL IN THE LATROBE LIBRARY.

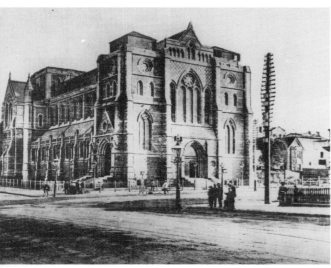

St Paul's Cathedral, consecrated in 1891. The spires were added in 1929-32.

PHOTO: FROM THE ORIGINAL IN THE LATROBE LIBRARY.

In 1920 Clarke attended the sixth Lambeth Conference of Bishops and while there, resigned his See. He left the Diocese much more effectively organised, increasingly staffed by local clergy, and with no dominant party ringing the changes.

In its search for Clarke's successor, the Archbishopric Election Board lighted briefly upon George Bell, later Dean of Canterbury and Bishop of Chichester, but finally rested on the Vicar of Swansea, Harrington Clare Lees. Lees, an evangelical with broad sympathies, came with a reputation as a preacher and this was enhanced in Melbourne and Victoria. He was in constant demand as a speaker by Anglicans and other denominations and was one of the first to use the new radio medium effectively. He had a facility for friendship that impressed all he met and he was both well known and popular.

His episcopate coincided with the decade of post-war community optimism based on S.M. Bruce's triad 'men, money and markets'. A major extension of welfare activities funded by the sale of much of St John's Church Lands was achieved by the Mission of St James and St John under Archdeacon George Lamble. This followed the formation of St John's Homes for Boys under Eric Thornton. The movement to

evangelicals swept the field, most factional energy was directed to developing the characteristic Melbourne arrangement of parallel structures, one 'High', one 'Low', serving their different constituencies. Thus we find in theological education two colleges – Trinity and Ridley; two missionary societies – the Australian Board of Missions and the Church Missionary Society; and in welfare, two agencies – the Mission to the Streets and Lanes and the Mission of St James and St John.

13

Melbourne Church Congress in 1906.

complete St Paul's Cathedral by the addition of spires and tower was begun in 1925 and steady progress achieved in 'church planting' in the suburbs of Melbourne and Geelong.

On Lees' sudden death in 1929, the Sub-Dean of Liverpool Cathedral, Frederick Waldegrave Head, who had an established reputation as an historian, who had been a Guards' chaplain, and was an experienced pastor and organiser, succeeded as Archbishop. Hard upon his arrival he had to face the challenge of the Great Depression which brought not only a blighting of community and family life, but also a grave crisis in diocesan and parochial finance caused partly by the acquisition of a number of girls' schools.

Head believed that his diocese's major contribution to recovery lay in strengthening parochial life and in pressing on with the completion of the cathedral.

In this last campaign the leadership of the Registrar, A.E. McLennan was vital. By preaching, teaching and visitation, by regular meetings with country bishops and with his own archdeacons and rural deans, and by the appointment of J.J. Booth as the first Melbourne coadjutor bishop in 1934, he strove to equip clergy and parishes for the difficult times they faced. Church societies received his active encouragement, particularly the Church of England Boys' Society for its camping program especially at Frankston and the Church of England Men's Society for its evangelistic and beach missions. The Brotherhood of St Laurence, a religious community founded in 1931 by Gerard Kennedy Tucker, moved at his invitation to Melbourne from Newcastle, New South Wales, in 1933, and R.G. Nichols, 'Brother Bill', was strongly supported in his settlement work at St Mark's, Fitzroy.

Head supported moves to secure a constitution for the Australian Church. Under his leadership and that of E.C. Rigby, Melbourne adopted the successive drafts prepared by the General Synod Constitutional Convention and its Continuation Committee led by Bishop J.S. Hart of Wangaratta. In the referenda on prohibition held in 1930 and 1938,

Head joined Protestant leaders in campaigning, unsuccessfully, for a 'yes' vote. In matters ecumenical, Head was chairman of the local committee of the World Faith and Order movement and initiated a series of conversations with Victorian Methodists.

Head, while lacking the bubbling *bonhomie* of his predecessor, was held in high regard in every section of his diocese and the Victorian community. He believed wholeheartedly in the British Empire and declared at his welcome by 10 000 Anglicans in the Exhibition Building, 'I love the Empire, I want to serve it and keep it Christian'.[8] A scholar himself, Head invited a series of overseas scholars to Melbourne and spoke frequently on platform and radio on historical and apologetical subjects. Despite his Establishment background, he knew no distinction of class or education and impressed the community as a man of engaging modesty and unfailing courtesy.

The combination of Head as Archbishop and Booth as coadjutor served the diocese well and hence it was no surprise that, following Head's death late in 1941 as a result of a motor accident, Booth succeeded as Archbishop in 1942. His proven capacity for business, his intimate knowledge of

the diocese, and his reputation as a military chaplain all combined to make him a popular and logical choice. His knowledge and experience of the wider Anglican Communion was less than any of his predecessors, but this deficiency was largely remedied when he attended the 1948 Lambeth Conference and the 1954 Pan Anglican Congress at Minneapolis. John David McKie, appointed Bishop coadjutor in 1946 brought contrasting gifts to the leadership of the Diocese.

Under Booth's leadership the Diocese of Melbourne, together with the rest of the Australian Church and community, faced the challenges of war-time shortages and post-war reconstruction and development. It took until 1950 before the transition from war-time arrangements was completed, just in time to face the phenomenal expansion of Melbourne and Geelong that followed the Korean War and the resumption of immigration.

Along with the raising of funds to finance clergy training and church extension in new areas went other new initiatives. A Department of Youth and Religious Education was established under Robert Dann. The Melbourne Diocesan Centre was given responsibility for parishes and institutions in the inner city and under Geoffrey Sambell it pioneered new initiatives in hospital chaplaincy. At Camberwell, 'Broughton Hall', the first Anglican Elderly People's home, was initiated by Canon P.W. Robinson and Mr R.L. Gair of St Mark's parish. Visits by Archbishop Geoffrey Fisher of Canterbury and Canon Bryan Green of Birmingham stimulated in the diocese an awareness of its Anglican inheritance and encouraged more effective evangelism. The successful introduction by G.H. Codrington of the 'American Wells Every Member Canvass' system of fund-raising gave promise of a more adequate financial basis for parish programs. Booth also worked to develop provincial initiatives, particularly in the selection and deployment of ordinands but with only short-term success.

On Booth's retirement in 1956, the Electoral Board began with a preference for an Australian cleric. None commended themselves, so eventually the Archbishop of Canterbury was invited to submit some names. He offered only one - Frank Woods, Suffragan Bishop of Middleton, in the Diocese of Manchester, who was duly elected and enthroned in December, 1957. Woods, the son, nephew and brother of English diocesan bishops, had an impressive record of ministry: curate of St Mary's,

Portsea, chaplain of Trinity College, Cambridge, vice-principal of Wells Theological College, army chaplain, vicar of Huddersfield and assistant bishop. He came to a diocese well served by its clergy and specialised agencies. Though lacking the massive endowments of its Sydney sister, its resources had been carefully husbanded by Booth, by H.W. Buckley, Chairman of the Finance Committee and by Registrars E.T. McDermott and R.C. Wardle. If it had a fault it was complacency and Woods, fresh from involvement with the most forward-looking elements in the Church of England, soon dispelled this.

A survey of the Diocese indicated potential growth areas and under Archdeacon Geoffrey Sambell a diocesan-wide 'Forward Move' was launched. A good response was achieved which allowed expenditure to be increased on clergy training, new area parishes and hospital and institutional chaplaincies. In tandem with this went a four-year study program entitled 'Forward-in-Depth'. New expectations of pastoral care and community participation by bishops led to Sambell's appointment as a second bishop-coadjutor with Bishop Donald Redding in 1962. These major initiatives were sustained, not only by increased

giving from parishes, but also from the increased income derived from the proceeds of the sales of the St James' Buildings.

Woods' episcopate was also marked by growth in ecumenical understanding and joint action. It saw growing participation in the Australian Council of Churches, and new ventures in industrial mission under Canon Lawrie Styles. The influence of Vatican II was soon felt in personal and theological dialogue with Roman Catholics and, at the level of theological education, in the formation in 1969 of the United Faculty of Theology at Parkville.

In 1971, following a far-reaching review of diocesan life by a series of broadly based and representative committees, Synod approved the establishment of three Regions of Episcopal Care. Beginning in 1971, the three Bishops Coadjutor, R.W. Dann, J.A. Grant and G.B. Muston, each took responsibility for a 'geographical area' comprising approximately one third of the parishes of the diocese together with 'functional areas' for the diocese as a whole. The arrangement worked well and testified to the quality of mutual trust that characterised the diocese. However, an unforeseen outcome was the diminishing role of the other senior clergy

Bishops participating in the Consecration of St Paul's Cathedral, 22 January, 1891.
Top row: Bishop of Adelaide, Bishop of Melbourne, Bishop of Sydney, Bishop of Tasmania, Bishop of Ballarat
Bottom row: Bishop of Riverina, Bishop of Goulburn, Bishop of Bathurst

in this new line management model.

In 1955 the General Synod adopted what proved to be the final draft Constitution for the Church of England in Australia. This required acceptance at diocesan level. In Melbourne, the motion for its adoption was moved successfully by Bishop J.D. McKie. But it was 1962 before the first General Synod under the new Constitution was convened in Sydney. From the outset Melbourne representatives assumed national leadership in a number of key areas. Geoffrey Sambell was appointed co-ordinator of the Australian MRI (Mutual Responsibility and Interdependence) program and as such, was responsible for the establishment of the Diocese of the Northern Territory and the National Home Mission Fund. Felix Arnott, Bishop Coadjutor from 1963, made major contributions to the work of the Liturgical and Theological Education Commissions. The election of Woods as Primate in 1971, of Sambell as Archbishop of Perth in 1969 and Arnott as Archbishop of Brisbane in 1970, was recognition of Melbourne's role in the wider national Church.

In education, apart from a considerable expansion in parish kindergartens, no new 'church school' had been founded for almost forty years. In the 1960s two were successfully launched, Peninsula and Yarra Valley, and all existing Anglican schools expanded considerably. In part, this was due to the availability of State aid, first for laboratories and libraries, and then generally. But more significant was parental disenchantment with State high schools and the preparedness of many women to work to ensure for their children a 'good education'.

In welfare, the existing agencies consolidated their operations, building extensively, improving professional standards for staff and gaining increased government funding. The Church of England Social Services Advisory Council (CESSAC) was established to co-ordinate the work of the agencies, but suggestions of amalgamation were vigorously rejected. Not even the Whitlam Government's offers

Old St James' Cathedral, corner of William Street and Collins Street, Melbourne, 1842-1914, thereafter erected on the corner of King and Batman Streets, West Melbourne. Architects: Robert Russell and Charles Laing.

St Peter's, Eastern Hill. Architect: Charles Laing, 1846.

of largesse moved the agencies from their isolation, though there was some rationalisation in the location of programs. The Avalon Community established at Lara in 1967 by the Reverend Vernon Cohen offered less structured pastoral care to a range of needy and troubled folk.

Woods' episcopate saw the church move from its traditional role of 'hallowing the Establishment' and providing care and carers through its institutions, to one of offering a more radical critique of society. The Brotherhood of St Laurence, under Sambell's leadership, in addition to providing new services such as family planning, established a vital Research and Social Action unit. On issues such as capital punishment, poverty, and Australian involvement in the Vietnam War, the church in Melbourne, officially at least, was in the vanguard of public opinion.

Ecumenically, the influence of Vatican II was soon felt. Theologically, John Robinson's questionings in *Honest to God* fuelled those of the 'Melbourne Agnostics' of 1967. Parochially, 'Parish Life Conferences' promoted by the General Board of Religion Education encouraged a sharper focus in parochial activity. At the same time, the experience of the 'Parish and People Movement' over several decades influenced the course of liturgical change and the development of new pastoral strategies, especially in Christian initiation. The Mothers' Union under the leadership of Jean Woods, Mary Britten and Jean Pratt modified its policy on divorce and despite many working wives, maintained a substantial membership.

The 1970s saw a massive decline in Sunday School enrolments, in youth work and in nominal adherents. But this was paralleled by a greater commitment at every level by those who continued to identify themselves as Anglicans. There was no sense of panic, and the approach which had characterised the Diocese since Moorhouse was maintained and enhanced by Woods. Intellectually, theologically, ecumenically, pastorally and spiritually he contended for an 'open' position. He encouraged a similar stance among his clergy through his Ordination and Retreat addresses, through a series of notable Synod Charges, and through sponsoring visits by leading contemporary theologians.

As Primate, Woods was perhaps more appreciated by other churches and the wider community than by his own church's establishment. He did not relish meetings of the General Synod and its Standing Committee. But his primatial visits, especially to outback dioceses, brought inspiration and encouragement to clergy and laity alike.

His particular strengths had always been as a teacher and spiritual guide and these were brought together in his pre-retirement 'Let's Pray Better' course. This picked up some of the aspirations of the earlier 'Forward-in-Depth' program and applied them in a more contemporary style. Woods' retirement functions in April 1977 demonstrated how well this very English Archbishop had gained the affections of his Diocese.

The appointment in 1977 of Robert Dann as Archbishop in succession to Woods signalled no fundamental departure in diocesan policy. The first Australian-born Archbishop of Melbourne, he had left school early and known privation in the Great Depression. Convinced of his vocation, he had matriculated and put himself through college. He was ordained as a mature-age candidate in 1945 and proved a trail-blazer in the areas of youth ministry, Christian Education, parish renewal and church extension. Following Woods' election as Primate in 1971, he became *de facto* administrator of the Diocese.

The enthronement of Archbishop Frank Woods, 17 December, 1957.

Now, as Archbishop, he was able to establish a thoroughly professional program of supervised field education for ordained and lay ministers under Stephen Ames and sponsor a visit from Loren Mead of the Alban Institute in Washington DC to resource new initiatives in parish ministry. The diocesan Immigration Department under Helen

Hunter was given a extended charter to work with refugees and ethnic communities and within the community he was able, from his own experience, to articulate, powerfully, the plight of the increasing number of unemployed, especially the young. Bishop David Shand, who had taken the courageous step of promoting the amalgamation of his Diocese of St Arnaud with the Diocese of Bendigo, was appointed a Regional Bishop in 1978.

Major surgery in 1980 took its toll, so it was no surprise that Dann retired on his sixty-ninth birthday, 1 November 1983, one year ahead of the statutory retiring age.

Changes made in the *Archbishopric Election Act* allowed the Electoral Board to convene forthwith. Its first decision was to circulate a questionnaire to all parishes and to invite submissions for candidates to the Archbishopric. This procedure did not command universal support - what the majority wanted might not necessarily be what was needed - but there was a good response. Not unexpectedly, the Diocese was looking for a leader of broad sympathies, prepared to venture into the public arena, and with an ability to communicate and commend the Gospel within contemporary

St John's, Camberwell; architect Louis Williams, 1957.

culture. In particular, the issues of evangelism, church growth, multiculturalism and youth ministry were seen as needing a higher priority. Despite its early start, the Board made only slow progress and it was May 1984 before David Penman, the Western Regional Bishop, was named as seventh Archbishop of Melbourne.

A New Zealander who had served as a missionary of the Church Missionary Society in Pakistan and Lebanon, he came to Melbourne in 1976 as Principal of St Andrew's Hall, the CMS federal Training College. Here his gifts, particularly as a biblical expositor, were soon recognised, not least by Archbishop Dann. In 1979 he returned to the parish of Palmerston North in New Zealand whence he was recalled in 1982 to succeed Gerald Muston as Assistant Bishop.

A diocesan Partners-in-Mission Consultation was already planned as part of a provincial program, and this took place just before Penman's enthronement. With the help of external consultants, most notably Bishop John Reid, Assistant Bishop of Sydney, and Bishop-elect Bruce Wilson of Canberra, the operations of the diocese were reviewed and evaluated. The Report identified a need for Melbourne to move from a 'maintenance' to 'a mission mode' and called for a more intentional and participatory leadership. It was to provide the blueprint for the Penman episcopate.

Once enthroned, Penman soon made his presence felt. Possessed of a natural facility and working closely with his media officer, Angela Grutzner, he quickly established good relations with the media, commenting frequently and effectively on a range of issues. His own experience and his continuing contacts with the church overseas, symbolised by the presence of the Bishop in Jerusalem at his enthronement, enabled him to speak with authority on both international affairs and the Church's mission.

The new regional bishops, John Stewart, Robert Butterss and John Wilson, an additional bishop for the Inner City, Peter Hollingworth and a new Dean, James Grant, were in place within six months. The senior clerical staff was further enlarged by the appointment of sector archdeacons, Charles Bailey for Chaplaincy and Marjorie McGregor, Australia's first woman Archdeacon, for deacons.

Given his overseas missionary experience it was not surprising that one of his first initiatives was to convene a 'Christ across Cultures' conference in January 1985. Its Report, *A Garden of Many Colours*, spelt out a multicultural vision for the diocese which Helen Hunter, as Director of the Department of Multicultural Ministry, was charged with realising. Penman's own commitment to a multicultural Australia was recognised by his Government appointment as the chair of the Australian Institute of Multicultural Affairs.

That same year, following a Report to Synod in 1985, a youth strategy began to be developed under Michael Goodluck, Youth Chaplain within the Department of Christian Education. The appointment in 1988 of Stephen Hale as Director of Anglican Youth Ministries ensured that Youth Affairs once more featured prominently on the diocesan agenda.

As suggested in the Report of the Partners-in-Mission Consultation, a group convened by Peter Corney produced, in August, 1985, 'A Plan for Mission and Growth'. Its main recommendation was for a new Department of Evangelism and Church Growth. This was duly established with Peter Corney, now an Archdeacon, as director.

Another was for the appointment of a Mission Priorities and Strategy Committee. This worked to produce a blueprint for restructuring the diocesan administration to comprehend all the multifarious activities of the Diocese within five divisions: Pastoral Care, Administration, Parish Development, Community Care and Mission Agencies and Ecumenism. Alan Nichols, appointed Archdeacon of Melbourne in 1986, carried the main responsibility for establishing the new structure. However, inadequate resources, powerful personalities, conflicting interests, unnatural groupings and the absence of a clear definition of the respective spheres of Regions and Divisions inhibited the full completion of the new scheme.

But if the structures proved intractable, Penman's personal impact was unquestioned. Within the community his interests ranged from Afghan refugees through Carlton Football Club to the National AIDS council. Support for persecuted and suffering churches overseas found practical expression in the formation of the Archbishop's International Relief and Development Fund. In the Australian Church he was seen as the leading advocate for women to be ordained to the diaconate and the priesthood. As to the former, success came in 1985, but the latter was not accomplished in his lifetime; however, his conviction of its rightness was open and consistent.

Within the Province of Victoria, the appointment in 1985 of Bishop David Shand as part-time Bishop in Geelong and part-time Provincial Officer worked wonders for the cohesion of the Province. Sadly, funds were not forthcoming to continue a provincial appointment at this level. Instead, Shand's successor, John Bayton took up a full-time appointment as Bishop of the Geelong and Western Region while John Stewart as Vicar-General moved to a new, smaller, Northern Region. Within parishes, both in Melbourne and South Africa, Penman's evangelistic missions, undertaken in association with the Network Music Group, were appreciated and effective.

Penman suffered a massive heart attack in July and died on 1 October, 1989. The public grief in church and community was unprecedented and testified to how attractively and how faithfully he had commended the Gospel.

In reaction to the long delay before Penman's election, Synod in 1987 gave to the members of Synod, rather than a Board, the responsibility of electing the next Archbishop. At the first attempt in February 1990 Synod members confounded expectations by dividing, not on the issue of the ordination of women, but on

Evangelical/Catholic lines. At the second attempt in July, Archbishop Keith Rayner of Adelaide allowed himself to be nominated and in due course secured the required two-thirds majority of both clergy and laity. A major influence in the success of the new process was the chairmanship of the Administrator, Bishop John Stewart.

To the position of Archbishop of Melbourne, Rayner brought unequalled episcopal experience and a formidable intellect. Born, educated and ordained in Brisbane, he was elected Bishop of Wangaratta in 1969, translated to Adelaide in 1975 and had been Acting-Primate since 1989. Awarded a PhD for his study of the Anglican Church in Queensland, he was also a considerable theologian and had served as Chairman of the Inter Anglican Theological Commission.

His first concern, both as Archbishop and Primate (from 1992) was to resolve the long-running controversy over the ordination of women to the priesthood. Recognising the failure of several attempts to provide directly for the ordination of women, a draft canon was finally prepared which, while not directly authorising such ordinations, allowed those dioceses which adopted it to proceed. With Rayner's strong support this was finally enacted in November, 1992: one month later thirty-three women deacons were ordained priest in St Paul's Cathedral.

Within the Diocese a series of deficits, due largely to lower interest rates and reduced income from property, forced reductions in a number of Penman programs. There was little resource for new initiatives and attention was focused on clergy reviews and parish restructuring. The five division structure was abandoned in 1992 in favour of two divisions, the Administrative division under registrars John Lester, and then Leigh Mackay, and Diocesan Services under Archdeacon Howard Dillon. Dillon quickly concluded that effective co-ordination was impossible so long as the several departments were dispersed across Melbourne. With the co-operation of the Cathedral Chapter, the co-location of the whole Division within the Cathedral Buildings - now renamed the Anglican Centre - was achieved early in 1996.

Meanwhile, in 1994, partly to compensate for the loss of lay input through the Divisional Policy Committees and partly to fulfil what had been envisaged when the Regions of Episcopal Care were inaugurated, four Regional Councils were established charged with identifying needs and setting priorities - but not expending a budget - for each region. As part of a concern to maintain the lay element in Synod in the face of the increasing proportion of non-parochial clergy, the membership of Synod was expanded dramatically. Not surprisingly, this brought calls for regional assemblies to function in tandem with a smaller representative Synod.

That same year, Rayner convened for the first time ever a residential diocesan Clergy Conference. Designed by the Strategy Committee of the Archbishop-in-Council, it sought to bring home to the clergy the changed and changing context of the Church's Mission - secular, multicultural Australia - and the diminishing effectiveness of inherited models of ministry and parish life. It also provided the Archbishop with the opportunity to promote his vision for the Diocese as it approached the new century. It had been expected that agreed goals and strategies would have emerged. Rather, the diversity of ministries operating in the diocese was starkly revealed. Nonetheless, broad support was gained for a Parish Viability Study over the whole diocese.

One of the significant elements of the 150th Birthday program in 1997 has been the preparation of this volume. The Electoral Synod of 1990 and the Clergy Conference of 1994 underlined what has been true of the diocese for over a century - its diverse character. So, the question has been asked and needs to be asked again 'Would a monochrome diocese have been a more effective instrument for God's mission in Melbourne?'

On the one hand, Melbourne has been characteristically Anglican in allowing the development of contrasting excellences amongst parishes and institutions. On the other, there has been a tendency to be content with lower expectations of effectiveness. The challenge for Melbourne Diocese has been, and is, not to rest content with a range of options, but to enhance the performance of all its constituents. Along with its celebration of diversity, if it is to face the future with any degree of confidence, Melbourne needs to pursue a higher level of all-round effectiveness.

The Sesquicentenary of the Consecration of Bishop Perry affords an opportunity to do two things: to celebrate what has been achieved, since 1847 and to embrace, positively, the future.

1   See comments by 'Partners', especially John Reid, Bruce Wilson, in *Report of the Melbourne Partners-in-Mission Consultation*, Anglican Media, Melbourne, 1984.

2   K J Cable, Good Government in the Church, Inaugural Bishop Perry Memorial Lecture, Melbourne Anglican Evangelical Association of Victoria, Melbourne, 1983, p. 1.

3   Quoted from the *Edinburgh Review*, October 1855, p. 282, in Vivienne Parsons, The Church of England during the episcopate of Bishop Perry, MA Thesis, University of Melbourne, 1969

4. Perry's 'Rules', quoted in George Goodman, The Church in Victoria, Melville, Mullen & Slade, Melbourne, 1892, p. 344.

    Never to ordain, or admit into the
    diocese, a man, who, I had reason
    to believe, held the doctrine of
    Christ's presence, in any sense
    whatever, in the bread and wine
    upon the Lord's Table after
    consecration; or who would
    encourage auricular confession
    with the object of receiving
    private absolution...'

5   Quoted in A. de Q Robin, *Charles Perry, Bishop of Melbourne*, University of Western Australia Press, Nedlands WA, 1967, p. 180

6   1855-56; 1863; 1874-77; 1886-87.

7   *Church of England Messenger*, 8 December, 1886.

8   *Argus*, 24 December, 1929.

CHAPTER TWO

DAVID HILLIARD

The first meeting of General Synod outside Sydney, held at Melbourne Grammar School, 1995.

Intellectual Life
in the Diocese of Melbourne

The Diocese of Melbourne has come to see itself as representing a moderate and comprehensive Anglicanism, theologically more diverse than any other major diocese in Australia and open to new ideas. The Diocese has not always had this reputation and it is hard to see an unbroken linear development over the past 150 years. Anglican intellectual life and theology in Melbourne have had many different expressions. They have been the product of the interaction of Anglican thinkers and writers with a particular urban and social environment and of the ideas and policies fostered by successive bishops. This essay examines Melbourne Anglicanism in relation to some of the theological movements and controversies of the last 150 years.[1]

The religious culture of the first generation of Anglicans in Victoria was firmly Protestant and predominantly evangelical. In this it was much the same as every other Australian colony. The distinctive teachings of the evangelicals were the supreme authority of Scripture, salvation through the atoning death of Christ on the cross, the necessity of personal conversion, and the need to spread the faith. Within the Church of England at home, the evangelical movement achieved its greatest influence just after the middle of the nineteenth century, soon after Charles Perry's appointment in 1847 as Bishop of the newly created Diocese of Melbourne.[2] Perry himself was an evangelical, as was his Archdeacon and Dean, Hussey Burgh Macartney, and the great majority of Anglican clergy in Melbourne in the mid-nineteenth century. Perry's vision for the Church of England in Melbourne was that of a church that was firmly anchored to the doctrines of the Reformation and the teachings of the Thirty-nine Articles 'in their plain and full meaning', unfragmented by parties or factions. At the meeting in Sydney in 1850 of the six bishops of Australia and New Zealand, he declined to assent to a joint statement on baptismal regeneration but issued his own minute, in which he stated his view that spiritual regeneration required personal repentance and faith.[3]

Like other Anglican bishops of his generation, Perry was compelled to define his position in relation to the emergent Oxford Movement, or Tractarianism. The ecclesiology, sacramental teaching and spirituality of the Tractarians grew out of, but diverged from, the old high church tradition and raised 'the doctrinal temperature of the Church of England'.[4] There was no doubt about Perry's opposition. He saw the teachings of the Tractarians as unscriptural and doctrinally subversive, 'calculated to pave the way for a return to the doctrine and practice of the Church in England previous to the Reformation'.[5] He therefore refused to ordain or admit into his Diocese any clergyman who, in his words, 'held the doctrine of Christ's presence, *in any sense whatever*, in the *bread* and *wine* upon the Lord's Table after consecration; or who would encourage *auricular confession* with the object of receiving *private absolution*'.[6] However, a few influential clergymen with Tractarian sympathies notably J.H. Gregory of All Saints, East St Kilda, and H.H.P. Handfield of St Peter's, Eastern Hill – stood firm against episcopal pressure, so that the Diocese of Melbourne was 'less monochrome than its bishop desired'.[7]

At the same time, evangelical orthodoxy was being challenged from another direction. Like the Tractarians, Perry and the evangelical clergy saw the principal hostile force of the day as philosophical liberalism, or 'infidel' latitudinarianism. By this they meant the idea that doctrinal differences and 'error' were of little importance, for absolute truth in religion was unattainable by human minds, and that the traditional creeds of the church were obstacles in the quest for truth. These views were frequently expounded in the editorial pages of Melbourne's rival daily newspapers, the *Age* and the *Argus*. Colonial liberals saw Perry as out of touch with modern thought, and indeed in his old age he admitted he was 'not fond of reading, for its own sake' and had read 'very few' theological works.[8] Armed with an intellectual training in mathematics, he sought to defend Christianity as a body of revealed and objective truth against those who were arguing that old doctrines needed to be restated in the light of modern scholarship and the changed intellectual climate.

The intellectual challenges to traditional Christian beliefs and doctrines in the late nineteenth century were wide-ranging. Four main areas may be identified. In the first place, there was a new approach to Scripture, which sought to treat the Bible like any other book. It was argued that the 'Word of God', having been written in human language and transmitted like other human documents, should be studied free of church control or dogmatic assumptions, using the same techniques as scholars were applying to other ancient writings. This 'higher criticism' produced new and unsettling theories over the dating and authorship of biblical books, the historical accuracy of events recounted in Scripture - such as physical miracles - and much else. The new biblical scholarship led to a second area of debate: the historical Jesus. When the gospels were treated simply as historical documents was it possible to see a Jesus who was not the founder of a religion or an ecclesiastical system? This Jesus was a first century Jewish teacher, a perfect man, a moral exemplar, but not a divine saviour. Thirdly, there was 'science' and in particular the questions raised by Charles Darwin's *Origin of Species* (1859).[9] Darwin's theory of evolution was profoundly disturbing, for it seemed to threaten the historical accuracy of the creation account in the book of Genesis, the role of God as benevolent designer, for natural selection involved waste and suffering, and the special place of humanity in

God's created order. For if there was no historical 'first Adam', what about the Fall and the need for Redemption? Finally, there was a new way of perceiving the world, which was no longer satisfied with the old external and 'objective' evidences of the truth of Christianity. A very popular work was William Paley's *Natural Theology* (1802), which justified a universe of design and purpose; it was a textbook for Anglican theological students in Melbourne until the 1860s. From the mid-nineteenth century there was a perceptible shift away from Christianity as an objective revelation at a particular point in time towards the concept of a God who was active in the world, within history and nature - 'divine immanence' -, and the idea that religious truth could develop and change.

Nowhere in the Australian colonies in the late nineteenth century was the crisis of faith more obvious than in Melbourne.[10] In the generation after the gold rushes of the 1850s, Victoria was 'briefly the most educated society of the Empire'.[11] A middle-class intelligensia emerged, comprised mainly of professional men, civil servants and journalists. Many of them were prominent members of the Church of England, whose adherents then numbered one-third of the population.

They enjoyed books and explored intellectual questions in periodicals such as the *Melbourne Review* and the *Victorian Review*. For the unrestricted discussion of religion and other subjects the Eclectic Society was founded in 1867 and the Sunday Free Discussion Society, with meetings open to the public, began in 1870. Rationalists such as H.K. Rusden claimed that Christianity was based upon ideas and stories which no modern rational person could believe and sought to find a scientific basis for morality without religion. In 1867 the bookseller E.W. Cole published *The Real Place in History of Jesus and Paul*, which was a natural account of the origins of Christianity, without the divine or the miraculous.

The new spirit of enquiry led to a wave of religious unsettlement, especially among the educated elite, which peaked in the early 1880s. A historian of nineteenth century Victoria has observed that these were 'the years of tense excitement when men and women debated theology as never before or since'.[12] Among Presbyterians there was a storm over the unorthodoxy of Charles Strong, minister of Scots Church in Melbourne. He was expelled from the ministry of the Presbyterian Church of Victoria and in 1885 formed a free religious fellowship called the Australian Church.[13] As with almost every area of Melbourne cultural life, local debate was conducted within the framework set by the parent society.[14] The arguments on each side were much the same as in Britain, but usually with a time lag of five or ten years.

Among the leaders of Melbourne Anglicanism there were many different responses to the new intellectual climate. At one extreme was Digby Berry, a combative and blinkered evangelical clergyman, who tried to prove, from elaborate mathematical calculations, that the world was made in six days, as recorded in the book of Genesis, and who argued that higher criticism was both blasphemous and a literary fraud.[15] Bishop Perry was a scholarly conservative, concerned to defend with rational arguments the supreme authority and inspiration of Scripture, which could never be undermined by human knowledge. In 1869 he personally entered the debate with a two-hour public lecture on 'Science and the Bible'.[16] Having read some of the major works on evolution, he was unconvinced and argued that the truth of the biblical record of creation, six thousand years ago, was unaffected by

the new scientific discoveries and theories:

> The evidence which we have of the whole Bible being inspired of God, and, therefore, substantially true, is so conclusive, that we cannot conceive of any facts discovered by Science, or any theories grounded upon such facts, being able to invalidate it.[17]

Perry misunderstood Darwin, but in his critique he was in good company, for the majority of scholars in the Australian colonies at the time were very cautious about evolutionary thought. One of them was Frederick McCoy, an Anglican layman, palaeontologist, Professor of Natural Science at the University of Melbourne and founder of the National Museum of Victoria, who on scientific grounds strongly rejected both evolution and natural selection.[18] On the opposite side in the university was another Anglican, William Edward Hearn, Professor of History and Political Economy. In his book *Plutology* (1863) he applied the concept of evolution, as expounded by Darwin and Spencer, to political economy; it gained him an international reputation.[19]

Middle-class lay Anglicans with intellectual interests and enquiring minds were open to the new scientific and literary

critique of religion and more likely to be dissatisfied with the answers given by traditional orthodoxy. They were attracted to the idea that Christianity should develop and change. Some were prominent in the public debate on religion. One of them was George Higinbotham, an independent-minded Supreme Court judge and parishioner of St Andrew's, Brighton, who in 1883 caused a sensation with his lecture, given at Scots Church, on 'Science and Religion'. This was a call for a new and enlightened Christianity, without dogmas or creeds or dogmas - 'the most dangerous and insidious enemies of the religion of Christ' - that would be acceptable to the 'educated thinking laity'.[20]

Lay liberals found a few allies among the clergy. Among them was Dr John Bromby, first headmaster of the Church of England Grammar School. In a series of public lectures in the late 1860s and early 1870s, under the auspices of the *Early Closing Association*, he set out to challenge conventional religious ideas. There were, he said, many 'current notions' which

> though only floating in the minds of believers, have come to be looked upon as a portion of the Church's creed, and which, yet, are at once

rendered exceedingly questionable by a more extensive acquaintance with the original languages of Scripture, or by the progress of scientific discovery. This is one reason why inquisitive minds have never been popular with ecclesiastics.[21]

Another liberal Anglican clergyman was the Reverend H.N. Wollaston of Holy Trinity, East Melbourne. On the question of the inspiration of Scripture, he challenged the popular theory of 'verbal inspiration' and expounded the view that the Bible contained the 'Word of God', but was 'not constituted of all the words of God'.[22] This distinction meant that it was possible to be a Christian – as good a Christian as others – without believing every word in the Bible. Among people in the pews such views became a subject for discussion and argument. In Henry Handel Richardson's novel *The Getting of Wisdom*, which is set in a Melbourne girls' boarding school in the 1890s, the half-believing Laura is confronted by the firmly orthodox Mary Pidwall:

'You don't want to say, I hope, that he [Laura's father] didn't believe in the Bible?'

Laura drove back the: 'Of course not!' that was all but over her lips. 'Well, not exactly', she said, and grew very red. 'But you *know*, M.P., whales don't have big enough throats *ever* to have swallowed Jonah.'

'Little girls shouldn't talk about what they don't understand. The Bible is God's Word; and God is Truth.'[23]

The confidence of Anglicans was much boosted by Bishop James Moorhouse, who in 1876 was appointed from England to the see of Melbourne.[24] Moorhouse saw it as the duty of a bishop who was head of the largest church in the colony, and also of parish clergymen, to confront in public the 'present crisis of unbelief' and to assist ordinary Christians in relating the 'vast and familiar accumulations of secular knowledge' to 'the faith once delivered to the Saints'.[25] He had the ability to put across scholarly ideas in an assimilable form and he had a commanding presence and unprelatical style which colonial lay people found attractive. From the time of his arrival in the colony he issued pastoral letters, wrote articles and delivered lectures on a huge range of topics; he seemed to be an authority on everything. Each autumn,

to reach Melbourne's business and professional classes, he gave (without notes) a series of lunchtime lectures. These began with 'Messianic Prophecies' in 1877 and ended with 'The Galatian Lapse' in 1885.[26] As the audience grew, the lectures were transferred to the Town Hall, which seated several thousand. Moorhouse's public addresses were published in full by the Melbourne press and taken up by other colonial newspapers, so that his reputation spread far beyond Victoria.

The underlying theme of Moorhouse's lectures and sermons was that orthodox Christianity, if slightly adjusted, could accommodate contemporary thought. He had none of Perry's defensiveness. In 1879, addressing the Melbourne Church Assembly, he urged the clergy and laity to meet the intellectual and social problems of the day with confidence:

Brethren and fathers of the Church of God, I have no fear; I dread no light. I rejoice in every advance of real knowledge, for although the future formal solution of our difficulties may perhaps be different from mine, yet most firmly do I believe that we hold in our hand the key of the great mystery.[27]

Moorhouse rejected the conventional either-or defence of Christianity. Contrary to the claims of the secularists and other critics of Christianity, he argued that modern scholarship and 'true science' contained much that verified or was consistent with orthodox truth. God's revelation though Jesus Christ was 'final and complete', but the church's understanding of Christ's revelation could grow and develop: 'articles of faith can be altered and gradually conformed to the demands of increasing knowledge'.[28] Unlike evangelicals, he accepted the findings of 'moderate' biblical criticism, regarded the doctrine of substitutionary atonement as 'a false theory', invoking the words of Jesus on the question of eternal punishment of the wicked, he hinted at universalism: that all would be 'saved'. However, in opposition to advanced liberals such as the Melbourne Unitarian Church, the judges Higinbotham and Hartley Williams, and the secularist Marcus Clarke, he defended Trinitarian orthodoxy and the uniqueness of Christ as saviour, described miracles as both 'possible' and 'probable', and taught that 'science can never disprove the existence of the soul and God'.[29] His synthesis of Christianity and modern thought did not always convince his opponents,

but, as Archdeacon Hancock recalled: 'He made the Christian Faith acceptable to numbers of thoughtful men perplexed with doubts and difficulties.'[30]

Moorhouse's progressive orthodoxy fitted well with the optimism and expansiveness of 'Marvellous Melbourne', which by the 1880s had become a 'boom metropolis', the largest and wealthiest city in Australia. He encouraged in the Diocese a liberality of intellectual outlook. When he returned to England in 1886 to become Bishop of Manchester he left many disciples, among both clergy and lay people. Later, a sum of two thousand pounds was subscribed to commemorate his remarkable episcopate. This took the form of an occasional series of lectures which were to be delivered in St Paul's Cathedral and later published as a book. The first of the Moorhouse Lectures was given in 1907.

It was consistent with Moorhouse's approach that he should forge links between the Church of England and the University of Melbourne. He was Chancellor in 1884 to 1886 and in 1878 he founded a theological school at Trinity College.[31] To this he attracted some gifted young university graduates and took a close interest in their academic progress. So

did the first warden of Trinity, Dr Alexander Leeper (1876-1918), who lectured them in Biblical Greek. From then on the University of Melbourne had a significant influence on the Anglican clerical elite. Those of the clergy who studied there absorbed quite a lot of its prevailing ethos - patrician, humanist, reformist, mildly progressive, sympathetic to notions of religious as well as social evolution.[32] In the department of Philosophy, for example, there was a long tradition of idealist philosophy, which held that ideals such as truth and right really existed, reflecting something of the mind of God. It was an environment that was not inherently antagonistic to religious faith.[33]

A few Anglican clergymen became university teachers or examiners. One of them was Canon Robert Potter, a graduate of Trinity College, Dublin, incumbent of St Mary's, North Melbourne, then of All Saints', East St Kilda, who lectured in Theology at Trinity College and examined in English and Philosophy at the university. He was also the author of a book of sermons, a closely argued essay on religion and ethics - 'The essence of religion is the moral idea' - a number of controversial pamphlets, and the first Australian example of a science fiction novel.[34]

Through the graduate clergy associated with Trinity College, the liberal intellectual culture of the university entered the mainstream of Melbourne Anglican intellectual life. The initial group included Thomas Henry Armstrong, Arthur Vincent Green, William Hancock, Ernest Selwyn Hughes, John Francis Stretch and Reginald Stephen. In the early twentieth century they became the first generation of locally trained church leaders and their personal influence persisted until the 1930s. By then about one quarter of the clergy in the Diocese had been educated at the University of Melbourne and Trinity College.[35] The great majority of them looked for inspiration to Moorhouse rather than to Perry.

The second identifiable period in the intellectual history of the Diocese ran from the mid-1880s to the end of the First World War. During these years the prevailing tone of the Diocese began to change. There were two connected trends: heightened churchmanship and broadening theology. Neither trend went to extremes, for most Melbourne Anglicans did not take to extremes, and they were part of much wider movements within Anglicanism.

Whereas Bishop Perry had done all he could to limit the influence of the Oxford Movement in his Diocese, his successors were prepared to accept and even to welcome a certain amount of theological pluriformity. Moorhouse set the Diocese in a new direction. Bishop Field Flowers Goe, who succeeded him as Bishop in 1887, was a gentle and eirenical evangelical who abhorred party spirit.[36] 'To him was not given the statesmanship and brilliancy of his predecessors', observed a Melbourne evangelical paper after the news of death was received in 1910, 'but he possessed a certain and effective vein of spirituality which was peculiar to himself.'[37] His sermons were homely and he avoided controversial issues. The church, moreover, was badly affected by the Depression of the early 1890s and the devastation caused by the bank crash of 1893. Church members who had invested in 'Marvellous Melbourne' lost large sums of money, parish income declined, and there was an erosion of confidence in that Protestant world-view which had emphasised the moral and theological foundations of social progress and prosperity.[38] With reduced funds, Goe could not afford to recruit evangelical clergy from England or Ireland who shared his theological views. During these years the evangelical tradition planted by Perry was diluted rather than reinforced.

The trend continued under Henry Lowther Clarke, who arrived from England as Bishop in 1903 and became Melbourne's first Archbishop from 1905. He was a scholarly but abrasive non-party churchman, whose outlook and piety were hardly influenced by either evangelicalism or Anglo-Catholicism. 'Call me, if you will, broad', he told the Synod in 1909.[39] After his death in 1926, his son recalled:

Philosophy was a closed book to him, and he had no patience with theological subtleties. The half-lights and nuances of modern speculation were meaningless to him. Talking to his son about the Incarnation, he would brush aside all arguments, laying down his pipe and saying, with profound reverence: 'He is God'.[40]

His own interests were in the rather dry area of ecclesiastical constitutional history. On this subject he published two books, the most substantial scholarly works written by any occupant of the See of Melbourne.[41]

From the 1890s, largely as a result of the influence of the Oxford Movement, a growing number of Melbourne churches adopted patterns of worship, symbolic ornaments and 'correct' ceremonial which were seen as expressions of Catholic doctrinal truths. The indicators of what was seen as standard Anglican practice went up every decade.[42] The service of consecration of St Paul's Cathedral in 1891 included a mixture of old and new, which reflected the theological shift. Bishop Goe celebrated Holy Communion from the 'north end' at an 'altar' which was vested with an embroidered frontal and surmounted with four vases of flowers.[43] Changes in styles of worship and theological emphasis produced sharp tensions. The years from 1900 to 1920 were marked by personal quarrels among the clergy and public controversy.

At the same time the intellectual initiative was passing to a new generation of clergy who had been influenced by the liberal Catholic tradition stemming from *Lux Mundi*, published in England in 1889.[44] This collection of studies in 'the religion of the Incarnation', edited by Charles Gore, marked a line of theological division between the older Tractarians, who had regarded secular thought as the enemy, and the younger generation who wished 'to put the Catholic faith into its right relation to modern intellectual and moral problems'. The *Lux Mundi* essayists were open to contemporary thought and accepted the legitimacy of 'moderate' biblical criticism. In a shift from the old emphasis on divine transcendence, they stressed divine immanence, for the God of Truth (the Logos) was at work in the whole created order. *Lux Mundi* and Gore's 1891 Bampton Lectures on the Incarnation were seminal works for the liberal wing of the Anglo-Catholic movement.[45] So was the Christian Social Union, founded in England in 1889, which advocated study of the social problems of the day, for the religion of the Incarnation should be applied to the whole of life. It was a proudly English and nationalist Catholicism, based on the idea that the Church of England was the ancient church of the English people which had maintained its Catholic identity at the Reformation and that the *Book of Common Prayer* should be interpreted in a Catholic sense. These 'Prayer Book Catholics' were as hostile to the papal claims as any evangelical and they disapproved of Anglo-Catholics who followed Roman Catholic devotions and ritual practices.[46]

In Melbourne the school of liberal Catholicism was particularly associated with St John's Theological College, which had been founded in 1906 by Lowther Clarke at East St Kilda to prepare non-graduates for ordination.[47] It was closed in 1919. The first Warden of St John's was Reginald Stephen, who in 1910 was also appointed Dean of Melbourne.[48] He was later succeeded in both posts by John Stephen Hart.[49] Both men became bishops: Stephen was elected Bishop of Tasmania in 1914 and Hart went to Wangaratta in 1927. Both of them delivered Moorhouse Lectures which were published as books: Stephen on *Democracy and Character* (1908) and *Ancient Law and Modern Morals* (1935), Hart on *Spiritual Sacrifice* (1915) and *The Gospel Foundations* (1930). Influenced by the ideas of the Christian Social Union, both of them saw it saw it as their duty to declare 'social principles' from the pulpit and to criticise aspects of the social order, and their views were often quoted in the press. In 1908 Stephen gave a paper on labour conditions in Australia at the Pan-Anglican Congress in London.[50] When the newly ordained William Temple, later Archbishop of Canterbury, visited Melbourne in 1910, Stephen was one of a small group of clergy and laymen interested in social questions who sponsored a breakfast meeting in a city café after an early celebration of Holy Communion in the cathedral. In his address Temple made 'a thoughtful plea for a Social Theology' in the church which 'would enrich her life and enable Churchmen to press forward more confidently in social reform'.[51] The ideas of the Christian Social Union did not win wide support among the generality of Melbourne Anglicans, but they influenced a section of the lay and clerical leadership.

Evangelicals became aware that they were losing their old position of dominance in Melbourne. Some became edgy and combative.[52] The majority avoided controversy and concentrated on the building up and nourishing of faith within their own congregations through biblical preaching, support for evangelistic endeavour and foreign missions. Many were influenced by the holiness teaching of George Grubb, a Keswick preacher who had visited the eastern colonies in 1891: that Christian believers could experience 'victory' over sin and live a Spirit-filled life in union with Christ. They sought 'sudden sanctification' and prayed for revival. In cooperation with evangelicals of other Protestant denominations, they planned, supported and gained strength from the evangelistic missions of R.A. Torrey, Charles Alexander and Wilbur J. Chapman (1902, 1909 and 1912).[53]

In 1902 a group of prominent evangelical clergymen with scholarly interests founded the 'Parker Society' (modelled on an English society founded in 1840), as a brotherhood of clergy 'who desire to maintain the cohesion and promote the spiritual development and expansion of the Church of England upon the basis of the Reformation Settlement'.[54]

Tensions erupted in Melbourne, as in England, over the New Theology controversy. This was triggered by the English Congregationalist R.J. Campbell, whose rather facile book *The New Theology* appeared in 1907. Lowther Clarke was not sympathetic. Against wayward liberals, he appealed to the Christian faith which had been taught by the Church from the beginning, formulated in the ancient creeds and proved by Scripture. He deplored that biblical criticism which is 'destructive, vain, and irreverent', but praised the work of 'devout scholars, whose labours have overthrown the antiquated fortresses of defence':

The Bible has not been overthrown, but scholarship and history have illustrated its meaning, and have introduced other and more truthful methods of interpreting its words.[55] In his readiness to accept biblical

criticism, and his cautious willingness to allow the possibility of new interpretations of old doctrines, Lowther Clarke reinforced the broad church tradition implanted by Moorhouse.

Evangelicals in every Protestant denomination were very disturbed by anything which appeared to put the human mind above the Word of God. In July 1907 they held a big meeting in the Melbourne Town Hall, 'to protest against the rationalistic teaching of the day' and 'to reaffirm those fundamental truths of God's Word which, though revealed in the Scriptures, are now being largely denied'.[56] The only Anglican bishop on the platform was Bishop Pain of Gippsland. One of the speakers was C.H. Nash, vicar of Christ Church, Geelong, who responded to the New Theology in terms very different from the Archbishop. In both the historic Christ and the Holy Scriptures, he claimed, there was 'a perfect unity of revelation':

There is not one page, not one chapter, not one true word that I would sacrifice out of the unity which God the Holy Ghost has wrought together in that book.[57] It was a call to arms.

Within a few years, however, as in England, there were signs of a divergence between conservative evangelicals such as Nash who insisted on the infallibility of Scripture - a much stronger doctrine of inspiration than had been held by earlier evangelicals - and 'liberal' evangelicals who were prepared to modify traditional evangelical doctrines and views of biblical inspiration in the light of what appeared to be the findings of the best modern scholarship.[58] They differed from conservatives not only in their view of the Bible, but also in their more positive attitudes towards the 'social gospel', the arts and popular amusements (such as dancing and the cinema), and the extent to which the Church of England should tolerate a degree of theological and ceremonial pluralism. They were concerned more with the 'mind of Christ' and personal devotion to him as saviour than with doctrinal precision or theological controversy. A representative figure of the liberal evangelicals was Cassian Crotty, vicar of the important church of St Luke in South Melbourne.[59] At Ridley College, founded in 1910, the new outlook was exemplified by the first principal, G.E. Aickin (Dean of Melbourne, 1927-32), who in his Moorhouse Lectures for 1916 on 'The Kingdom of God and the Nations' declared that he was prepared to see something

of 'divine light and leading' in the best minds of ancient Greece and Rome.[60]

To preserve their identity and defend the faith against 'modernism', conservatives from every Protestant denomination formed during these years a cluster of organisations that were committed to the historical evangelical doctrines and brought together evangelicals for common action. These included the Upwey Convention (1918), the Melbourne Bible Institute (1920), and the Bible Union of Victoria (1923).[61] The latter was formed specifically to 'resist the various attacks' made upon the inspiration and authority of Scripture as 'the written word of God'.[62] At the centre of this network during the interwar years was C.H. Nash, who had resigned his Anglican church appointments in 1912 after (unproven) allegations of sexual misconduct. He later became founding principal of the Melbourne Bible Institute. Described by a historian of Australian evangelicalism as 'the evangelical colossus', Nash 'seemed to have more than a finger in every evangelical pie' and had a profound influence on thousands of young lay people.[63]

The great majority of churchgoing Anglicans did not think of themselves as

belonging to any 'party', but as ordinary 'C of E'. From the 1920s to the 1950s the tone of the Melbourne Diocese tended to be 'low' rather than 'high'. It embodied a restrained and moderate Anglicanism, broadly Protestant in sympathy, conservative politically, though with a sense of social responsibility, cautiously open to change, and proudly imperialist. These values both reflected and helped to define the political culture that dominated Melbourne, and the state of Victoria, for a long period. For only a few years was Labor in power. The city's conservative establishment, closely linked through the greater private schools, the university colleges and Freemasonry with the Anglican and Presbyterian churches, was 'quietly confident because unthreatened', reformist and even idealist.[64] Anglicanism was also in harmony with the Melbourne middle-class, with its social confidence, emotional reticence, concern for hard work and personal respectability, and respect for intellectual and moral achievement.[65] Anglican parishes, and the social networks around them, flourished in the well-to-do eastern and southern suburbs, where lived most of the senior clergy and leading lay people of the Diocese.

The Anglican temper, wrote Archdeacon

Hayman in 1924, 'in time of crisis, places duty to King and Country in the forefront of human obligation'.[66] Anglican churches and schools were permeated with the belief that the British Empire was the standard bearer of civilisation and that the Church of England in Australia was a guardian of English traditions. Among Melbourne Anglicans this imperial loyalism was especially intense, in reaction against the Irish nationalism of the Roman Catholic community, led and symbolised by the controversial figure of Archbishop Daniel Mannix. The editor of the diocesan paper, Dr Alexander Law, vicar of St John's, Toorak, was a vocal supporter of the British-Israel movement, which taught that the 'Anglo-Saxon race' was the successor to Israel as God's chosen people.[67] The historian Manning Clark, who attended Melbourne Church of England Grammar School from 1928, recalled that in the chapel services he had 'the impression that God had some special relationship with the British . . . In the chapel I never heard of Australia, or its people.'[68] St George's Day was observed at St Paul's Cathedral every year with a special service attended by members of patriotic societies. Banners and flags were carried in procession and the archbishop or some

other church dignitary expounded the achievements, traditional virtues and ideals of the 'English race' – 'fidelity, honour, chivalry, and devotion to duty' – and its place in the divine plan.[69] In 1951 Dean Roscoe Wilson, in welcoming to a service at the Cathedral the Lord Chancellor of England and the Master of the Rolls, proudly referred to St Paul's as 'a little bit of England in Australia'.[70]

In reaction to the polarisation and party strife of the previous decades, the theological climate of the Diocese in the interwar years was dominated by an emphasis on cooperation, mutual tolerance and 'fellowship'. The frequency with which these values were stressed indicates that tensions were never far below the surface. Liberal evangelicalism made the running, especially among the clergy.

This outlook was fostered by Harrington Lees who in 1920 was appointed as archbishop in succession to Lowther Clarke. In England he had been a regular speaker at the annual Keswick Convention and he had written a number of popular religious works with comforting titles such as *God's Garden and Ours* and *The Divine Master in Home Life*. His Synod addresses steered clear of practical or intellectual issues. Each of them, from 'The Building of a

Living Church' in 1921 to 'The Freshness of a Living Church' in 1928, was intended to encourage devotion and uplift the heart to God. It was a version of Christianity that many Melburnians found attractive; St Paul's Cathedral was crowded whenever the archbishop preached at Evensong. Although in 1923 Lees had given an address at a Melbourne 'Conference on Fundamentals', to promote the conservative cause, he increasingly took positions that were at odds with the more militant evangelicals. 'No school can claim monopoly of place or action', he told the diocesan Synod in 1925: 'The whole church must find room and welcome for all her workers to express their contribution and share their hearth fire.'[71] In 1927 he welcomed the prospect of the *Revised Prayer Book* in England, which sterner Protestants saw as a betrayal of Reformation principles.[72].

After Lees' sudden death in 1929 the leadership of the Diocese did not change direction. Lees's successor, Frederick Head, had previously been on the staff of the new Liverpool Cathedral, which was one of the most visible centres of English liberal evangelicalism. In 1931, at the patronal festival of St Peter's, Eastern Hill, he rather reluctantly consented to wear a cope and mitre, the first Archbishop of Melbourne to do so. A Sydney evangelical paper claimed that his wearing of this 'tawdry millinery' had given 'great shock' to 'sober, devoted Churchmen of Victoria and elsewhere'.[73] When the Diocese commemorated the centenary of the Oxford Movement in July 1933 Archbishop Head preached at the opening service in the cathedral. In his praise for what the 'Church Revival' had achieved he went further than many evangelicals would have approved, but he also, pointedly, did not endorse the claim that the teachings of the Tractarians were the only legitimate expression of Anglicanism:

> Our heritage is Reformed as well as Catholic, and we should not be ashamed of the title Protestant, nor allow it to be monopolised by those who have given up Episcopacy. We retain the historic Episcopate, but we must not un-Church those who have given it up. We want to be inclusive and not exclusive.[74]

It was an approach that had come to be very characteristic of Melbourne. Any one of Head's successors would have said the much the same.

A minority of Anglicans was quite out of sympathy with this comfortable, middle-to-low-church consensus. Conservative *Evangelicals* wanted a firmer stand against both liberalism and Anglo-Catholicism. In 1933 the secretary of the Melbourne branch of the Anglican Church League, a body committed to defending the Protestant basis of the Church of England, wrote of Archbishop Head: 'We in Melbourne are just a little tired of importing *Evangelicals* from England, who when they settle here, find that they left their backbone behind, and want to be all things to all men.'[75] Conservative evangelical laity who shared these views, while remaining attached to the Church of England, tended to throw their energies into interdenominational evangelical societies and conventions. In Melbourne, lay Anglicans, rather than clergy, during these years assumed leadership of the evangelical movement.[76]

Another dissident was Farnham E. Maynard, vicar of the leading Anglo-Catholic church, St Peter's, Eastern Hill, from 1926 to 1964. Maynard was a liberal Catholic in theology, widely read in history, economics and psychology and editor of an Anglo-Catholic journal, the *Australian Church Quarterly*. He wrote many articles and tracts, several works of social theology and also a historical defence of English Catholicism against the papal claims.[77] In politics he was an outspoken socialist and hosted the 'Red Dean' of Canterbury, Dr Hewlett Johnson, when he visited Melbourne in 1950 to open a conference of the Australian Peace Council. One who grew up at St Peter's in the 1950s recalled: 'If there's a gospel which I associate with Father Maynard, it would be the one about casting the Money-Changers out of the precincts of the Temple.'[78] Maynard regarded the Diocese of Melbourne as sunk in a 'Protestant slough of despond'.[79]

For every denomination in Australia the 1950s was a decade of ecclesiastical expansion and untroubled orthodoxy. In every capital city new congregations and parishes were founded in the expanding post-war suburbs. Buildings were seen as having a higher priority than theology. Joseph Booth, a product of Ridley College and the Depression, who was elected archbishop in 1942, reflected the prevailing mood of Melbourne Anglicanism. Booth's Synod addresses, his biographer observed, typically dealt with 'practicalities rather than flights of fancy'; he was a man of common sense, not a man of ideas.[80] The popular religious writings of the period – in paperback editions for the first time – were those that expounded traditional doctrines with fresh insights and imaginative examples. England was still the main source of theological ideas. In 1951 Canon Bryan Green of Birmingham conducted two missions in Melbourne and gave the Moorhouse Lectures on 'Practical Evangelism' which attracted huge congregations.[81] His book *The Practice of Evangelism*, based on these lectures, was read by many clergy and keen lay people throughout the decade.[82] The works of John Stott and J.I. Packer had a big readership among evangelicals, while Anglo-Catholics preferred Michael Ramsey and E.L. Mascall. Christian popular apologetics were dominated by C.S. Lewis. Alan Richardson introduced a generation of theological students to the ideas of biblical theology and during a visit to Australia and New Zealand in 1960 he gave a series of lectures in Melbourne.[83]

In the second half of the 1950s the Diocese of Melbourne gained a reputation in Australian Anglicanism as a nursery for reformist ideas and progressive policies, a place where new thinking was not stifled. In areas such as ecumenical activity, liturgical reform, marriage guidance, religious education, theological education within an ecumenical framework, and specialised ministries in hospitals, universities and industry (through the Inter-Church Trade and Industry Mission), Melbourne led the way.

This was partly a matter of environment. In Melbourne, in the Presbyterian and the Methodist churches, there was already an influential group of theologians and ministers who were open to the new theological scholarship from Europe and deeply involved in the ecumenical movement: J. Davis McCaughey of Ormond College was the outstanding figure. At the University of Melbourne there had been since the 1930s a strong liberal Christian presence, centred on the Student Christian Movement (SCM) and the church-related colleges.[84] At a time when the university was more accessible than ever before, and when religious societies attracted a significant level of loyalty and support from undergraduates, the socially reformist and ecumenical ideas of the SCM influenced another generation of young lay people. Many of them achieved positions of leadership in the church and the professions in the following decades.

Some of the impetus came within the Diocese from creative individuals who encouraged exploration of the broader implications of Christianity. Younger evangelicals responded to the leadership of Stuart Barton Babbage, who was principal of Ridley College from 1953 to 1963, as well as part-time Dean of Melbourne from 1954 until 1962. He lifted the academic standard of Ridley and from the cathedral built bridges to the wider community through lectures, musical recitals and special services. His views on religious and political issues were often reported in the newspapers.[85] Another influential figure in the 1960s was Geoffrey Sambell, director of the Brotherhood of St Laurence from 1956, director of the diocesan Home Mission Board from 1961 and Coadjutor Bishop from 1962.[86] He provided theological underpinning to the cause of social justice and encouraged the diocese as a whole to look beyond ecclesiastical concerns to its 'mission in the world'.[87] In 1969 he was elected Archbishop of Perth.

The new mood was fostered by Frank Woods, who arrived from a suffragan see in Manchester to be Archbishop in 1957.[88] Woods, came from an English episcopal dynasty. With the religious self-confidence engendered by an upper class and liberal evangelical background – 'I can never remember a time when I doubted the truth of the Christian faith'[89] – he was well read, open to new ideas and encouraged a certain amount of experiment in church life. He had a good eye for clergy whose talents were not being fully utilised where they were and encouraged them to come to Melbourne.

Among those who came into the diocese from the 1960s were Felix Arnott, Barry Marshall, Max Thomas (Archbishop's Consultant Theologian, 1969-75) and John Gaden (Archbishop's Consultant Theologian, 1976-85). All of them, at various times, were associated with Trinity College. Intellectually they were a lively group, closely attuned to the city's cultural life and able to talk knowledgeably with writers, artists and agnostic academics. In 1964 the Canterbury Fellowship, a congregation of university and professional people which worshipped in the Trinity College Chapel from 1938, held its first art exhibition.[90] But like many other Australian thinkers of the post-war years - who were described as 'disappointingly unprolific of any work of substantial proportions'[91] - the clergy associated with Trinity College, apart from the historian James Grant, published very little of original scholarship.[92] Their influence spread through their preaching and lectures, their membership of the General Synod Commission on Doctrine, their contributions to liturgical revision and church music, and the annual Trinity School of Theology. This was first held in 1968 and brought a stream of international figures to Melbourne: for example, John Macquarrie in 1969 and Hans Küng in 1971. There was a new readiness to look beyond England as the primary source of theological ideas. Thomas and Gaden, who had done postgraduate degrees at General Theological Seminary in New York, were deeply influenced by their exposure to progressive American theologians. Barry Marshall, who spent the year 1967 in Paris studying at the Institut Catholique, brought back to Melbourne the insights of contemporary French theology and stimulated new thinking on Christian initiation and the significance of the eucharist, as the central act of a worshipping community.[93]

A very different theological tradition was represented at Ridley College by Leon Morris (principal from 1964 to 1979), who from the 1950s gained an international reputation as a New Testament scholar. His studies, fine examples of the grammatico-linguistic approach to the New Testament, centred on the person and work of Christ. He wrote extensively on the doctrine of the atonement and produced substantial commentaries on St John's Gospel and other books of the New Testament. Morris was a very significant figure in the post-war resurgence of evangelical scholarship. By the time he retired in 1979 he was the most published and most respected evangelical biblical scholar in Australia.[94] In Melbourne, however, he worked almost alone and he was closer to evangelical biblical scholars overseas than to local centres of intellectual life. At Ridley he did not seek to establish a 'school', but a tradition of evangelical biblical scholarship was continued by Colin Kruse, David Williams and John Wilson.[95]

The decade of the 1960s was a time of religious upheaval, not only in Australia but throughout the Western world. Received religious traditions came under attack and seemingly secure religious subcultures fragmented, so that the theological scene became much more diverse and confused. Phrases such as 'the new Reformation', 'the death of God', 'ferment in the church' and 'post-Christian era' entered the popular religious vocabulary. The religious turbulence interacted often explosively with the debate over the Vietnam War and the emergence of the counter-culture in the late 1960s. Some claimed that Jesus was a political revolutionary. Melbourne was the Australian centre of almost every radical and progressivist movement of the period, and the demonstrations against the Vietnam War in 1970 were the largest in the country.[96]

In English religion, the book that more than any other summed up the theological questions of the decade was *Honest to God*, by John Robinson, Bishop of Woolwich. Within three years of its publication in 1963 more than a million copies of this paperback were sold; it was widely read and discussed in Australia.[97] Robinson's fundamental contention was that there was a need to recast traditional Christian doctrines so that they could be 'real' and 'meaningful' for people in the modern secular and scientific world. He proposed a new image of God ('the ground of our being'), a new Christology (Jesus as a model for humanity, 'the man for others'), and a new Christian ethic ('the new morality').

In Melbourne the responses of Anglicans, and other Christians, to the 'new theology' of the 1960s were generally more positive than those in most other parts of Australia. Evangelicals, as elsewhere, were not impressed by the claim that traditional beliefs and doctrines should be modified

GODLESS EDUCATION.

Bishop of Melbourne.—NEARLY HALF OUR CHILDREN NEVER ENTER A SUNDAY SCHOOL, NOR, SO FAR AS WE KNOW, RECEIVE ANY RELIGIOUS INSTRUCTION AT ALL.

Bishop Punch.—I BEGIN TO THINK, MY LORD AND YOUR GRACE, THAT THERE IS SOMETHING IN WHAT YOU SAY, FOR, SINCE THE APPEARANCE OF MY LAST CARTOON, I HAVE BEEN DELUGED WITH LETTERS AND INQUIRIES FROM NUMBERS OF PEOPLE—WHO OWN BIBLES, TOO—ASKING ME WHAT NUMBER 666 MEANS.

'Melbourne Punch', 21 October 1881, page 61.

in order to be meaningful to 'the modern mind'. Leon Morris, then in England as warden of Tyndale House, Cambridge, published a stringent critique of 'religionless Christianity' and the ideas that lay behind it; in his view the new movement did not retain the 'essential gospel'.[98] In 1965 he wrote a series of articles in the diocesan paper on 'The Ferment in the Church' which likewise concluded on a sober note:

> It is certain that the orthodox have some hard thinking to do. But it is also clear that those who follow the Bishop [Robinson] most closely have yet to show that what they are teaching is authentic Christianity. They, too, have some hard thinking before them.[99]

Anglicans in the liberal Catholic tradition, on the other hand, were rather more likely to be attracted to the ideas of the radicals, seeing signs of 'a real advance in Christian thinking and practice'.[100] Peter Hollingworth, chaplain (later director) of the Brotherhood of St Laurence, described Harvey Cox's *The Secular City* as 'one of the few really successful attempts to recast the Gospel so that it relates to contemporary society'.[101] A few, combining social, political and religious radicalism, took up the American 'Death of God' theology, which enjoyed a brief fashion in the mid-1960s. In April 1968 two young clergymen, David Pope and Peter Lane, announced to the press that they found the concept of the supernatural 'irrelevant' and were agnostic on the existence of God. For a few weeks the case of the Melbourne agnostic clergy was national news which tested even the tolerant limits of Melbourne Anglicanism. The diocesan bishops promptly issued a pastoral letter to reassure churchgoers that 'these opinions are but old heresies dressed up in new clothes' and that priests who believed such things should resign.[102] Both men soon dropped out of the ministry. More conventional Anglicans elsewhere in Australia were not really surprised that such heresies had appeared in 'trendy' Melbourne.

In several of his Synod presidential addresses during these years, Woods took up the questions that the radicals were asking. He was sympathetic to their contention that the historic faith needed constant reinterpretation and he recognised the 'extreme difficulty' of communicating traditional Christian images and theological statements to 'the modern mind':

> When any movement in theology, ancient or modern, tries or tends to overthrow the reality of the Christian faith, by all means let us oppose it. But if a movement is trying to help us to regain a reality that has been lost, then at least let us consider it with care and avail ourselves of such insights as it may have.[103]

His approach was shared by many of the clergy and the more articulate lay people.

After the 1960s Melbourne Anglicanism was not quite the same. Some of the landmarks that once defined the church were dissolving. Anglicans were being exposed to a greater range of ideas and movements than ever before. By the 1980s they were involved in widely diverse causes and organisations, ranging from the charismatic movement, American-inspired church growth seminars and the well-established evangelical Belgrave Heights Convention to the traditionalist Prayer Book Society, the ecumenical Victorian Council of Churches, Catholic Renewal and the Movement for the Ordination of Women. As elsewhere in the Anglican world, the old division between 'high' and 'low' became rather less important than the division between conservative and liberal. An Anglo-Catholic cleric, who had come to the Diocese from Adelaide, found 'great freedom' in Melbourne, along with 'the stimulation that comes with the great variety of styles', but he also detected an 'intolerance to even hearing the conservative voice in debate'.[104]

In the area of theology several distinct trends may be detected. The first was the dissolution of what had once been a fairly cohesive Anglo-Catholic party, which from the early 1980s became sharply divided over the question of women priests. The majority of Anglo-Catholic clergy and lay people in Melbourne, on the liberal wing of the movement, supported the move, but a minority remained fiercely opposed.[105] Melbourne evangelicals were also divided but not to the same extent. Secondly, there was the impact of Christian feminism. From the 1970s, for the first time, Anglican women began to study and write theology, and in the United Faculty of Theology within the Melbourne College of Divinity John Gaden introduced students to feminist theology. Thirdly, there was the advance of evangelicalism, but with a distinctive style. It was more accommodating and less insistent on theological correctness than in Sydney.

The concerns of Melbourne evangelicals largely dominated and were reinforced by the first National Evangelical Anglican Congress held at Monash University in 1971, but behind the scenes a powerful group of Sydney conservatives attacked a chapter on 'What do evangelicals believe' in a conference booklet *What is an Evangelical?* as 'misleading and inadequate'.[106] In the late-1990s there are signs that a more militant evangelicalism, influenced by Sydney, is gaining ground in Melbourne. Fourthly, there was a continued exploration of the social dimension of Christianity, with a concern to relate scripture and tradition to present-day ethical, political and social issues. This was encouraged by Archbishop Robert Dann (1977 to 1983). It was influenced by the idea popularised in the 1960s that the church is the fellowship of those who are ready to 'serve the world' at the points of human need,[107] and reinforced by the revival of evangelical social commitment that began in England in the 1970s. In this 'new evangelicalism' it was common to speak of evangelism as being integrally related to social responsibility.[108]

The latter trends fused in the person of David Penman who was elected Archbishop of Melbourne in 1984, but died five years later.[109] During his short episcopate he became the best known Anglican in Australia. Among progressive evangelicals he was a hero figure and pace setter, though many conservatives thought that his theology was inadequate, soft on the doctrines of the Reformation.[110] Penman initiated new policies on multicultural ministry in Melbourne and gave strong support to the ordination of women.[111] In 1985 the diocesan Synod was the first in Australia to approve the ordination of women deacons.

Behind the shifts and changes of the last 150 years, is it possible to see the emergence of an intellectual outlook or style that is distinctive of Melbourne Anglicanism?

In the first place, more than any other diocese in Australia, Melbourne has been representative of a wide spectrum of Anglicanism, a place where different traditions have met or confronted each other. It is a pragmatic church. The Diocese, less concerned than many others to impose uniformity of either doctrine and practice, has accepted theological diversity as a fact of life and has acclaimed this as a source of strength. Moreover, with more than two hundred parishes, it has been large enough to sustain almost every theological movement and to enable many different causes to gather supporters and achieve an institutional base. Secondly, since the 1870s the ambience of Melbourne has provided a hospitable environment for a liberal tradition in theology, which is sceptical of unqualified appeals to scripture and churchly tradition, open to intellectual movements within the wider society and disinclined to regard the secular world as an enemy to be shunned. This outlook has in turn influenced the temper and style of both Anglican evangelicalism and Anglo-Catholicism. A liberal and pluralist intellectual tradition, combined with social prestige and proximity to power, has been for Melbourne Anglicanism a source of strength and distinctive identity. However, the social and intellectual landscape is changing. In the next generation it is likely that the theology of the Diocese will be more influenced by those who emphasise the proclamation of a collective faith and reject the assumptions and conclusions of modern secular thought.

Research for this essay was assisted by the Australian Research Council through its Small Research Grants Scheme, as part of a larger project on the history of Anglicanism in Australia.

1 Ruth I. Sturmey, 'Women and the Anglican Church in Australia: Theology and Social Change', PhD thesis, University of Sydney, 1989, pp. 66-8. A pereceptive analysis by a sociologist of the character of Melbourne Anglicanism.

2 A. de Q. Robin, *Charles Perry, Bishop of Melbourne: The Challenges of a Colonial Episcopate, 1847-76*, Nedlands, WA, 1967. Recent studies of the history of British and Australian evangelicalism include D. W. Bebbington, *Evangelicalism in Modern Britain: A History from the 1730s to the 1980s*, London, 1989, and Stuart Piggin, *Evangelical Christianity in Australia: Spirit, Word and World*, Melbourne, 1996.

3 Perry's statement is in Robin, pp. 199-201; and R.A. Giles, *A Constitutional History of the Australian Church*, London, 1929, pp. 244-5.

4 Peter Benedict Nockles, *The Oxford Movement in Context: Anglican High Churchmanship, 1760-1857*, Cambridge, 1994, p. 311.

5 Quoted in Robin, p. 159. See also Austin Cooper, 'The Oxford Movement and Australia', PhD thesis, Monash University, 1973, pp. 275-86, on Perry and Tractarianism in the Port Phillip colony.

6 Quoted in George Goodman, *The Church in Victoria during the Episcopate of the Right Reverend Charles Perry, First Bishop of Melbourne*, Melbourne, 1892, p. 344.

7 James Grant, 'The Diocese of Melbourne (and Victoria)', in Brian Porter (ed.), *Colonial Tractarians: The Oxford Movement in Australia*, Melbourne, 1989, p. 69.

8 Perry to Handfield, 9 January 1891, TS copy, St Peter's Eastern Hill Archives.

9 Barry W. Butcher, 'Darwinism and Australia, 1836-1914', PhD thesis, University of Melbourne, 1992.

10 Geoffrey Serle, *The Rush to be Rich: A History of the Colony of Victoria, 1883-1889*, Melbourne, 1971, ch. 4; Francis Barrymore Smith, 'Religion and Freethought in Melbourne, 1870 to 1890', MA thesis, University of Melbourne, 1960, and F. B. Smith, 'Spiritualism in Victoria in the nineteenth century', *Journal of Religious History*, vol. 3, no. 3 (1965), pp. 246-60; Jill Roe, 'Challenge and response: religious life in Melbourne, 1876-1886', *Journal of Religious History*, vol. 5, no. 2 (1968), pp. 149-66.

11 Janet McCalman, *Journeyings: The Biography of a Middle-Class Generation, 1920-1990*, Melbourne, 1993, p. 29.

12 Serle, p. 127.

13 C.R. Badger, *The Reverend Charles Strong and the Australian Church*, Melbourne, 1971.

14 Graeme Davison, *The Rise and Fall of Marvellous Melbourne*, Melbourne, 1978, p. 131.

15 For example, D.M. Berry, 'Dates of creation and the flood', *Church of England Messenger*, 5 April 1889, pp. 56-7; and the response by H. P. Handfield, 3 May 1889, p. 76.

16 Goodman, pp. 432-7.

17 Charles Perry, 'Science and the Bible: A Lecture …Delivered by Request, on Monday, September 20, 1869', Melbourne, 1869.

18 Butcher, 'Darwinism and Australia', ch. 4.

19 J. La Nauze, *Political Economy in Australia: Historical Studies*, Melbourne, 1949, pp. 59-65, and his 'Hearn on natural religion: an unpublished manuscript', *Historical Studies*,

vol. 12, no. 45 (1965), pp. 119-22.

20 George Higinbotham, *Science and Religion: or the Relations of Modern Science with the Christian Churches . . .*, Melbourne, 1883; and a response by an Anglican clergyman: Reverend AW. Cresswell, 'Science and Religion: An Address Delivered in St John's Church, Camberwell, on Sunday Evening, 19th August, 1883', Melbourne, 1883.

21 J.E. Bromby, 'Beyond the Grave: A Lecture Delivered at the Town Hall, on Tuesday, 15th November, 1870', Melbourne, 1870, p. 2. See also his lectures 'Pre-Historic Man', Melbourne, 1869 and 'Creation versus Development', Melbourne, 1870.

22 H.N. Wollaston, 'Biblical inspiration', *Melbourne Review*, vol. 2, 1877, pp. 149-57.

23 Henry Handel Richardson, *The Getting of Wisdom*, new ed. 1931, London, 1910, p. 216.

24 Edith C. Rickards, *Bishop Moorhouse of Melbourne and Manchester*, London, 1920, chapters 7-14.

25 J. Moorhouse, *Church Work: Its Means and Methods*, London, 1894, pp. 25-6.

26 Moorhouse's lectures on 'The Galatian Lapse' were published with others in his book *Dangers of the Apostolic Age*, Melbourne, 1891.

27 Presidential address to the Melbourne Church Assembly, 16 September 1879, *Church of England Messenger*, supplement, 8 October 1879, p. 1.

28 'Presidential address to the Melbourne Church Assembly, 28 September 1883', in *Church of England Messsenger*, 11 October 1883. p. 9.

29 'What is Religion? A Controversy between the late Marcus Clarke and Dr Moorhouse',

Melbourne, 1895; *Church of England Messenger*, 5 June 1883, p. 13.

30 *Church of England Messenger*, 19 November 1937, p. 572.

31 James Grant, *Perspective of a Century: A Volume for the Centenary of Trinity College, Melbourne, 1872-1972*, Melbourne, 1972, pp. 103-11.

32 Geoffrey Blainey, *A Centenary History of the University of Melbourne*, Melbourne, 1957.

33 S.A. Grave, *A History of Philosophy in Australia*, St Lucia, Qld, 1984, chapters 2 and 4.

34 Robert Potter's published works include: *Voice from the Church in Australia*, London and Cambridge, 1864; *The Relation of Ethics to Religion: An Introduction to the Critical Study of Christianity*, London, 1888; Robert Easterley and John Wilbraham (pseud. of Robert Potter(, *The Germ Growers: An Australian Story of Adventure and Mystery*, London and Melbourne, 1892. See also obituary in *Church of England Messenger*, 24 July 1908, p. 227; Robin Sharwood, 'The Doughty Champion: Canon Robert Potter, 1831-1908', Address at St Mary's, North Melbourne, 22 September 1985, TS, St Peter's Eastern Hill Archives.

35 Barbara Brinsley Darling, 'The Church of England in Melbourne and the Great Depression, 1929 to 1935', MA thesis, University of Melbourne, 1982, p. 149.

36 J.A. Grant, 'Field Flowers Goe. The bishop: myths and a ministry', *Royal Historical Society of Victoria Journal*, vol. 54, no. 2, 1983, pp. 17-25.

37 *Victorian Churchman*, 8 July 1910, p. 201.

38 Renate Howe, 'Protestantism, social Christianity

and the ecology of Melbourne, 1890-1900', *Historical Studies*, vol. 19, no. 74 (1980), pp. 59-60.

39 Henry Lowther Clarke, Seventh Address, 1909, in his *Addresses delivered to the Synod of the Diocese of Melbourne, 1909-13* Melbourne, 1914, p. 159.

40 W.K. Lowther Clarke, 'Henry Lowther Clarke, First Archbishop of Melbourne', *Church of England Messenger*, 7 October 1926, p. 462.

41 H. Lowther Clarke, *The Constitutions of the General, Provincial and Diocesan Synods of the Church of England in Australia*, Melbourne, 1918; and *Constitutional Church Government in the Dominions beyond the Seas and in other Parts of the Anglican Communion*, London, 1924.

42 In 1891 there were thirteen churches in Melbourne where services were conducted with 'correct' ceremonial and Holy Communion was celebrated in the eastward position, instead of the traditional 'north end'. *Banner and Anglo-Catholic Review*, Sydney, 1 August 1891. See generally Colin Holden, *Awful Happenings on the Hill: E.S. Hughes and Melbourne Anglo-Catholicism before the War*, Melbourne, 1992.

43 *Banner and Anglo-Catholic Review*, 2 February 1891.

44 Charles Gore (ed.), *Lux Mundi: A Series of Studies in the Religion of the Incarnation*, London, 1889. See also Geoffrey Wainwright (ed.), *Keeping the Faith: Essays to Mark the Centenary of Lux Mundi*, Philadelphia, 1988, and Robert Morgan (ed.), *The Religion of the Incarnation: Anglican Essays in Commemoration of Lux Mundi*, Bristol, 1989.

45 Charles Gore, *The Incarnation of the Son of*

God: being the Bampton Lectures for the year *1891*, London, 1891.

46   For example, Father Cyril Barclay, at St John's, Latrobe Street and later at St Mary's Mission in Fitzroy. In 1918 a storm broke over Barclay's teaching on the Virgin Mary, which was attacked on all sides for its 'incipient Mariolatry' and disloyalty to the doctrines of the Church of England. A. Law, *An Australian Protest against False Catholicity: The History of the Melbourne Movement of 1918*, Melbourne, 1918.

47   Stuart Edward Blackler, 'Henry Lowther Clarke and Educational Policy in the Anglican Diocese of Melbourne, 1903-20', PhD thesis, University of Melbourne, 1991, pp. 120-6.

48   John Clarke, 'The Life, Ministry and Episcopate of the Right Reverend Reginald Stephen, MA, DD (1860-1956)', Sydney Smith Memorial Lecture, St Paul's Cathedral Chapter House, 18 November 1992.

49   T. B. McCall, *The Life and Letters of John Stephen Hart*, Sydney, 1963.

50   Pan-Anglican Congress, 1908, Reports, vol. II, Section A, *The Church and Human Society*, London, 1908, pp. 87-8.

51   *Church of England Messenger*, 16 September 1910, p. 1131.

52   For example, Rev Digby M. Berry, author of *Altar, or Table? A Question for Members of the Church of England*, Melbourne and Sydney, 1887; and *The Eastward Position: Its Origin and Meaning*, Melbourne, 1903.

53   Darrell Paproth, 'Revivalism in Melbourne from federation to World War I: the Torrey-Alexander-Chapman campaigns', in Mark Hutchinson and Stuart Piggin (eds), *Reviving Australia:*

Essays on the History and Experience of Revival and Revivalism in Australian Christianity, Sydney, 1994, pp. 143-69.

54   Darrell Neil Paproth, *C.H. Nash and his Influence*, PhD thesis, Deakin University, 1993, p. 149.

55   Henry Lowther Clarke, Presidential address to Melbourne Diocesan Synod, 30 September 1907, in *Church of England Messenger*, 4 October 1907, supplement, p. 4.

56   *Victorian Churchman*, 12 July 1907, p. 278.

57   *Victorian Churchman*, 9 August 1907, p. 323. Nash's address 'His Seamless Vesture', which his first biographer erroneously attributes to this meeting, was delivered in January 1923. David H. Chalmers, *Tempest Tost': The Life and Teaching of the Rev. C. H. Nash, M.A., Founder and First Principal of the Melbourne Bible Institute*, Melbourne, 1959, pp. 173-81.

58   The main features of liberal evangelicalism are usefully summarised in Kenneth Hylson-Smith, *Evangelicals in the Church of England, 1734-1984*, Edinburgh, 1988, pp. 250-2.

59   See his sympathetic review of the influential book of essays 'Liberal Evangelicalism: An Interpretation by Members of the Church of England', London, 1923 in *Church of England Messenger*, 19 July 1923, pp. 442, 444.

60   George Ellis Aickin, *The Kingdom of God and the Nations*, Moorhouse Lectures, 1916, TS, Mollison Library, Trinity College, Melbourne. See also his address on 'Evangelical Religion', *Victorian Churchman*, 23 June 1911, pp. 182-3.

61   Darrell Paproth, 'The Upwey Convention and C.H. Nash', in Lucas: *An Evangelical History Review*, no. 16, 1993, pp. 23-42; Piggin,

Evangelical Christianity in Australia, pp. 98-100, 142-8.

62   David Parker, 'The Bible Union: a case study in Australian fundamentalism', *Journal of Religious History*, vol. 14, no. 1, 1986, pp. 71-99.

63   Stuart Piggin, 'Not a little holy club': lay and clerical leadership in Australian Anglican evangelicalism, 1788-1988', in W. J. Sheils and Diana Wood (eds), *The Ministry: Clerical and Lay Studies in Church History*, vol. 26, Oxford, 1989, pp. 378-9. For a full account of Nash's career, see Paproth, C. H. Nash and his Influence.

64   James Jupp, 'The "bourgeois" and "proletarian" variations', in Jim Davidson (ed.), *The Sydney-Melbourne Book*, Sydney, 1986, pp. 79-88.

65   Janet McCalman, *Journeyings;* and 'Private life in the garden suburbs between the wars' or 'What will people say?', in Graeme Davison, Tony Dingle and Seamus O'Hanlon (eds), *The Cream Brick Frontier: Histories of Australian Suburbia*, Clayton, Vic., 1995, pp. 51-61.

66   *Church of England Messenger*, 25 September 1924, p. 454.

67   For example, 'The Anglo-Saxon destiny', in *Church of England Messenger*, 29 November 1918, p. 564; A. Law, (n.d.), *Prophecy Reveals Britain's Destiny*, Melbourne.

68   Manning Clark, *The Puzzles of Childhood*, Ringwood, Vic., 1989, p. 181.

69   For example, Archbishop Lowther Clarke, *Church of England Messenger*, 2 May 1919, p. 821.

70   *Church of England Messenger*, 7 September 1951, p. 282.

71 Archbishop Lees, presidential address to Synod, 12 October 1925, in *Church of England Messenger*, 22 october 1925, p. 507.

72 Archbishop Lees, presidential address to Synod, 10 October 1927, in *Church of England Messenger*, 20 October 1927, p. 477-83.

73 *Church of England Messenger*, 10 July 1931, p. 317; *Australian Church Record*, Sydney, 30 July 1931, p. 1.

74 *Church of England Messenger*, 21 July 1933, p. 318.

75 Thick to Corish, 1 May 1933, Anglican Church League records, Moore Theological College Library, Sydney. The Anglican Church League was founded in Sydney in 1909 and the Melbourne branch was formed in 1929.

76 Piggin, pp. 378-82.

77 Farnham Maynard, *Economics and the Kingdom of God*, Melbourne, 1929; and *The Continuity of the Church of England: A Story of the Kings and Popes of the Sixteenth Century*, Melbourne, 1939; David Adrian Pear, Two Anglican responses to the depression and Second World War in Melbourne: a study in churchmanship, MTh thesis, Melbourne College of Divinity, 1985. The Anglicans concerned are F. E. Maynard and R.G. ('Brother Bill') Nichols.

78 Peter Bryce, TS transcription of address to the Melbourne branch of the Australian Church Union, early 1980s, St Peter's Eastern Hill Archives

79 St Peter's Church, Eastern Hill, *Parish Paper*, Winter 1955.

80 A. de Q. Robin, *Making Many Rich: A Memoir of Joseph John Booth, Fourth Archbishop of Melbourne*, Melbourne, 1978, p. 66.

81 *Church of England Messenger*, 13 July 1951, p. 212, 27 July 1951, pp. 229, 232.

82 Bryan Green, *The Practice of Evangelism*, London, 1951.

83 The lectures that Alan Richardson gave at Ormond College in Melbourne formed the basis of several chapters of his book, *The Bible in the Age of Science* London, 1961.

84 See, for example, Owen Parnaby, *Queen's College, University of Melbourne: A Centenary History*, Melbourne, 1990, pp. 215-17, 232-34.

85 While principal of Ridley College and Dean of Melbourne, Stuart Barton Babbage published three books: *Man in Nature and in Grace*, Grand Rapids Michigan, 1957; (with Ian Siggins), *Light beneath the Cross: The Story of Billy Graham's Crusade in Australia*, Kingswood and Melbourne, 1960; *Puritanism and Richard Bancroft*, London, 1962.

86 Anne Porter, 'Archbishop Geoffrey Sambell: the making of a social conscience', in John Tonkin (ed.), *Religion and Society in Western Australia*, Studies in Western Australian History, vol. 9, Nedlands, WA, 1987, pp. 54-62, and her Biography of Geoffrey Tremayne Sambell, 1914-1980: Archbishop of Perth, 1969-1980, MPhil thesis, Murdoch University, 1990.

87 As director of the Primate's Committee on Mutual Responsibilty and Interdependence, formed after the 1963 Toronto Congress, Sambell wrote many articles and study guides expounding this theme. See, for example, *Responsive Obedience: A Source Book for Clergy*, Melbourne, 1965.

88 Frank Woods, *Sermons and Addresses: Forward in Depth*, Melbourne, 1987.

89 Ken Harrison, 'Frank Woods: humble servant of the King of Kings', *Southern Cross*, Sydney, April 1977, p. 5.

90 *Church of England Messenger*, May 1964, p. 72.

91 Vincent Buckley, 'Intellectuals', in Peter Coleman (ed.), *Australian Civilization*, Melbourne, 1962, p. 100.

92 James Grant's publications include (with Geoffrey Serle) *The Melbourne Scene*, Melbourne, 1956 and *Perspective of a Century: A Volume for the Centenary of Trinity College, 1872-1972*, Melbourne, 1972. John Gaden's papers were published posthumously: John Gaden, *A Vision of Wholeness*, (ed. Duncan Reid), Sydney, 1994.

93 See, for example, his four lectures on 'Christian Initiation' (1969), Leeper Library, Trinity College, Melbourne. In 1970 he went to England to become principal of Pusey House, Oxford, but died following an accident only a few weeks after his arrival.

For a perceptive assessment of the man and his thought: Robin Sharwood, Barry Marshall and the Armour of Light 12th Barry Marshall Memorial Lecture, 1982, tape, Leeper Library.

94 Robert Banks (ed.), *Reconciliation and Hope: New Testament Essays on Atonement and Eschatology presented to L. L. Morris on his 60th Birthday*, Grand Rapids, Michigan, 1974. The select bibliography of Morris's publications from 1947 to 1973 runs to six pages. His most important works are *The Apostolic Preaching of the Cross*, Leicester, 1955, 3rd ed., 1965; and *The Gospel according to John*, Grand Rapids, Michigan, 1971. See also Robert Banks,

'Fifty years of theology in Australia, 1915-1965', part 2, *Colloquium: The Australian and New Zealand Theological Review*, vol. 9, no. 2 (1977), pp. 7, 11.

95 Their published works include: Colin G. Kruse, *The Second Epistle of Paul to the Corinthians: An Introduction and Commentary*, Tyndale New Testament Commentaries, Leicester and Grand Rapids, Michigan, 1987; David J. Williams, *Acts*, New International Biblical Commentary, Peabody, Mass., 1985, and *1 and 2 Thessalonians*, New International Biblical Commentary, Peabody, Mass., 1992; John W. Wilson, *Ezekiel: God's Commentator*, Wanniassa, ACT, 1990.

96 Jupp, pp. 82-3.

97 John A.T. Robinson, *Honest to God*, (London, 1963); David L. Edwards (ed), *The Honest to God Debate*, London, 1963. For a survey of the debate, see Keith W. Clements, *Lovers of Discord: Twentieth-Century Theological Controversies in England*, London, 1988, ch. 7.

98 Leon Morris, *The Abolition of Religion: A Study in 'Religionless Christianity*, London, 1964.

99 Leon Morris, in *Church of England Messenger*, April 1965, p. 4.

100 Review of John A.T. Robinson, 'Christian Morals Today', *Church of England Messenger*, February 1965, p. 10.

101 *Church of England Messenger*, November 1965, p. 11.

102 'A Letter to the Clergy and People of the Diocese of Melbourne, 28 April 1968', Melbourne Diocesan Archives; *Age*, 29 April 1968, p. 1; See, June 1968, p. 6.

103 Archbishop of Melbourne, *Charge to Synod*, 1968, p. 35.

104 David Farrer, 'Orthodoxy down under', in *Tracts for our Times*, 1833-1983, St Mary's, Bourne Street, Annual for 1983, London, 1983, pp. 64-5.

105 For a statement of the conservative case, with several contributors from the diocese of Melbourne, see David Wetherell (ed.), *Women Priests in Australia? The Anglican Crisis*, Melbourne, 1987 and his 'Archbishop Rayner and the Anglican Church', *Quadrant*, no. 303 (1994), pp. 68-73.

106 Anglican Church League Council minutes, 3 November 1970, 2 February 1971, Anglican Church League records, Moore Theological College Library, Sydney.

107 Ideas expounded by the Australian Methodist Colin Williams in his books *Where in the World?*, 1963; and *What in the World?*, 1964.

108 David Bebbington, 'The decline and resurgence of Evangelical social concern, 1918-1980', in John Wolffe (ed.), *Evangelical Faith and Public Zeal: Evangelicals and Society in Britain, 1780-1980*, London, 1995, pp. 175-97.

109 Obituary in *Age*, 2 October 1989; See, November 1989; Alan Nichols, *David Penman: Bridge-Builder, Peacemaker, Fighter for Social Justice*, Sutherland, NSW, 1991.

110 D.B. Knox, taped interview with Stuart Piggin and Margaret Lamb, 17 June 1988, Centre for the Study of Australian Christianity, Sydney.

111 Diocese of Melbourne, *A Garden of Many Colours: The Report of the Archbishop's Commission on Multicultural Ministry and Mission*, Melbourne, 1985.

Sketch of Melbourne's first Pioneer Church. The church was used as a school on weekdays.

PHOTO: FROM THE ORIGINAL IN THE LATROBE LIBRARY.

Architecture, music, art, and liturgy
in the Diocese of Melbourne

The general lack of recognition in Australia of any kind of relationship in matters of thought, art, politics, or religion does not augur well for an essay on the subjects enumerated above.[1]

Yet somewhat surprisingly, Samuel Marsden wrote in the early days of European settlement that evangelistic work should be preceded by some practical knowledge of the arts of civilization. He did not outline his definition of 'the arts', but clearly he saw the field of human imagination and enterprise preparing the ground for evangelising:

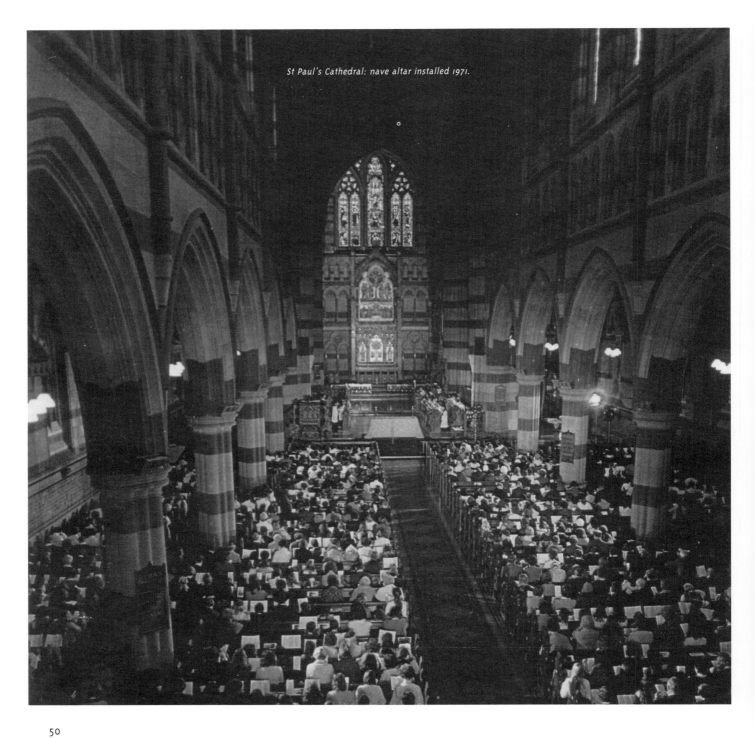

St Paul's Cathedral: nave altar installed 1971.

Since nothing in my opinion can pave the way for the introduction of the Gospel but civilization; and that can only be accomplished among the heathen by the arts...The arts and religion should go together.[2]

* * *

The European settlement of the Port Phillip District could only be described as haphazard. It did not even have the grim planning of a penal settlement, and that degree of haphazardness is reflected in the utilitarian and prosaic nature of the architecture of the first settlement in what we now call Melbourne. The first tents pitched gave way to rough timber and canvas shacks, then to timber houses, and finally to brick dwellings. The first brick house was not built until 1837.

The immediate need was for shelter from cold and heat, wind and rain. In addition, little was known about the building materials at hand. Many early buildings were erected with faulty materials – timber and sandstone in particular. There was also a lack of professional builders and artisans, often resulting in faulty designs and workmanship, for these early days were the days of the amateur builder.

But from the 1850s on, the gold discovery in the colony transformed the settlement in every way – politically and socially. There was an enormous change in the usage of proper building materials, properly supervised use of the correct kind of timber and stone, and the provision of bricks and slates. Moreover, immigration brought professionally trained artisans – carpenters and joiners, bricklayers, masons, metal workers, gold and silver-smiths, instrument makers – those agents of the arts of civilization that Marsden had mentioned.

This change in the community was reflected in the church, especially in the first Anglican churches to be erected for what was to become the Diocese of Melbourne. Moreover, the manner in which the first churches were erected reflects some of the same expectations and problems between church people and architects that have persisted for 150 years.

In 1836, Dr Alexander Thomson pitched his circular Indian tent under a large gum tree on what was to become the site for the present Cathedral Church of St Paul. In this tent Christian services, read from

1. Architecture

the *Book of Common Prayer*, were the first such services to be held in this corner of the globe.[3] The same Dr Thomson, a Presbyterian medical doctor and missionary to the Aborigines, claimed to have been the person who designed the first church – a wooden structure, usually known as the Pioneers' Wooden Church.[4]

As regarding architecture for this building – there was none. It was essentially a shelter and by reports, a fairly inadequate shelter at that. Built of weatherboard, slab walls, with an earthen floor and a shingle roof, it could accommodate eighty people in what has been described as 'draughty discomfort', heat or cold.[5] Extensions in 1838 seemed to have made it no less uncomfortable.

Built by open subscription from settlers of all kinds and creeds, this wooden church witnessed an early ecumenical spirit, as it was shared by several denominations for their worship, but unfortunately the building became the source of dissension when Bishop Broughton claimed its sole use for the Church of England. Other denominations bitterly resented that they could no longer use a property to which they had contributed. Small wonder that it was by all reports an unlovely and unloved building. After

the building of St James Church it was no longer used as a church, though it continued as a school until replaced by another building, and finally disappeared unlamented in 1853.

The building of a more permanent construction, that of St James' Church, seems to have inherited the opprobrium of the Melbourne populace from the Pioneers' Church. The present building, though standing on a different site, is now treasured as an historic relic of the city's earliest days, and it is hard to realize that for the 19th century and much of the 20th, this same church was ridiculed and despised by Melbourne's people. It was known none too affectionately as 'the old pepper pot of Collins Street'.

The design and building was entrusted to Robert Russell, formerly the Clerk of Works for the young settlement. It was to be his first and only church building. The whole enterprise was fraught with difficulty and opposition, a portent perhaps of things to come. Charles LaTrobe laid the foundation stone in 1839 shortly after his arrival in the district, but it was 1842 before it was opened for worship. Lack of funds curtailed Russell's plans, and the proposed steeple was never completed. A certain Dr Palmer engineered the replacement of a spire with a domed

tower, hence the nickname in later times of 'Dr Palmer's Pepper Pot'. The architect Charles Laing is credited with completing the building after Russell was paid out. Garryowen wrote that the tower was 'to be bonneted with an abortion of no known order of architecture in existence'.[6] The whole sorry story is unfortunately typical of much of the record between church and architects still to come. Lack of sufficient finance, and ill-informed interference by clergy and laity in matters in which they had little or no knowledge or understanding, led to difficulty for architects and congregations alike.

The 1840s saw the rise of further churches in the infant town – St Peter's on the Eastern Hill and St John's in the outer settlement of Heidelberg. The present nave of St Peter's, built by Laing shows very well the trend towards a full Gothic design. The addition of transepts and galleries by Charles Vickers in 1853, and the further addition of sanctuary and vestries by Terry and Oakden in 1876, completed the present church in a fuller Gothic style. St John's, Heidelberg, designed by John Gill, was erected in 1849-51 and has a distinct resemblance to St Peter's, without the later additions.

The earliest full Gothic style is outside

Old St Andrew's Church, Brighton.

The old St Paul's church on the site of the present cathedral.

St James' Old Cathedral, Melbourne.

the city of Melbourne though still within the Diocese: Christ Church, Geelong, designed by Edmund Blacket from Sydney, in the Perpendicular Gothic style, begun in 1847 and largely completed in 1855.

These four churches are the only ones to be built in the 1840s, and are established around the first centres of human settlement, but it could not be maintained that they served the population well. Both Serle and Lewis have commented that the reports of crowded churches was not so much due to the increase of church-going, but to the absence of enough churches to hold those who desired to attend.[7]

For Anglicans the great incentive for establishing parishes and building churches came after the appointment of Charles Perry as the first Bishop of the Diocese in 1847, and his subsequent arrival and installation in 1848. Perry at once set about the proper organisation of the Diocese and the arduous task of soliciting funds for building. Here, he was hampered by the reluctance of Anglican laity to recognise their duty of financially supporting their church, being used to state support for their religious belief and practice.

After the discovery of gold, the huge increase in population, and the founding of the Colony of Victoria by its separation from New South Wales, the building of new churches rapidly takes place. With the confidence in public life from the gold rush and its profits, the churches built in the following decade were nearly all intended to be on a grand scale, and nearly all intended to be replicas of the town and village churches of England. By the mid century the Gothic style, with few exceptions, reigned supreme for all denominations, but particularly for Anglican churches.[8]

The establishment of architectural societies such as the Camden society in Cambridge, began to influence the architects of the era, especially in the Gothic style of architecture being considered as the correct architectural style, as well as in ecclesiastical matters pertaining to ornaments, furnishing, and liturgy. Many architects who came to Melbourne to pursue their careers had brought with them concepts of this ecclesiastical architecture then reigning foremost in Europe, and especially in England. Melbourne did not share the influence of the Colonial Georgian architectural style as found in the Dioceses of Sydney and Tasmania, apart from St James Old Cathedral, which is the only strictly Georgian building in the Diocese. The later churches of St Peter's, Eastern Hill and St John's, Heidelberg, show the transition from the Regency style into Gothic by the end of the 1840s, and especially in the former with the additions later in the century.

From the 1850s, the proliferation of churches through the Diocese was immense and cannot be given full treatment in the scope of this essay. As the population increased and spread, new parishes sprang into being and with them the necessary erection of churches, vicarages, and schoolhouses. Most of these erections were close to the centre of the present city, though there were some like St John the Less, East Brighton, (the small church and schoolroom building now in the grounds of St Mark's); St Andrew's, Brighton; St Paul's, Westmeadows; and Holy Trinity, Oakleigh; which were on what were then the outskirts of the city. And of course, it is necessary to remember that at this time, the Diocese of Melbourne extended throughout the whole of Victoria.

Compared with the four churches commenced in the 1840s, the decade of the 1850s saw the erection of no less than 29 churches - 14 in the actual boundaries of the city of Melbourne, 10 in country districts, and 5 in places such as Geelong, Bacchus Marsh and Ceres, still within the diocesan boundaries.

A few more were brought into being in the following decade of the 1860s, 32 churches in all. Six of these in the city environs, 9 in the present diocesan boundaries, and 18 throughout the whole State. By the time that Bishop Perry left the Diocese and returned to England, he had been responsible for the building of no less than 71 churches, ten of these in the last five years of his episcopate.

Few of these churches were to be completed as they had been initially envisaged, and many of them were never completed, and remain as such to this day. A tour of the Diocese reveals towers awaiting spires, nave walls awaiting transepts and porches, naves awaiting chancels and sanctuaries, or chancels and sanctuaries awaiting naves. There are obviously temporary timber walls to be seen awaiting a more permanent conversion in some churches.

Following the first architects, Robert Russell and Charles Laing, there have been many distinguished persons working as architects for the Diocese, not without the traumas experienced by their forerunners. When plans were being discussed about the erection of a building on the Cathedral site in East Melbourne as a church for the local Anglican population, a suggestion was made that as the building was to be only temporary, either in brick or stone, the window frames should be made of wood, so that they could later on be adapted to any form of general ornamentation and architecture that an architect might happen to choose. So much for an understanding of architecture or the role of an architect. Another suggestion was made that Bishop Perry should procure designs for a cathedral whilst in England, and that therefore these were bound to be Gothic, so that any temporary building erected should be as 'Gothicky' as possible.[9]

The following were amongst the more important church architects for the Anglican Diocese of Melbourne. Charles Laing was wholly or in part responsible for the building of St James', Melbourne (the completion of Russell's designs); St Peter's, Melbourne; St Paul's, Geelong; All Saints', East St Kilda; All Saints', Northcote; St George's, Malvern; St Stephen's, Mt Waverley.

Charles Webb was the architect for St Paul's , Melbourne (the first church on the site of the existing Cathedral);

St. Andrew's, Brighton (with Lloyd Tayler); Christ Church, South Yarra; (Webb and Taylor); St Mark's, Fitzroy; St Stephen's, Richmond (later work); Christ Church, Dingley.

Leonard Terry was the Diocesan Architect from 1860 and as such played a prominent role in the rather stormy history of the building of the present Cathedral. He was the architect for the first extensions to St Mark's, Fitzroy in 1865. Charles Webb was also involved with later extensions in 1876, this church being attributed to James Blackburn Jnr from 1853. Terry's own work, and later with his partner, Percy Oakden, is found at Holy Trinity, Williamstown; St John's, Ballarat; Christ Church, Beechworth; St Mary's, Sunbury; St Peter's, Mornington; Christ Church, Daylesford; St Paul's, Geelong; St Saviour's, Collingwood; St Matthew's, Prahran.

Purchas and Swyer, the latter being the architectural adviser to Bishop Perry for a time, were the architects for one of the unique churches in the Diocese namely, Christ Church, Brunswick, a distinctive Italianate renaissance church. Smith and Watts were responsible for the chancel and transepts and the very attractive campanile tower. This intriguing Italianate

setting became the home of Anglo-Catholic activity in later years, but in the more restrained tradition of Sarum usage rather than the ultramontane character of *Ritual Notes*. Frederick Wyatt was the architect for the sanctuary of Christ Church, as he was also the architect for Holy Trinity, Beechworth; Christ Church, Hawthorn; and for the east end of All Saints', East St Kilda in 1873-5.

Nathaniel Billings was the first architect for All Saints, East St Kilda, (1858-61) reputed to be one of the largest parish churches in the Southern hemisphere. Billings' churches are also to be seen at All Saints, Northcote; St George's, Malvern; St Stephen's, Mt Waverley; St Stephen's Richmond (additions of 1863, and 1868-76.) St Paul's Cathedral, Sale; St Thomas', Winchelsea; St John's, Cranbourne; St Margaret's, Eltham; St John's, Port Fairy; Christ Church, Warrnambool.

Many architects were responsible for only a single building, and mention must be made of the only Anglican church designed by the Roman Catholic architect, and eminent student of Pugin, William Wardell: this is St John's, Toorak. Notable also as one of the most distinguished architects of 19th century Melbourne was Joseph Reed, an exponent of polychrome

William Butterfield (1814-1900), principal architect of St Paul's Cathedral.

brick designs such as at St Jude's, Carlton, but also responsible for more traditionally based concepts as St Mary's, Caulfield; Holy Trinity, Balaclava; the Chapter House of the present Cathedral, and of course, his role as the Honorary Architect, completing the present Cathedral to William Butterfield's designs. In some cases, the architect is unknown, and possibly designs for the building emanated from a member of the congregation, or local community. Over twenty architects were each responsible for one only Anglican church building erected in the 19th century, and though some of them undertook buildings for other denominations, their work for the Anglicans is constrained to these single examples.

All of these churches of the 19th century were entirely or principally Gothic, and usually of stone. Most of them were of Early English or Decorated Gothic style. Some were erected in polychrome brick, as St Jude's, Carlton; St Barnabas, Balwyn; St James, Drysdale; St Margaret's, Eltham; St Martin's, Hawksburn.

Some notable timber churches erected in this period exist to this day – Christ Church, Tarraville; All Saints, Blackwood; The Epiphany, Meredith; All Saints, Stanley; St Cuthbert's, Menzies Creek; St Paul's,

Clunes; All Saints, Lorne. The first church erected at Bacchus Marsh, was one of the pre-fabricated iron buildings sent out to the colony in its early days, still standing, though no longer in use as a church.

The influence of the Gothic style continued into the new century, and parish churches tended to adopt their style of worship to accord with Cathedral traditions emanating from this architectural style. Large parish choirs were the order of the day, as the fading photographs in many church vestries display, hence the necessity of extensive chancels and choir stalls. Later development of parish life frequently saw the parish worship as a copy and modification of cathedral-style worship.

The erection of churches lessened considerably towards the end of the 19th century and at the beginnings of the 20th century. This was partly due to the plateau reached in the development of the metropolis, and for the Diocese the need to extend existing buildings and consolidate property. It was also partly due to the serious economic difficulties that had beset Melbourne in the last decade of the 19th century, in which many parishes throughout the Diocese were struggling financially, and what funds were available were needed for the establishment and consolidation mentioned above. As new areas were opened up they were serviced by temporary structures which have long since disappeared, or become the new parishes of this century.

Of importance for the Diocese of Melbourne, the area of the Diocese had considerably diminished by the new century, the Diocese of Ballaarat (sic) being founded in 1875, the Diocese of Bendigo in 1901, and the Dioceses of Wangaratta and Gippsland in 1902.

Before leaving the 19th century, mention must be made concerning the erection of the present Cathedral, and the tremendous difficulties that occurred between the cathedral authorities and the architect, resulting in the resignation of William Butterfield, and the appointment of Joseph Reed as honorary architect to complete the building.

Many problems had arisen over the site, and misunderstandings concerning the actual construction, which Butterfield was determined to oversee though adamantly refusing to travel to Australia. Problems about the choice of stone exemplified the situation between architect and client, and there was fault on both sides. The Melbourne authorities refused to comply with Butterfield's instructions regarding the quarrying of the stone and its proper storage until being used, as well as his requirements for its laying, but Butterfield likewise refused to submit the samples of stone he had been sent to any analysis, though being warned that the composition of sandstone in Australia was markedly different from that in Europe.

Greater sensitivity might also have been exercised in the selection of Leonard Terry as the Melbourne representative for Butterfield, and the chief overseer of his designs and their implementation, for Terry had already submitted two designs for a cathedral, both of which had been rejected. Furthermore Terry's partner, Percy Oakden, was decidedly unsympathetic to Butterfield's design and intentions. After several recriminatory letters had passed between Melbourne and London, Terry was dismissed as the Melbourne architect. But further trouble developed over instructions to the Head of Works, and eventually Butterfield's third resignation left a half-completed cathedral to be finished. Fortunately, Joseph Reed offered his help to the authorities, claiming to complete the building according to Butterfield's plans, and with some exceptions this was achieved, so that the present cathedral stands as a notable example of a very notable architect of the Gothic revival.[10]

The history of the building of the Cathedral does reflect on some of the misunderstandings and difficulties that have occurred between congregations, Diocese and architect over the 150 years, though of course exacerbated in this case by the 'tyranny of distance' in the matter of communication. There is an important reverse side to this negativity. The erection of St Paul's Cathedral on such a grand scale has provided the Diocese of Melbourne with a building that has nobly served not only the Diocese but the city and the nation as well. Cathedrals at their best are able to reach out into the non-church community on a level that parish churches simply cannot do. This service to the 'secular' as well as the 'sacred' is not always understood by church people.

The twentieth century has far fewer prominent architects at work in church building. Alexander North is a notable example, though his own works are few. The Church of the Epiphany at Meredith is a timber Gothic construction built in 1913. North was joined by Louis Williams as a junior partner, and together they were responsible for some of the best church architecture of the twentieth century, Williams in particular continuing well into the century. He died in 1980.

North and Williams were responsible for the unique semi-circular apse of All Saints', Newtown. The crowning achievement of their work together is found with two chapels. The first is that of Trinity College, within the University of Melbourne, a notable example of the Arts and Crafts tradition. This is a term applied to buildings and furnishings with an open and honest use of materials and construction[11], as the exterior and interior of this chapel well illustrate. The other building is the chapel of All Saints at Geelong Grammar School, Corio, begun in 1915 by Hudson and Wight, and modified and completed by North and Williams from 1917 to 1928.

Another notable example of the Arts and Crafts style is St Mark's, Camberwell by Rodney Alsop, built in 1927-8.

Louis Williams became almost legendary as a church architect throughout Australia but alas, some of his churches have disappeared or ceased to function as a church. St Andrew's, Clifton Hill was demolished, St Stephen's Darebin, and St Luke's, Brighton are now in private hands, and St Paul's, Malvern has been wilfully desecrated by modern treatment. St George's, Flemington remains as a good example within the Diocese of Williams' work, and particularly of the growing necessity in the middle of the century to erect a building that could serve as church and hall. Williams built the new church

St Faith's, Burwood.
Architects: Mockridge, Stahle and Mitchell, 195

Side chapel, St Faith's, Burwood.

of St Andrew's, Brighton after the disastrous fire there, incorporating as a chancel, the original nave by Charles Webb which had remained intact. Williams was also responsible for the re-building of St John's, Camberwell after a similar disastrous fire. The suburbs of Melbourne contain many examples of Williams' workmanship, and his work spreads far beyond these boundaries.

The latter part of the twentieth century has seen a change from the Gothic style. This has no doubt been forced by changes in the liturgy of the church, and the greater role now accorded to the participation of the laity. Many churches designed for the parochial/cathedral style of worship have been altered to suit

modern tastes and practices, with varying degrees of success. One of the most successful alterations was that made by Gary van Trompf to St Linus', Merlynston. Some changes have come into effect by sensitive treatment from parishioners, to modify their inheritance for altered circumstances, such as at All Saints, Preston.

Several entirely new churches have been built with current liturgical concepts in mind. The firm of Mockridge, Stahle and Mitchell has been responsible for many new buildings within the diocese. St Faith's, Burwood; St George's, Reservoir; the extensions to Holy Trinity, Doncaster; St Stephen's, Mt Waverley; St Michael's, Beaumaris; the chapel of Ridley College, Melbourne; the chapel of Ivanhoe Grammar School.

St George's, East Ivanhoe is the work of Grounds, Romberg and Boyd, whilst Wystan Widdows has been the architect for All Saints, Rosebud, and All Saints' North Footscray. John Rosenthal was the architect for St Aidan's, Noble Park.

The real threat to existing churches in the Diocese is the shift in population and the decline of congregations, which forces the closure of some churches. The problem then remains for the Diocese to consider the proper approach to these buildings, many of which are fine examples of ecclesiastical architecture, and many of which are an integral part of our social history.

St Philip's, Collingwood; St Andrew's, Clifton Hill; and St Matthias', North Richmond; have all disappeared under the wreckers' hands. Some churches have been sold to other denominations, especially those of the Orthodox Churches. Some are destined to become studios, professional rooms, residential apartments, restaurants, or devoted to some commercial activity.

There is a great problem facing the church in the matter of these redundant buildings, and sometimes the quick decision proves to be a false one. St Philip's, Collingwood was abandoned and demolished under the belief that the suburb was becoming devoid of residential population and more and more emerging as an entirely industrial suburb. This process was arrested. Not only were several high-rise residential apartments built in the parish, but much of the remaining housing has been gentrified. The industry has diminished rather than increased, and the church is now called on to exist in the midst of this new community with very reduced plant and facilities.[12]

Similarly, there is a great problem in the adaptation of existing buildings to modern needs without defacing and destroying a building with inappropriate additions and alterations. Demolishing a stone or brick wall and replacing it with plate glass does not increase the interest of passers-by to the extent that they wish to join the church, and picture-window views of the passing traffic can be detrimental in the extreme to devotion, worship, and community.

The Diocese of Melbourne has a rich heritage in its cathedral and parish churches, a heritage which needs careful understanding and care. There are generations to come that need to be served as well as our own. Architects need to have a sound and proper briefing of the requirements of the congregation, and congregations need to have a proper understanding of the mission of the church, as a centre of worship and pastoral care, as well as a meeting place between God and humanity. Education on all sides in needed.

1   Kenneth Henderson, 'Anglicanism in Australian Life', *Anglican Review*, No. 4, October 1948, pp. 27. seq.

2   Ross Border, *Church and State in Australia 1788-1872*, London, 1962, p. 38, quoted from Henry Jacob, *Colonial Church Historians*, New Zealand, 1889, p. 6.

3   Alexander Sutherland, *Victoria and its Metropolis - Past and Present*, facs.ed. Vol. IIB, Melbourne, 1888, p. 532.

4   J.M. Freeland, *Melbourne Churches 1836-51*, Melbourne, 1963, p. 45.

5   *Ibid*, pp. 46-7.

6   Albert McPherson, That Uncomfortable Genius: a study of the building of St Paul's Cathedral, Melbourne, and the role of its architect, William Butterfield, 1878-1884, MA thesis, University of Melbourne, 1980, p. 14; *Port Phillip Gazette*, 9 February, 1848; J.M. Freeland, op. Cit., p. 51; Maie Casey, *Early Melbourne Architecture*, Oxford, 1953, p. 76.

7   Miles Lewis (ed), *Victorian Churches: their origins, their story and their architecture*, National Trust, Melbourne, 1991, p. 6. Geoffrey Serle, *The Golden Age*, Melbourne, p. 336,

8   References to churches of the Diocese in the rest of this chapter are extracted from the invaluable record of Miles Lewis and his associates in Victorian Churches.

9   Albert McPherson, op. cit., p. 19. *Minutes of the Church Assembly 1: 466*, 15 January 1864, 1. 481, 482, 21 January, 1864.

10 Paul Thompson, *William Butterfield*, London, 1971; Albert McPherson, op cit., p. 206.

11 Miles Lewis, *op cit.*, p. 158.

12 John Henwood and Tom Hazell (eds), *The Future of our Historic Churches*, National Trust, Melbourne, 1988.

At the laying of the foundation stone of St John's Church, LaTrobe Street in 1854, it is recorded that the Band of the 40th Regiment played the National Anthem and a selection of vocal and instrumental music.[1] No mention of any hymns, nor of what the musical items were, but this is an interesting comment on the music chosen for special liturgical occasions.

It is evident that music played an important part in the worshipping life of the church in this settlement of Melbourne from its earliest years, though the records are rather meagre with their information. In the *Church Record* of 1855, there is an article commending music in worship, but in rather non-specific terms,[2] though as another article a year later indicates there could be a somewhat dismal appreciation of the role of music:

> art is short, and time is fleeting, and our hearts, though stout and brave, still like muffled drums are beating funeral marches to the grave.

The article elaborates in this mood claiming that 'Christian musicians should be "born again", for music is couched only in terms of the heavenly choir, and meanwhile we walk as it were in the crypt or subterranean chamber of life.'[3] One hopes that the writer never composed any music.

In 1858, a new hymn book was sought for the parish of Prahran, and a suggestion was made that there was a need for an Australian Hymn Book, a book for use with the consent of all the dioceses.[4] This was a rather surprising suggestion this, seeing that it took over a hundred years to come to fruition and then not in a strictly Anglican hymnal but in an ecumenical dimension. The 1850s revealed that music was coming to play an increasingly important role in worship, not only in hymn singing and the use of music for congregational responses, but also in the establishment of choirs, though some writers of the period expressed antagonistic views regarding individual singing and singers.[5]

There were three factors influencing the role of music in the early life of this Diocese. Firstly, the beginnings of the Diocese were also the beginnings of a revival of music in the Church of England. After a prolonged period of dereliction in matters liturgical and musical, the established church began to rediscover its musical heritage in the mid 19th century. Secondly, the role of cathedrals played

2. Music

a major part in the recovery of an authentic musical life of the church, though this did not apply in Melbourne Diocese until the erection of the present cathedral and its opening in 1891. Before that date, the revival of music in worship had been taken by leading parish churches throughout the Diocese. Thirdly, the 19th century was the era when the organ became dominant over all other forms of musical accompaniment, and instrumental music almost entirely disappeared from regular services. The acquiring and building of organs begans to gather pace in the 1850s.

From the very beginning of the Diocese, church musicians played an important part in the general musical life of the community, for until the Great Exhibition of 1880 there were no established orchestras, and few orchestral concerts of any note. Concerts were mainly devoted to choral music and individual singers. A good deal of music making was largely domestic and private. Musicians earned their living by teaching, and a few of them found spasmodic employment playing in the orchestras of the various theatres. Sometimes, lengthy seasons of opera, provided them with better opportunities, such as occurred with the Lyster Opera Company and other companies, in their frequent seasons in Melbourne.[6] Many leading singers of visiting opera companies sang in churches, though mainly in Roman Catholic churches.

It was an era when church musicians, none of them in full time employment, and few of them paid anything like a livable salary, eked out their livelihood by teaching, training choirs, examining music students, conducting, and promoting concerts and recitals wherever possible. This was also an era of many choirs, both within the community, and within the various parish churches. To this day when visiting a parish, or when perusing their records or written histories, photographs of choirs of all sorts and sizes invite examination. Some are mixed, male and female; some are the traditional cathedral composition of men and boys; some are small in number, some quite large, with thirty to forty members. Moreover, most of these choirs wore some form of liturgical dress, usually cassock and surplice, or gown, and for the women, a kind of mortar-board or similar cap.

In accordance with the traditional form of Gothic architecture which pervaded the Diocese, with the placing of antiphonal choir stalls between altar and people, most parishes formed some sort of choir. Some of the leading parishes formed very good choirs which often provided the basis for secular choirs. The 19th century was an age of choral music; many oratorios and cantatas being written by first-line composers, and dozens of them by second-rate composers. A few of them, by both lots of composers, exist to this day. One of the early Precentors of the Cathedral, Alfred Wheeler, composed numerous cantatas, secular as well as sacred, for Sunday Schools, some of which endured well into this century.

In Melbourne, the choral tradition in parishes commenced quite early, and Bishop Perry in a famous incident after his visit to St Stephen's, Richmond in 1857, wrote passionately against the intonation of responses at Morning and Evening Prayer, and the singing of anthems. Unless the setting was extremely simple, he wrote, it should not be used, and as for anthems they were best restrained to those places so designated in the Prayer Book *Quires and places where they sing*, which in Perry's opinion meant Cathedral churches and not parishes.[7]

Perry berated his protege, Henry Handfield, for introducing a surpliced choir into St Peter's, Eastern Hill, and

St Paul's Cathedral organ, built by T.C. Lewis,
one of the greatest organ builders of the second
half of the nineteenth century; restored 1991.

boycotted visiting the parish for some seven years.[8] Nevertheless, music in the Diocese began to flourish in spite of him, not because of him. St Peter's by its development of musical ideas from the Oxford Movement , and under the guidance of Canon Handfield, introduced music more and more into the liturgy.[9]

One of the notable parish churches with a fine choral tradition was All Saints, East St Kilda, which played a vital role in the forming of the choir of the present cathedral. Other parishes were also noted for their musical tradition, and many church organists and musical directors were also part of the staff at various academies, schools, and the conservatoria of music.

The influence of church musicians and the heritage they passed on was predominantly that of England, though continental influence from Europe cannot be discounted. Dr George Torrance had great success as a musician before he studied for holy orders, including studies in Leipzig. He came to Melbourne in 1869, and held positions at Christ Church, South Yarra; St John's, LaTrobe Street; All Saints, Geelong; and finally at Holy Trinity, Balaclava. He was Acting Principal of Trinity College and brought his musical gifts to bear in the founding days of that institution. In 1888, he was instrumental in choosing and forming the cathedral choir in preparation for the opening of the cathedral in 1891, and supervising their training and singing alongside All Saints choir, East St Kilda.

After the opening of St Paul's Cathedral, the Cathedral organists played a significant part

Dr A.E. Floyd, organist of St Paul's Cathedral, 1915-47.

64

in the musical life of Melbourne. The first organist, Ernest Wood, commenced regular organ recitals which are still a feature of the musical program of the cathedral to this day. Wood is also accredited with the first performances in Melbourne of Bach's 'Passion according to Matthew', Brahms' 'German Requiem' and Stainer's 'The Crucifixion'.[10]

Dr A.E. Floyd widened the repertoire of the choir introducing a good deal of Tudor music. Floyd also achieved great fame as a broadcaster with his famous session 'The Music Lover' until almost the time of his death in 1972. Floyd was the inheritor of the best in the English tradition of church music, being associated at Cambridge with A.H. Mann (King's College), Sir Charles Villiers Stanford (Trinity College), and George Garrett (St John's College). Aside from this Cambridge inheritance, Floyd had also been the pupil of G.B. Arnold at Winchester Cathedral. His links thus went back to S.S. Wesley.[11] Floyd's influence on music in Melbourne and indeed throughout Australia was immense. Apart from his radio broadcasts he gave lectures to the Workers' Educational Association, founded Bach-Handel festivals at the cathedral in 1946 with Sir Bernard Heinze, and was the general music critic

for the Melbourne *Argus* for many years. He brought to the cathedral choir an international reputation, but alas, disagreements over the re-building of the Lewis organ, and constant irritations between the organist and chapter led to his resignation amid great acrimony. It was not one of the Cathedral's finest hours, nor, in some measure, was it one of Floyd's.[12]

A similar influential musician in Melbourne was the long-time organist and musical director at St Peter's Eastern Hill, Arthur Nickson, who was also a general music critic for the Melbourne *Age*. He studied in England with Sir Walter Parratt, who was the pupil of George Cooper, who was the pupil of Attwood, who had studied with Mozart. Nickson (or Nicky as he was popularly known) was also a great friend of Karg-Elert, himself a pupil of Reinecke and Jadasshon, the former being a pupil of Mendelssohn and Schumann, the latter a pupil of Liszt. So the English tradition was by no means insular, but had many links with Europe.[13] Nickson taught from 1901 – being a teacher and lecturer at the Conservatorium within the University of Melbourne, the organist and choir master of St Peter's, Eastern Hill, a foundation examiner for the Australian Music

Examination Board, and musical director of Melbourne Grammar School.[14]

Since then no other church musicians have had such great influence upon the general musical life of Melbourne and beyond.

The weekly broadcast of Choral Evensong from an Australian cathedral was a popular feature of the ABC for many years, and was withdrawn not without considerable protest. After the Second World War, this influence of church musicians on the wider musical world has diminished very much. This was already happening with the introduction of radio in the 1930s and the consequent disappearance of many amateur choirs and musical groups. With the establishment of fully professional orchestras in all capital cities, and the proliferation of high quality, concert programs, a full time musical profession became available outside church circles. Most states now have full- or part-time opera companies, highly accomplished instrumental groups, and choral singing has reached higher standards of performance than were once widely possible. The general populace is no longer dependant as it once was on the church for a musical outlet, and the disappearance of church choirs has speeded since the 1940s. Parish churches such as All Saints'

East St Kilda; Christ Church, St Kilda; Christ Church, South Yarra; St John's, Toorak; St Mark's, Camberwell; St Andrew's, Brighton; St John's, Camberwell; Holy Trinity, Kew; Holy Trinity, Surrey Hills; St Dunstan's, Camberwell; Christ Church, Brunswick; St Peter's, Eastern Hill; to name but a few, all had choirs of considerable expertise. Now some of these choirs have ceased, and most of them are persisting under changed circumstances and great difficulties, struggling to maintain standards, and only a few continue with consistently notable achievement. Nowadays one frequently meets older men throughout the Diocese, some no longer associated with the church, who trace back their religious connection to the days when they sang as a treble in one of the several choirs of the Diocese. They seem to be a rapidly disappearing breed.

St Paul's Cathedral has maintained a daily choral Evensong since its foundation, but this is done amidst great and increasing difficulty, and mostly without the appreciation or notice of the Diocese, though high praise and appreciation often comes from non-church circles. Regular organ recitals by local and visiting organists are given and several recordings of the organ and choir have been made.

If this unique tradition of a cathedral choir should disappear, it would be a great loss to Melbourne, and one which would be very difficult to replace or revive.

It could be argued that standards of music in the parish churches had sadly deteriorated for several reasons by the early 20th century. A good deal of the music composed was of an inferior quality, and the standard of direction and performance often left much to be desired. Some choirs became just incapable of performing some music. A good deal of blame for this situation must lie with the church itself, particularly in the matter of theological education, and many priests were ordained without the slightest appreciation of the nature of the ministry of music in the church.[15] This crucial matter of theological education has not improved much, if at all, to the present time, though the introduction of the Royal School of Church Music into the Diocese in 1933 greatly improved matters on the musical side, and has to a degree arrested the deterioration. Each year many church musicians in the Diocese attend the annual conference of the RSCM and try to bring the knowledge gained into parish music. There is much conflict in all parishes between the role of the choir and congregational participation, between conservative, traditional values in music, and modern approaches, but the work of the RSCM is trying to provide an answer.

Most importantly, there has arisen a serious gap between music for the public and music for the church. For far too long, too many serious musicians have disdained to compose 'church' music, and the church tended to cling to the 19th century until well into the present century. A few settings for Morning and Evening Prayer and for the Holy Communion, plus some motets and anthems, have not produced a great abundance of enduring music, and much that was written for churches has already passed into oblivion. Composers who write orchestral, instrumental, vocal or operatic music, do not often turn their attention to the church and its liturgy. There may be some truth in the allegation that modern composers do not understand the church, its theology and its liturgy, but they could be guided. There is no record that Mozart, Bach, Haydn, Montiverdi, Palestrina, or for that matter Stainer, Stanford and Wesley were told that their music did not fit the church, or required theological cleansing. The absence of many Australian composers of stature composing for the church is alarming. There is a great need for someone to study why this gap between secular and sacred music has occurred, and mostly in this century.

If you want to hear a good deal of the rich heritage of church music today you must go to the concert hall, or listen to recorded music rather than expecting to hear it in the church. Some of our attitudes regarding our music need to be re-examined, and there are surprising anomalies. We are told by theological and liturgical experts that young people will not tolerate plainsong or Gregorian chant. Yet a recent release of Gregorian chant by some monks has been top of the charts, and the writer last heard it being played at the Myer Music Bowl in winter, for hordes of young people ice-skating!

There are some signs that this gap is being bridged, as church musicians, choirs and congregations come to grips with modern musical forms. In the early 1970s the Cathedral experimented for some time with rock Masses and rock Evensongs, attracting huge congregations of young people. Rock operas featuring leading pop singers of the day also brought large crowds. Unfortunately, there was rarely any rapport

St Peter's, Eastern Hill Choirboys' picnic, late 19th century.

between these congregations and other assemblies at different service times.

The disappearance of choirs from most of our churches, and the expense of building a pipe organ in the newer churches, has meant that congregations have come to rely on other musical instruments, and other types of music. Some forms of accompaniment, however, such as the guitar, are not always fully supportive of congregational singing.

All this has had the unfortunate result of creating a hostile division in the church, not least by partisan congregations as well as musicians, between classical music

and popular forms such as jazz , folk, and rock; and between natural performances and electronic styles. Some places are trying to bridge this gap by special services at appointed times with one form of music or the other. Some churches try to make a combination of various styles within the one service.[16] Some churches have resolutely refused to

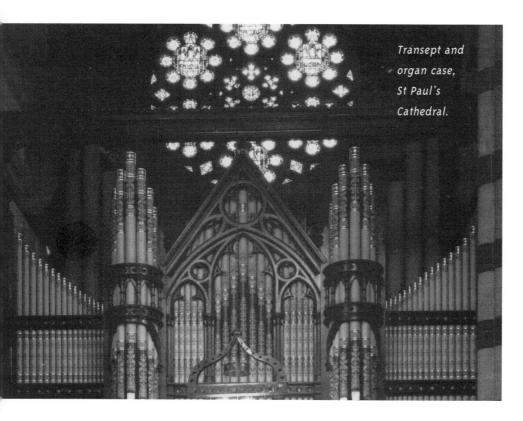

Transept and organ case, St Paul's Cathedral.

countenance any but their own particular favourite style. Some places expunge any form of music that does not facilitate congregational participation, but not all forms of modern music are suitable for this, any more than elaborate settings or difficult classical harmonies. A suggestion has been made that the problem will not go away until we have a system of proper training and appreciation for both clergy and musicians, and one might add, for congregations too.[17] A good deal of musical presentation in the Diocese is lacking in adequate talent, and when the talent does exist, lacking in adequate preparation and rehearsal. This is a common fault with all non-professional forces.

The development of organ building in the young colony was an interesting matter as it was nurtured principally by the churches and their perceived need of a proper musical accompaniment according to the latest tastes in church music. In the commencement of the settlement, it seems that the music of services (mainly hymns) got under way with the help of a Precentor or hymn-starter. Sometimes, flutes or recorders seem to have been used, and a seraphine was used in some early churches as at St James Church until the installation of a pipe organ from overseas in 1842.[18]

Organ builders were at work in Melbourne as early as 1842, assembling organs imported from England. One such builder was James Moyle, who erected a Bevington organ in St Stephen's, Richmond in 1853, and was responsible for the first locally manufactured organ - the Moyle Organ, now restored at St Linus' Church, Merlynston.[19]

Peter Hurlstone, who was a miller and timber merchant, built organs including one at St Andrew's, Brighton.[20] The most notable of the early builders was George Fincham, whose descendants carried on his firm into the latter part of the 20th century. Fincham can be said to have established the local organ building industry in Melbourne.[21]

The Victorian Organ Society was inaugurated by Herbert Davis in 1938, and most Anglican organists throughout the Diocese became members. The first choral/organ festival was held in St Paul's Cathedral in 1944 with an attendance of

I 700. These developments led to the establishment of the Australian College of Organists in 1966, the Melbourne Harpsichord and Organ Festival from 1971, and the Organ Historical Trust of Australia in 1976.[22] The latter organisation has fought to retain and restore notable organs throughout the country.

A rather confused picture emerges of the relationship of music in this Diocese at the end of the 20th century. There is a reluctance on the part of the church to pay for adequate musical resources, which pertains to this Diocese as to any other. Many of the organs of the Diocese fell into disrepair, necessitating huge sums of money for restoration, when an ongoing commitment to regular maintenance might have saved much finance and anguishing over costs.

With a few exceptions, the church has not encouraged the writing of new music, especially by commissioning Australian composers, and there seems to be no resource for doing so, nor much interest in establishing such. The Diocese in its theological education pays almost no attention whatever to the musical training of its clergy, but puts them into positions within the Diocese where they can exercise great influence and authority over music - its performance and its performers.

Furthermore, the church very often does not pay its organists and musicians anything like an adequate remuneration. Church vestries and diocesan authorities have no hesitation paying for architects' fees, builders' fees, paying for plumbing, plastering, painting, lighting, furnishings, and printing, but when it comes to the performing arts in particular, the argument too often goes 'surely the artist will contribute their livelihood as a gift to God?' The church has always maintained the New Testament injunction that the labourers are worthy of their hire when applied to clerical stipends, but it needs to review this when it comes to matters of adequate reward and adequate training in one of the most important aspects of the church's worshipping life.

1   *Messenger*, March 1854, p. 91.

2   *Church of England Record*, September 1855, p. 18.

3   *Ibid.*, May 1856, p. 89.

4   *Ibid.*, April 1858 p. 43.

5   *Ibid.*, October 1858, p. 116; November 1858, p. 138.

6   John Byrne, *Echoes of Home: Music at St Francis'*, Melbourne, Melbourne, 1995.

7   Arthur de Q Robin, *Charles Perry: Bishop of Melbourne*, pp. 136-7.

8   *Ibid.*, p. 160.

9   Paul Harvie, The First Sixty Years of Music at St Paul's Cathedral, Melbourne, 1887-1947, M. Mus thesis, University of Melbourne, 1983.

10 *Ibid.*, p. 19.

11 *Ibid.*, p. 22; Bruce Naylor, 'Musical Melbourne 50 years ago' *Victorian Organ Journal*, October 1986. pp. 26-7; William. F Chappell, 'A.E.Floyd' *Victorian Organ Journal*, Vol. 2, No. 11, September 1974, p. 9.

12 *Chapter Minutes*, Sept 1946, June 1947, St Paul's Cathedral archives; *Herald*, June 7, 1947.

13 Ian Mair, 'A.E.H. Nickson' *Victorian Organ Journal*, Vol. 7, No .5, April 1979, p. 8.

14 Bruce Naylor, *op. cit.*, pp. 26-7.

15 David Cole, *Problem of Culture as Communication: Pastor and Cantor Roles in Australian Churches Today*, lecture at Symposium on Church Music in Australia, Sydney, 25 May 1991.

16 Reita Mason, 'Church Music - integrity and idiom', *Church Scene* 9 September 1994.

17 David Cole, *op. cit.*, passim.

18 E.N. Matthews, *Colonial Organs and Organ Builders*, Melbourne, 1969, p. 54.

19 John Maidment, 'Victoria's Oldest Organ?', *Victorian Organ Journal*, April 1984, passim.

20 J.M. Freeland, *op. cit.*, p. 24.

21 J.N. Matthews, *op. cit.*, p. 9.

22 Joy Hearne, 'Forty Years On'. *Victorian Organ Journal*, Vol. 6, No. 8, July 1978, passim.

3. Art

The range of subjects under this title is vast, and must include what some people would probably prefer to designate as craft, as well as embracing the performing arts. For those people who consider art in terms only of painting and sculpture, the Anglican Diocese of Melbourne does not contain great treasures.

There are few original paintings to be found in churches, and two notable examples of recent Australian artists are in the Cathedral. John Coburn's 'Missa Cantata', bought from one of the Blake Prize Exhibitions hangs in the Readers' Chapel of the Cathedral, and in the Chapel of Unity in the south aisle, iconic paintings of St Peter and St Paul by Wendy Stavrianos surround the bronze candlestick of unity by Michael Meszaros. The candlestick is the gift of Pope John Paul II presented to the people of Victoria to be kept in perpetuity in the Cathedral, and to mark his visit there in 1989, St Paul's being only the third non-Roman Church the Pope had visited at that time. A series of studies on the Stations of the Cross by the late David Fitts, hang in St George's, Reservoir, and these examples really comprise the collection of major paintings. Not many!

Other examples of painting around the Diocese tend to be of a minor order, such as the Nicholas Draffin panels in the pulpit of Christ Church, Brunswick, and the painted altar cross in Trinity College Chapel. Esther Paterson's Madonna hangs in St Silas', Albert Park. St Peter's, Eastern Hill contains several 19th century copies of well-known paintings such as Raphael's 'Madonna of the Chair' and Andrea del Sarto's 'Madonna', and two of the paintings are considered to be original, one by a follower of Reni, and another by Ferrata, from the 17th century.[1] Several churches have copies of the famous and ubiquitous Arundel Prints, in fact, reproductions of famous paintings abound in odd corners and corridors, and many a Sunday School was littered with reproductions of Margaret Tarrant and Elsie Anna Wood. This is not a great field of artistic merit.

Several times in recent years there have been art exhibitions of considerable merit, where priests and laity have tried to explore the nature of art and religion. A notable exhibition for some years has been the travelling Blake Prize, which the Cathedral sponsored for some time until finance ran out. Parishes such as St John's, Croydon; St Agnes', Glenhuntly; and several others frequently promote an art exhibition, usually as a part of some anniversary celebration. Unfortunately, the aim of

Three sculptures at Ivanhoe Grammar School.

above: The Boyhood of Christ by Eva Schubert.

right: The Holy Family by Paul Kucera.

far right: The Holy Trinity by Eva Schubert.

encouraging local art and artists has not met with a great response from the church.

Sculpture has fared somewhat better, though the examples tend to be mainly confined to relief work on architectural piers or walls. Notable are the bronze reliefs of the Stations of the Cross by Andor Meszaros and his son Michael, hanging in Trinity College Chapel, and in the chapel of Ivanhoe Grammar School, and several medallions by Andor Meszaros are memorial tablets in the cathedral. A good deal of sculpture exists throughout the Diocese in the form of marble, stone or cast metal relief in the various memorial tablets that cover the walls of the parish churches. M.P. Jageurs was the artist for the relief of Bishop Perry in the carving above the sedilia in the Cathedral, but in many cases the names of these artists are unknown. Walter McGill was the sculptor for the stone carvings on the corbels of the chancel arch in St John's, Port Fairy, and also for the font, carved in 1854-5, making St John's one of the earliest churches with sculpture.[2]

Carving, mostly in wood, is well represented in the furnishings of many churches, such as the work of McGill mentioned above in St John's, Port Fairy. William Howitt was a notable carver, his finest work being seen at the Cathedral in the carving of the pulpit, the throne, the litany desk, and the choir and canons' stalls. These furnishings were the design of Joseph Reed, and in keeping with the traditions of the Camden Society. The later addition of a rood screen was designed by Walter Butler, and carved by White and Joseph Kanaluik.[3] It is reputed that the distinguished carver, Robert Prenzel, worked on this screen, though this has recently been questioned. Prenzel certainly was responsible for the lectern in St Peter's, Eastern Hill, and for carving in St John's, Toorak. Howitt was also the carver for the fine reredos and frontal of the high altar of Holy Trinity, Kew.

Some fine carvings for the churches and chapels in the Diocese have been produced in recent years by such local artists as Minivitch, Schubert and Hans Knorr. St Peter's, Eastern Hill has one of the few statues in a church, a Christ figure, a replica of a carving by the Danish sculptor, Thorvaldsen, as well as the crucifix behind the pulpit by the Swiss carver, Emil Thoman.[4] Two small carvings of angels by Ola Cohn are placed on the pillars at the entrance to the Lady Chapel. St John's, Croydon; St John's, Sorrento; and Ivanhoe Grammar School Chapel have excellent examples of wood sculpture.

The Arts and Crafts Movement established in England in the latter part of the 19th century has exercised a great influence on ecclesiastical art in Australia, particularly at the beginning of this century, and the publication of *Instrumenta Ecclesiastica*, under the auspices of the Camden Society, later called the Ecclesiological Society, containing designs by William Butterfield has influenced greatly church furnishings, ornaments, and decoration.[5] The cathedral communion plate holds examples of vessels made to Butterfield's designs, presented to the first St Paul's Church in 1854, and passed on to the cathedral where they are still in daily use.[6]

Metalwork by gold and silversmiths was at first imported but then began to be made locally. Alongside individual artists, commercial firms such as Pelligrini's, Steeth, and Gaunt's were responsible for both imported and local artefacts, as churches sought crosses, candlesticks, communion vessels, lecterns, and bookstands. The work of individual artists has continued well into the 20th century with work by Emily Hope (Trinity College, St Anselm's, Middle Park, and private collections), Ian Rasmussen (nave altar candlesticks of the cathedral), Peter Gertler (processional candles of the cathedral, and croziers for Bishops Andrew

Curnow and Andrew St John), Robert Baines (communion vessels at All Saints, Greensborough), Ernest Fries (a considerable amount of fine, personal jewellery), John and Dan Flynn (Church of the Resurrection, Macedon), Marcus Skipper (processional cross and verger's wand), St Mark's, Camberwell.

Commercial firms such as Albion Metalware under the direction of Max Dewan, and Ecclesiastical Metalware under the direction of Rene Hampl, have been instrumental in providing many churches with distinguished communion plate and ornaments. William Marks made the very fine processional cross of the cathedral to a design of Louis Williams[7], one of the finest pieces of metalwork in the country. Steeth was the artist for some of the plate at St Peter's, Eastern Hill, and for vessels, cross and candles to the design of Louis Williams at St Andrew's, Brighton.[8] Unfortunately an inventory of the churches and their collections throughout the Diocese does not exist. In the early 1970s, the General Board of Religious Education at its bookshop in the heart of Bourke Street established a Religious Arts Department, and here local artists were encouraged to design for churches of the Diocese in metalwork, embroidery, and carving, whilst customer-

churches were urged to consider refraining from purchasing mass-produced objects, and commissioning or purchasing original objects from these local artists.

Within the category of metalwork are some very good examples of communion railings, such as those at Trinity College Chapel, and the cathedral (by F.C.W. Richards).

Mosaic and opus sextile work is a decorative feature of churches. The great reredos of the high altar in gold mosaic at the Cathedral was imported from the Murano Works of Venice, Italy, and designed by the London firm of Clayton and Bell.[9] Venetian mosaics were a part of the Great Exhibition of 1880, and mosaics found their way into St Peter's, Eastern Hill; St Mark's, Fitzroy; and St Agnes', Glenhuntly amongst others.[10]

A fine example of opus sextile work is seen at St John's, Toorak, and in the Readers' Chapel of the Cathedral. Many memorial tablets were executed in this style. Floor mosaics feature in the chancels of many of the earlier churches. The Cathedral is entirely covered with tiles from Maw Jackson of England and laid locally by Brooks, Robinson of Melbourne.[11] Wall tiling has largely passed out of fashion, and the wall tiling of the Cathedral is generally

considered to be obtrusive and contrary to Butterfield's concept or design.

Some of the 19th century churches are rich in decorative stencilling, a favourite form of decoration in the Victorian era. Notable are the two St Kilda churches of All Saints and Christ Church.

By far the greater art in Anglican decoration of churches is that of stained glass, and the Diocese is rich indeed in many fine examples of this art, from overseas as well as by local artists. The art of stained glass had not been favoured by architects of the classical style, and had declined until the Gothic Revival, when it was restored to favour very strongly, in domestic as well as public buildings.[12] The 19th century saw many firms making stained glass established in Melbourne, most of them now defunct, and when Melbourne achieved some prosperity after the gold discoveries churches could afford stained glass decoration.[13]

Local firms quickly established themselves. Such a firm was Ferguson and Urie, which started out as plumbing business and commenced stained glass work in the 1850s.[14] This firm produced some fine examples of grisaille glass, a notable example being the east window of St James' Old Cathedral. One of their earliest

*Processional Cross
by William Mark,
c. 1931.*

PHOTO: NATIONAL GALLERY OF
VICTORIA

compositions is the Prince Consort window at Holy Trinity, Kew. Another Prince Consort window was that of old St Paul's Church, now in St John's, Sorrento. Windows at St Peter's, Eastern Hill; All Saints, East St Kilda; St John's, Toorak; Christ Church, St Kilda and Christ Church, Brunswick are samples of this firm's expertise.

A highly successful local artist in stained glass was William Montgomery, with examples of his work at St Columb's, Hawthorn; St John', Heidelberg; St Jude's, Carlton; Christ Church, Hawthorn; Christ Church, St Kilda; Holy Trinity, Williamstown, and Christ Church, South Yarra.[15]

By the turn of the century, Brooks Robinson was the largest and most dominant firm in stained glass and remained so until the firm closed in the 1960s. At one stage the noted painter William Frater worked as an artist with this firm.[16]

Stained glass windows became almost the most popular form of memorial throughout the Diocese. Much stained glass was imported from abroad, that of the cathedral being acknowledged to be the most important single corpus of 19th century stained glass in Melbourne. Most of the work comes from Clayton and Bell, featuring the life of Christ in the nave windows of the south aisle, and the life of St Paul in the windows of the north aisle. The great Te Deum window of the (liturgical) West end of the cathedral is a masterly composition of colour and design.[17]

Clayton and Bell windows are also to be found in Holy Trinity, Balaclava; St George's, Malvern; St John's, Toorak; and All Saints, East St Kilda. Windows from John Hardman are in Christ Church, Hawthorn, and from another overseas firm, Gibbs and Howard in Holy Trinity, Balaclava, and Christ Church, St Kilda.[18].

Stained glass art has continued into the 20th century, though on a diminished scale. One of the foremost artists in stained glass was Napier Waller, whose work is represented in several churches of the Diocese, notably in St Peter's, Eastern Hill, and St Mark's, Camberwell. There was a close working relationship between Napier Waller and the architect, Louis Williams, and a further relationship of both men with Canon Maynard of St Peter's, Eastern Hill. Maynard extended this contact with the artistic world working closely with Andor Meszaros. Recent stained glass artists include Joseph Stansfield, formerly of Brooks, Robinson, Alan Sumner, and David Wright.[19], but many churches still cling to past patterns of design rather than venturing into the present era.

The Arts and Crafts movement was very influential within the Anglican church, and this has probably been instrumental in preserving the churches of the Diocese from ghastly mass-produced factory artefacts in vesture and furnishings. One result of this was the huge output of embroidery work across the Diocese. Vestments, copes, banners, altar frontals, hangings, kneelers, cushions have been lovingly, and at times with astonishing expertise, manufactured in the Diocese. Many parishes formed their own embroidery guilds, and several outstanding examples of work were imported from overseas, usually from some of the English women's communities of the church. The fine needlework of the 19th century and up to the Second World War is rarely repeated today, fine stitching having given way to applique work.

In the work of decoration, many people would include flower-arrangement, as being truly an art form, and one in which many parish flower guilds excel, greatly enhancing the beauty of various buildings and contributing to the beauty of worship.

Nor can the performing arts of drama and dance be ignored. Although it no longer exists, the Religious Drama Society did try to bring this art form into the worship life of the church. The late Archbishop Felix Arnott wrote with concern about this.[20] He deplored the prevalence of little pious plays of no merit let loose in the parish churches. Many plays were performed with little prophetic impact on the people in the pews. Some like *Bend Thy Boughs* by James Murray were couched in the style of meditation dramas like the famous play of Henri Gheon, *The Way of the Cross*. Secular plays written for the theatre, were sometimes transferred into churches, such as T.S. Eliot's *Murder In The Cathedral*, and Dorothy Sayers *The Man Born to be King*. Some of Christopher Fry's plays like *Boy with a Cart* were performed, and the cathedral had several of the *Porch Plays* of Coventry Cathedral at Evensong in place of the sermon. During the seasons of Advent and Lent, the cathedral commissioned several local playwrights to write significant plays for those seasons performed by local professional actors.

Drama mingled with music and dance was used in a series of recitals at Trinity College Chapel, in conjunction with the now defunct Ballet Victoria and several professional actors and musicians, and dance has been used to great effect at special services in the cathedral and in various parish churches. Many of these performances have employed professional actors and dancers, just as the church has from time to time employed professional musicians,. and just as it usually employs professional artisans. Archbishop Felix Arnott expressed a rare insight into Australian aboriginal corroborees with their ritual dance as a concept of drama and religion developing side by side. The effective use of drama and dance in worship has not really been fully explored in the Anglican churches, and sometimes the attempt has been undermined by using inadequately trained performers. Too many dancing groups (nearly always entirely women) tend to look like the leaping nuns of Norwich, which does not enhance the concept of dance as a real art form. Again, the church is reluctant to pay for what it needs. As a well-trained and effective choir can lead a congregation in the music of the liturgy, so a well-trained and sensitive dancing choir can lead a congregation to participate in movement and dance within worship.

During Lent in the 1970s, Archbishop Woods used Sunday Evensongs at the cathedral to engage in discussion several leading artists in various art forms - art educationists, painters, dance, film, literature, and drama. The artists found their contact with the Archbishop as stimulating as he found contact with them. The artistic field is a wide one, and one which often provides ordinary men, women, and children of a parish with the field to exercise their artistic gifts, often alas, ignored or unexercised. Nevertheless, the church cannot do without the presence, imagination, and skill of professional artists of all kinds. Such a relationship should be fostered by the diocese to enrich the next stage of our history.

1   Information from John Jones, artistic advisor to St Peter's, Eastern Hill.

2   Miles Lewis, *Victorian Churches*, p. 141.

3   Godfrey Kircher, *Cathedral Guide - St Paul's Cathedral Melbourne*, p. 19.

4   F.E. Maynard, *St Peter's, Melbourne*, Melbourne, 1947, p. 23.

5   Judith O'Callaghan, *Treasures From Australian Churches*, catalogue, Melbourne, 1985, p. 11.

6   Marie G Moore, Antipodaean Gothic, MA thesis University of Melbourne, 1984, p. 222.

7   Judith O'Callaghan, *op. cit.*, p. 49; Marie G Moore, *op. cit.*, p. 224.

8   Judith O'Callaghan, *op. cit.*, p. 55.

9   Marie G Moore, *op. cit.*, p. 196.

10   Roma Mathews, The Church of Saint Peter: Melbourne's Translation of the Anglican Liturgy 1846-1970, B.Litt (hons) thesis, University of Melbourne, 1992, p. 8.

11   Marie G Moore, *op. cit.*, p. 193.

12   Geoffrey Downs, 19th century Stained Glass in Melbourne, MA thesis University of Melbourne, 1975, pp. 23-4.

13   John Held, Stained Glass window programme of St Paul's Cathedral, BA Hons thesis University of Melbourne, p. 246.

14   Geoffrey Downs, *op. cit.*, p. 62. seq.

15   *Ibid.*, p. 100.

16   *Ibid.*, pp. 89, seq.

17   Joan Held, *op. cit.*, pp. 177, seq; F.R. Godfrey, *A Guide To St Paul's Cathedral, Melbourne*, Melbourne, 1906. The chapter on stained glass windows (pp 26-35) gives the most exhaustiv examination and detailed account.

18   Geoffrey Downs, *op. cit.*, p. 117.

19   Bronwyn Hughes, Alan Sumner and Joseph Stansfeld: A comparative Study of 20th Centu Stained Glass, MA thesis, University of Melbourne, 1992, p. 63.

20   Felix Arnott, 'Church and Drama' *Anglican Review*, No. 1, Part I, August 1950. Nov 1950 No12- Part II

4. Liturgy

In the early records of Anglican services in the Diocese, little or no mention is made about the manner of the conduct of services. References to the worship of the church speak about attending Morning or Evening Prayer, hearing a sermon, the taking of communion or the conducting of baptism, and no comment is made as to the manner in which these ministrations of the church were conducted. Presumably these things were done in the manner of the late 18th century England that prevailed at the home churches the settlers knew. An early statement by Bishop Broughton records the care with which he conducted the services, preached a sermon, and prepared people for confirmation, but nothing further.[1]

The effects of the Evangelical Revival in the church seem to have pertained to the early years of the diocese with its first colonists, and the evangelical churchmanship of Bishop Perry was in contrast to that of some others of the episcopate of the time: Bishop Broughton in Sydney, Bishop Tyrrell in Newcastle, Bishop Short in Adelaide. Like all the early pioneer bishops, it was inevitable that Perry should stamp his own personality and theology upon the infant diocese.[2] By the 1850s, however, the effects of the Tractarian movement were beginning to percolate through to the diocese, and find receptive clergy to nurture them.

H.H.P. Handfield at St Peter's, Eastern Hill, a protege of Perry's, was certainly influenced by the teaching of the Tractarians, as was John Herbert Gregory at All Saints, East St Kilda. Music in the services was an issue that Perry felt led to a style of worship that was not consonant with his evangelical approach, as he saw it excluding congregational participation, and promoting excessive ritualism.[3] The Bishop also opposed the notion of introducing the Church Union into his Diocese fearing not only its 'high-church' attitudes but that it would also divide his Diocese.[4]

Not long before he left the Diocese, Perry warned that he would not tolerate clergy who embraced Tractarianism which, in his opinion, was aimed at returning the Church in England to a pre-Reformation position.[5] Handfield was embroiled in trouble with Perry over the matter of introducing a surpliced choir, and Gregory was reprimanded for presenting female confirmation candidates in white veils, both of these rather trivial customs appearing to Perry to be nothing but a return to Roman Catholic customs.[6]

Pontifical High Mass at St Mark's, Fitzroy.

Below left: Dr. G.W. Torrance, Acting Principal, Trinity College, 1872-76. Experienced late nineteenth century parish priest and musician.

Perhaps Perry may have been judged too harshly in some matters, but he certainly held catholic tendencies at bay in the Diocese during his episcopate. These reins were considerably lightened during the episcopate of Bishop James Moorhouse, a broad-churchman, and his successor, Field Flowers Goe, an acknowledged evangelical, but with a degree of tolerance not shown by Perry.[7] Tractarianism did not flow immediately into ritualism, but Perry's injunctions had made the transition in Melbourne more difficult than it might have been.

Throughout the 19th century the pages of the *Messenger* are full of letters and articles taking sides in the high-churchmanship and low-churchmanship controversies that occurred from the first days of the diocese, many of the letters portraying an ignorance of the subject as well as ingrained prejudices from the past, and little sensitivity or tolerance of differing points of view. Later commentators on these parties within the Diocese accentuate the high/low/broad adjectives, but forget that the most important word in these phrases is 'churchmanship'. Allowing for the differences between people, most Anglicans maintained a firm adherence to the church however they expressed their devotion in worship. The Tractarian teachings developed slowly into practice towards the end of the century. Vestments were worn first at All Saints, East St Kilda probably in 1882, though their regular use came at St Martin's, Hawksburn in 1887.[8]

The daily Eucharist was introduced in some parishes, vestments were worn, candles introduced, but until the end of the century not much more, and that not in very many parishes. Even the adoption by the celebrant at communion of the eastward position was seen by many to be a proclamation of Roman Catholic dogma. Altar candles at St Peter's, Eastern

Hill were placed but not lighted as late as 1896. Not until after Canon Handfield's death in 1900 did a fuller expression of a catholic liturgy come into force under E.S. Hughes. The vexed controversy between protestant viewpoints and catholic has been well handled in several treatises.[9] Certainly after the appointment of Hughes as incumbent of St Peter's in 1900 upon the death of Handfield, and particularly after the introduction of incense in 1906, controversy raged in the press of the day, and tempers were tried and lost.

Whatever the standard of liturgy and its ceremonial practice, the ritual used was that of the *Book of Common Prayer* 1662. Deviations from that were rare, and usually of a private nature, or as an extra motet such as the *Agnus Dei*, sung by the choir. In spite of such groupings as the Church Association, and their continual objections to liturgical practices by some high church parishes, the atmosphere of the Diocese of Melbourne was far more tolerant than in other places.

The reform of the Prayer Book in 1927-8 was an issue closely followed in Melbourne, though little direct contribution could be made to it in view of the constitutional link of the Australian church to that of the Church of England. Some churches had followed what was called the *Interim Rite*, mainly concerned with the use of the so-called prayer of oblation in conjunction with the prayer of consecration, and in some places, the saying or singing of the *Gloria* at the beginning of the Eucharist rather than towards the end, as in the *Book of Common Prayer*. The 1928 *Prayer Book*, though never officially sanctioned and only to be used with episcopal permission, did play a role in freeing, to a great extent, the 1662 liturgy. Even churches wary of being accused of Anglo-Catholic tendencies took advantage of permissible amendments and deviations.

About the time of the Second World War, the Parish and People Movement which had begun in England during the 1930s, began to exercise an influence throughout the whole Anglican Communion, and parishes in the Diocese of Melbourne began to experiment with a more relaxed liturgy than the usual formal style of worship. A service often called a 'Family Service' or 'Parish Communion' was held at an earlier hour, usually without formal choral music but with congregational hymns, and a certain degree of lay participation by readers. Some churches had long used a 'Children's Service or Eucharist' as a way of making the liturgy simpler for young people (and often for adults as well). After the war, churches showed growing interest in the meaning and practice of liturgy. When the Australian church achieved its own constitution in 1961, the moves for a distinctively Australian prayer book gathered momentum.

By this time, many parishes had produced a booklet setting out the structure of the liturgy as it was observed in their parish, and not intended for more extended use. Many devotional books such as *Adoremus* had a wide usage. In some parishes replaced the usual prayer book in the pews, containing as it did the essential outlines of the services. Permission could be obtained for churches to experiment with the revised rites of the Church of England: Series 2, Series 2a, Series 3. Some parishes experimented (not usually on Sundays) with such rites as that of South Africa. Much more interest was engendered in liturgy than in the past, and particularly amongst the laity through well-attended workshops and seminars.

Most importantly perhaps, though not always detectable in liturgical matters, is the age of ecumenism, and the greater understanding that it has brought into liturgical studies and discussions. Fortunately, this has also been very strong at the grass roots level, and many lay people attend churches of other traditions and come to appreciate other liturgies in a way that they never did in the past. A learning process from each other has hopefully brought a greater tolerance of differing ways. Important too is the growth of charismatic churches in the Diocese, though these tend to be depots for other nearby churches to experiment in a worship where no such provision is made closer to home. But they have brought, in many cases, a freeing of the liturgy from binding shackles of the past.

Since the introduction of *An Australian Prayer Book* (AAPB) in 1978, there has been a general lack of controversy between congregations of widely varying viewpoints concerning the book and its contents. There has been criticism of course, and rightly so, and much of this has been considered. Devotees of the *Book of Common Prayer 1662* are still staunch in their adherence to it in several parishes of the Diocese, though few people have ever had the experience of a pure, unadulterated version of the 1662 *Common Prayer Book* for a considerable time, if ever. The Prayer Book Society tries to exercise as much influence as it can, but there are many parishes where people are totally unfamiliar with the *Book of Common Prayer*, and this will undoubtedly increase.

The new prayer book, *A Prayer Book for Australia* (APBA) with its permissible options for certain liturgies and occasional offices from within the total book, will bring a new era to the church which is impossible to assess at this stage. As both the *Book of Common Prayer* and *A Prayer book for Australia* continue to be authorised liturgies, no longer will all services of the church be available in one book for all the people. There is also an acknowledgment that congregations must find their own way to a large extent in the ceremonial to be used. Increased lay participation, even the vexed question of lay presidency, are matters that loom large over the state of liturgy at this moment. Practical matters such as modern technology with electronic equipment will have a far-reaching effect on liturgy than the former assumption of common prayer, and the reputation of being a 'people of the Book'.

There will be a great need of tolerance and understanding, and indeed courage as the church in this Diocese threads its way through its liturgy into the years to come.

1   Quoted by J.A. Grant from *Church in the Colonies*, Vol. II, SPG, London, 1846, p. 31.

2   David Hilliard, *Anglicanism – Australian Cultural History*, No. 7, Cambridge University Press, 1988, p. 66.

3   Arthur de Q Robin, *Charles Perry: Bishop of Melbourne: The Challenge of a Colonial Episcopate 1847-76*, Western Australia, 1967, p. 137.

4   *Ibid.*, p.139.

5   *Ibid.*, p. 160.

6   *Ibid.*, p. 161.

7   J.A. Grant, *Colonial Tractarians: The Oxford Movement in Australia*, ed. Brian Porter, JBCE, Melbourne, 1989, p. 71.

8   Colin Holden, '*Awful Happenings on the Hill*': *E.S. Hughes And Melbourne Anglo-Catholicism Before The War*, St Peter's, Melbourne, 1992, p1 no.1 p. 125.

9   Lilla Brockelbank, *Canon Hughes: Priest of God, Friend of Man*, Cambridge University Press, Melbourne, 1944; J.A. Grant, *ibid.*; Colin Holden, *ibid.*; A. de Q. Robin, *ibid.*

There are no Gothic churches being built in the Diocese today, and many that are Gothic are being transformed as far as the architecture will permit, into a setting for the liturgy greatly different from mediaeval or post-mediaeval modes. The furnishings of our modern churches are more flexible than anything from our past, and the interior decoration of churches is often of a transitory nature with home-made banners and posters, sometimes effective, sometimes hideously obtrusive. In some places, the architecture of a church has been so domesticated that it is difficult to tell the place as a house of prayer and worship rather than some commercial enterprise. Yet there is also a reaction to this as people attempt to make their church a meeting point between the human and the divine, and to alert the visitor that this is no ordinary building but a highly special building for the activity of God, men, and women, and wherein may be celebrated all those points of significance in human life – birth, marriage, death, love, and where may be also brought the hopes and failures and achievements of the individual, the community and the nation.

Music itself is undergoing transformation, and it is to be hoped that there will be greater efforts to understand and embrace all that is good in music and its ministry, both of the past, and of the present. It might be hoped that the church will not entirely abandon its great heritage from the past, nor will it neglect to encourage and nurture our own composers and musicians to bring their talents to the service of the liturgy.

Likewise with the arts, new forms are rapidly emerging which hold out many possibilities to the church for evangelism, prophecy and proclamation. Modern art forms so often alert us, even disturb and shock us, and rightly so. Music, drama, dance, and the visual arts can bring imagination that confirms as well as confronts us. Modern technology will affect changes in public celebration and worship. One of the most potent art forms of this century, that of cinema, has not been referred to, for its use in liturgy has been restricted, mainly because it is such a powerful and dominating medium, but it is doubtful whether the church can ignore this vital art form for ever.

Liturgy itself, which enshrines so much of what we say, or sing, or do, and where we say or do it, is itself an ever-remaining but ever-changing element in the life of the church. That will be the crucial

5. Summary

challenge for the years to come in this Diocese: to hold on to the faith once given to the saints, and yet to transmit it in the faith of him who said, 'behold I am making all things new'.

In the 19th century when the Diocese came into being, architecture directed the liturgy, as did 19th century musical concepts and art forms. Formulas were governed by an inheritance from England, and within a context imposed from above. The laity had not had any part in the formation of the *Book of Common Prayer*.

Now, in the late 20th century, the situation in Australia is entirely different, and for the Diocese of Melbourne as for any other part of the Australian Church. The Anglican Church of Australia is now autonomous, existing in an ecumenical environment regarding the world-wide church; this Diocese exists in an intensely secular society; in a multi-racial, multi-cultural, multi-faith community, that now dictates to architecture, music, and art, the forms it desires. The situation is akin to that of the theatre, where 19th century theatres with their proscenium arches dictated the types of plays that were written and performed. Now with open stages an entirely different form of drama emerges. Architecture is tending towards a shape and space that allows for flexible arrangements and adaptability for differing circumstances.

A peculiar Anglican music no longer dominates the church, but it is music open to many cultural elements, along with art, and all of which must surely become more sensitive to the culture of our own indigenous people as well as many other influences which may be non-European. Liturgy itself is no longer superimposed, but rises from lay participation and experience.

There is continuity with the past 150 years, but there is also an era of new ways, and new beginnings. All culture is susceptible to the vast revolution of technology that is forming the way forward, and will bring to this Diocese, as to the whole church, many challenges and many opportunities.

CHAPTER FOUR

COLIN HOLDEN

Christ Church, Brunswick. Parish cricket match, late 19th century.

Parish and Organistional life
in the Diocese of Melbourne

Geographical parishes or gathered congregations?

Given the great diversity represented by the different parishes that have made up the diocese of Melbourne since its foundation, any treatment of parish development and organisation in as small a space as this essay is bound to be highly selective. At many points, I have treated the experience of a few parishes as representative of that of many others. Beginning with the post-World War II boom, when the parish system reached its operating peak, the essay progressively moves back in time. I have been particularly interested in the emergence of a worshipping population that was not affiliated with the local parish church, before returning to the period with which the essay begins, and commenting on the developments that followed it.

. . . .

As the following figures from diocesan Year Books show, there is a sense in which the two decades following the end of the Second World War might be regarded as the golden age of the parochial system:

Table One

Year	No. of parishes	No. of communicants	Acts of Communion at Christmas	Baptisms	Sunday School scholars[1]	Confirmees	Burials
1901	117	17 878	-	4029	28 163/ 20 466	844	3189
1910-11	132	23 429	-	4694	27 026/ 19 901	2122	2161
1920-1	149	35 631	-	5750	28 873/ 21 864	2256	2660
1930-1	174	45 473	-	5540	31 643/ 23 832	3151	2835
1940-1	161	49 784	-	5101	22 710/ 16 277	3201	3547
1950-1	161	55 720	-	8447	28 357/ 20 968	3007	6185
1960-1	179	82 076	-	10 346	48 666/ 37 486	6063	5993
1970-1	220	97 095	60 059	8654	37 339/ 26 987	4521	5513
1980-1	251	89,003	51 880	5110	10 484/ 8299	1852	4615
1990-1	242	21,293	42 215	3174	5652	1049	4016

Though the number of communicants continued to rise in the 1970s, the 1950s and early 1960s still represented the point at which Anglicans in the diocese had their greatest degree of contact with the institutionalised life of their parish churches, as the decline by 1970 in the number of baptisms, confirmations and Sunday school enrolments shows. The boom of the sixties is thrown into even higher relief by the dramatic decline in the decade between 1970 and 1980. By 1980, Sunday school attendances had dropped to less than a third of the figure ten years previously. Baptisms had declined by almost half the figure for 1970. The record of the rise and fall of confirmation is particularly noticeable.

If the end of the Second World War was accompanied by an understandable hope that a new and better order was at hand, Australians found some of that hope realised as the population increased, both from immigration and the 'baby

Table Two

Anglicans in Melbourne 1901-1991[2]

Census Year	Anglicans in Melbourne	Total Population of Melbourne
1901	187 608	483 548
1911	223 905	588 971
1921	320 127	766 465
1933	359 278	991 934
1947	456 586	1 226 409
1954	539 558	1 524 111
1961	593 469	1 911 895
1966	604 943	2 110 168
1976	548 409	2 604 036
1981	492 450	2 578 759
1986	432 110	2 645 484
1991	506 834	3 022 464

1 Of the two sets of figures for each year in this column, the first represents the number of children enrolled; the second the actual number in attendance. In themselves, these two figures indicate something of the tension between expectations of various kinds, and a more limited fulfilment.

2 I am grateful to Mr Peter Sherlock for compiling this census data from the Australian Bureau of Statistics. 'Melbourne' here is taken to mean metropolitan Melbourne as defined by the ABS since 1911. In 1901 the census defined Melbourne as the area served by the MMBW. The figures given for the total population of Melbourne are obtained from those listed within the tables on religion within each census report, and can only be taken as a guide: the figures for the population of the Melbourne Statistical District for each census given in the 1985 Victorian Yearbook are about 10 percent bigger than those given here.

boom'. The level of private car ownership continued to grow; television appeared in Melbourne in 1956. Secondary industries, including housing, mushroomed, and the resultant urban growth engendered and confirmed a sense of progress in the minds of Melbournians. Rapid growth took place in parishes that had been small and comparatively isolated before the Second World War: these were now being transformed from rural villages into part of the urban sprawl. One such was Boronia. The township tripled in population between 1945 and 1957, and figures of service attendances told a similar story. The Sunday average rose from 16 in 1945 to 1948 to 23 in 1949 to 1952, then to 36 in 1953 and 109 in 1963.

The stress on family life that was part of the post-war 'baby boom' years had its impact on parish life in the high numbers of baptisms, confirmations and weddings, and in the flourishing youth groups and sports teams that were also a characteristic of many parishes during this period. Those who were seeking a new age, or a better way of life, had not yet come to the point where they indulged in deep questioning of institutions and organisations. The focus on creating a new prosperity dulled the urge to probe in the way that became axiomatic in the 1960s and 1970s. Instead, those who had only a superficial attachment to the churches often seem to have accepted the inherited institutional structures without question, as though it were simply 'business as usual'.

Youth groups were sufficiently well stocked with members to make statewide and interstate organisational changes desirable. The Church of England Fellowship, which had branches in many parishes, merged with similar groups interstate to form the Young Anglican Fellowship in 1958. The new body amalgamated with various other similar groups interstate. At St Mark's Camberwell, a flourishing middle-class parish, a local youth fellowship ran a monthly dance, attended by an average of 250 youth, had an evening social and service, and a monthly corporate communion. Sports clubs, including a football team and a tennis club, flourished there at the same time. In the developing parish of Dromana, a locally devised youth club was replaced in 1960 with a branch of CEBS, and to provide for the girls, a gym club was established. In Boronia, the stimulus for the creation of a youth group came from an existing group in Croydon under Russell Clarke, some of whose members moved to Boronia. By 1952, it had about 40 members, and as it grew, an annual ball became a significant local function, forming the initial contact point for a number of future marriage partners. A branch of the Girls' Friendly Society was commenced in the parish in 1954, and the next year, another local creation, a club to cater for children too young to join the Young Anglican Fellowship. As in Camberwell, sports teams flourished at the same time: a tennis club commenced in 1964 and a basketball club in 1962. Such a large number of organisations allowed for varying degrees of association with the parish, but was also accompanied by greatly increased numbers of worshippers at occasional services, as the parish and the local community intersected at many points. Four hundred people attended a confirmation in mid 1957.

It was not only organisations for the young that grew in this period, but also locally created groups and branches of larger organisations for men and women. At Boronia in the inter-war period, a local women's guild was founded because the vicar's wife felt that the high level of rivalry and bickering created an unsuitable atmosphere for a branch of Mothers'

The marble font from St Katherine's Abbey Church, London, presented to St James' Old Cathedral in 1845 by Superintendent C.J. LaTrobe.

Union. A branch of this latter organisation was established there in 1953: had peace and harmony eliminated the earlier competitiveness? At St Mark's Dromana, when a Mother's Union branch was founded in 1960, it enrolled a large number of young women in its membership, but at St Mark's Camberwell, the image of Mothers' Union as a more senior group was well established, and a group for young mothers was founded there in 1956 as an alternative to the diocesan organisation.

Finance was another area in which the increasing strength of parishes in the post-war period was evident. As well as the general atmosphere of hope, it was the impact of two organisations that produced greater financial commitment. In the 1950s Lewis Wells, an American air force officer who had once considered entering the ministry of the Presbyterian Church, devised the Wells scheme and ran the Wells organisation. Australia's first experience of its workings came in 1954 when G.H. Codrington, then vicar of Brighton, requested a Wells campaign. 850 parishioners attended a loyalty dinner on 5 August, and the canvass resulted in a five hundred per cent increase in parish

Christ Church, South
Yarra, begun in 1856.
Architects: Webb and
Taylor, 1856.

income. Others quickly followed suit. In 1957, St Mark's Camberwell, hosted a Wells campaign. Church attendances increased by thirty per cent, the number involved in the envelope scheme increased from 100 to 550, and the parish income in 1958 was 9 000 pounds compared with 5 500 pounds in 1956. The initial enthusiasm with which some parishes embraced the scheme also revealed the extent to which parishioners had absorbed the stress on material values that was part of the new post-war prosperity. But a number of parishes that employed its services, such as St Paul's Boronia, also criticised the Wells organisation for equating membership with financial giving. The Diocese also ran its own planned giving organisation, the Department of Promotion; amongst its early directors were Wilfrid Holt, then vicar of St Barnabas' Balwyn, and William Weston. The era of organised campaigns did not mean the end of generous gifts by individuals. At St Mark's Camberwell, the Bott family made substantial contributions towards property development: this included the gift of a property which was sold in order to provide capital for another purchase of land.

A comparison between the growth that characterised the post-war period, and the situation of a number of parishes in the period between the two World Wars, highlights the way in which new factors were at work in many areas, as well as showing elements of continuity. St Mark's, Camberwell, illustrates the steady growth of a parish in a predominantly middle-class suburb. Its first structures were planned in 1913, and by 1923, it had a Sunday School of 223 and kindergarten of 70, also a Young Mens' society founded in 1921, and a cricket club, which was suspended during the First World War. Guides and Brownies had also been established, but flourished only briefly, lapsed, recommenced in 1931, only to lapse again; in contrast, a Scout troop, founded in 1925, had a stable existence. St Mark's was the centre for large scale services: in 1930, a confirmation was attended by 1100 people, the drawcard being the presence of the Archbishop. In the 1940s, the average Sunday attendance was 580. In 1943, when the Christmas carol service was broadcast on ABC radio, there were 820 in the congregation. By contrast, St Mark's Dromana, and St Paul's Boronia, were isolated rural communities. Not that they were incapable of raising a good congregation for a special event: in 1922, a confirmation for 10 candidates at St Mark's Dromana, brought a congregation of 112, but the average Sunday attendance then was 24. At Boronia, the initiative and popularity of Guy Brown accounted for the attendance of 180 people at a service in the local Progress Hall, a number that was not to be exceeded until the 1950s; the average Sunday attendance that year was 26.

A handful of organisations of English origin was present in many parishes: the Girls' Friendly Society (GFS), introduced to Melbourne in 1881, the Mothers' Union (MU), introduced in 1895, and the Church of England Men's Society (CEMS), commenced in 1909. If English Anglicans had founded CEMS to address a perceptible inbalance between male and female in many congregations, Australian Anglicans had to contend against a national mythology of the anti-authoritarian, anti-clerical male, with his heart centred on the land. If Melbourne Anglicans were disturbed by the claim of *Melbourne Punch* in 1906 that 'men don't go to church', the enthusiastic foundation of CEMS in 1909, with 47 branches and almost 1000 members within twelve months, did not lead to a sudden or even long term redressing of the balance. By 1940, admittedly a year when its ranks were thinned by service enlistments, the diocesan Yearbook referred to a membership of about one thousand. That year when sixty-five clergy were approached for expressions of interest in the organisation, not one responded positively; a decade before, in 1930, there were fewer branches than in 1910, nor was the membership large. A comparison between its membership with that of Mothers' Union makes the *Melbourne Punch* comment about men and church seem justified. In 1920, there were about 1800 members of MU in 50 branches; by 1930, this had risen to 2000 members and 74 branches, and that same year, GFS had 76 branches in the diocese, and ran two lodges, as well as providing training for domestic service at its Barry Street establishment. Was it that the local organisations for men had a greater attraction than CEMS? Some offered what appears to be a wider range of activities, ranging from smoke nights, musical evenings, competitions in billiards or snooker, to fitness programs. At St Peter's Eastern Hill, a representative of a local gymnasium addressed men on the importance of physical development; All Saints East Saint Kilda, went one better, as its 'Church Union' (a men's club, not

to be confused with the Anglo-Catholic pressure group) at the end of the nineteenth century had its own gym equipment.

Before the 1950s, regular giving was generally by means of envelope schemes which had been introduced into many Anglican churches in Melbourne in the First World War period. St Saviour's Collingwood, completed in 1876, was Melbourne's first church to be opened with all of its pews 'free', that is, unrented. In some centres, an envelope system and pew rents went on simultaneously, as in the case of Holy Trinity, Kew. Here, an envelope system was running by 1928, vigorously supported by Frank Shann, then head of Trinity Grammar. It began in response to specific and urgent needs in maintaining and refurbishing existing property, and soon it involved two hundred contributors. But pew rents were not finally abolished at Holy Trinity until the beginning of 1948, complete with a protective clause that enabled the last renters to retain their sittings. As well as regular giving, parish fetes played a significant role in fundraising, and offered opportunity for community involvement beyond the component of the parish that were regular worshippers. At St Mark's, Camberwell, the 1923 parish fete annihilated

the debt on the parish hall, and the following year, it raised 533 pounds. At St Peter's Eastern Hill, the setting up of the fete marquee brought members of the fire brigade from the fire station on the other side of Albert Street. The opening of a fete by a notable was another way of attracting potential buyers: in 1912, the wife of Andrew Fisher, the Prime Minister, opened the Eastern Hill fete. Such occasions included fairground style entertainment for children: at Eastern Hill in 1911 it included a concert and a farce, *The Ladies' Cook*, in which the chief characters included titled gentry. If Toorak and South Yarra were there, drawn by the denizens of Government House, the children of Fitzroy and Collingwood were there also, making less polite noises, and enjoying the way in which the parish comedians poked fun at what went on in society drawing rooms.

The life of parishes in the inter-war years, and beyond, that of the first decades of the century, grew in turn out of patterns that were established in law when Melbourne was only a tiny settlement, and a decade before it was given the status of a diocese. The concept of the parish as a geographical area, in which a church served a worshipping community located within its boundaries, underlay some of the first colonial legislation that dealt with parish structures, the *Church Act* 1836, and the *English Church Temporalities Act* 1837, passed under Governor Sir Richard Bourke. Under the first of these acts, a grant of up to 1000 pounds would be made on a pound for pound basis, once private, and (it was assumed) local subscribers, had pledged at least 300 pounds to funds managed by trustees for the future building. It also regulated the size of the government grant towards the stipend of the cleric, according to population. In an area where there were one hundred adults, the annual grant was 100 pounds, where there were two hundred, 150 pounds, and where there were five hundred or more, the largest grant, 200 pounds.

Certainly the migrant in colonial Melbourne gained comfort in seeing buildings in the alien and strange landscape that recalled the world he had left behind, as though its structures were being reproduced *in toto*. The first incumbent of St Peter's Eastern Hill, Daniel Newham, wrote with satisfaction that his brand new vicarage, a delightful Gothic cottage *ornee,* was easily identified by newly arrived migrants, many of whom treated it as a source of information about prospective employment, with the vicar functioning as the operator of an amateur labour exchange. Conversely, negative comments were made about the first iron-frame churches to be imported to the colony to provide facilities for worship in the wake of the gold rush. Notionally, they were cheaper than their brick or stone counterparts: one seating eight hundred cost 1250 pounds, a sum equivalent to the cost of a much smaller stone or brick church; in reality, costs of transport and erection eroded most of the supposed financial gain. The first, which arrived without floor or fittings, was put up in Williamstown in 1853. These buildings were designed for working class mission districts in the inner suburbs of English cities; their crude functionality denied them the power of association that emanated from the buildings they tried to reproduce.

For the newcomer, the illusion that it was 'business as usual' in the parish and its structures must have been reinforced by the the presence of schools as an integral part of the plans of many of the earliest of Melbourne's parishes. St James', the original St Pauls', St John's LaTrobe Street, and St Peter's all had schools attached to them. Further down the bay, at Brighton, the first parish building was a dual purpose one, serving as school and church, and on its erection, subscriptions were sought to ensure the income of an incumbent and a schoolmaster. At East St Kilda, a parish school was precursor to All Saints Grammar School, which closed in 1930. The pattern was to be perpetuated with variations into the present century in a number of middle-class suburbs, no longer reminders of the landscape left behind, but expressions of the comfortableness – or was it middle-class enterprise? – of the suburbs in which they sprang up. Trinity Grammar School, which was established on its present site under the headmastership of G.M. Long, began as a preparatory grammar school with 33 boys in the parish hall of Holy Trinity Kew, on the initiative of A. G. Hindley. Close by, in 1925, St Mark's Camberwell, had a day school with 70 children on its roll by 1925, and two years later, it had become a girls' grammar school in its new home, 'Torrington'. In its present form, the primary school attached to Christ Church, South Yarra is a post First World War development, but had a forerunner in a parish choir school established in the previous century.

The government aid established by

Bourke's Act certainly gave some stimulus to parish development. But the ceiling of 30 000 pounds set for church grants in 1842 for both of New South Wales and the Port Phillip district meant that as the population grew as the decade progressed, the grant became progressively more and more inadequate, and new communities could not rely on it for support. Later grants, for Victoria alone, in 1851 and 1856 fixed ceilings of 30 000 pounds and 50 000 pounds respectively. Committed Anglicans, whether clerical or lay, regarded the eventual and inevitable withdrawal of state aid, first for stipends, and then for schools, as crisis points, at which the real autonomy of the church would be dependent on the degree of financial support given by the laity. But while there was an extent to which church-state separation forced a degree of independence, there was also a degree to which parish growth reflected a body of laity with initiative and committment. It was in many cases the initiatives of committed laity that created the earliest patterns of worship in many centres, before the establishment of the structures that received legal recognition in the Bourke Act. At Brighton in the early 1840s, Henry Dendy conducted evensong in his first home on the corner of New and Wells Streets; in the early 1860s, parishioners of St Peter's met for regular worship in an East Melbourne schoolroom. And as city and suburbs developed, these patterns were repeated, particularly on the fringes.

In an area such as Fern Tree Gully, the smaller worshipping communities met in a number of private homes and schoolrooms until after the First World War.

The basic requirement for the staffing of a parish was a priest incumbent, who might be assisted by one or more curates, though it was exceptional for a Melbourne parish to have the kind of large staff of curates that was common enough in large city parishes in England before the First World War. Beyond this, there were a number of variations. For a short time, there was an attempt to staff Hastings on a bush brotherhood model commencing in 1917, but the Brotherhood of St Paul was brought to an end in 1921 when W. G. Hindley was Vicar-General, following Archbishop Clarke's departure. Clarke had also suggested that Fern Tree Gully might be run in this way, but in the end, F. W. R. Newton and George Cerrutty presided as 'warden' over a staff of clergy and readers, supplemented at weekends by visiting theological students.

A consciousness for the need to reclaim (or perhaps more accurately, claim) working people who had become alienated from the churches drove both Anglo-Catholics and Evangelicals, despite

St Alban's, North Melbourne, children's project, 1995.

Bishop James Grant, Dean of Melbourne since 1985, and Assistant Bishop Coadjutor 1970-85.

Canon Ray Hudson, born 1899, ordained 1923, the oldest priest of the Diocese in 1997.

All Saints', East St Kilda, Easter 1933. Architect: Nathaniel Billings, 1858.

differences of method and expression. In Melbourne, the Community of the Holy Name commenced its existence in 1888, working amongst the overcrowded inner-city population around Spring and Lonsdale Streets, and forging a long link with St Peter's, East Melbourne. The Brotherhood of St Laurence, introduced from Newcastle to Melbourne in 1933, came first to work in Fitzroy at St Mary's Mission, technically a daughter church of St Peter's Eastern Hill; by 1936, it was placed in charge of the parish of St Cuthbert's, East Brunswick. More recently, St Mark's, Fitzroy, was home for a short time to a religious community from 1975 to 1980 which formalised its existence in 1979 as a community of the Benedictine rule. At the other end of the churchmanship spectrum, detached members of the Church Army were working in Footscray and Caulfield by the beginning of the century, almost three decades before the Church Army commenced working in a structured way in Australia; it was commented at this time that the absence of a charismatic leadership hindered their effectiveness. By the 1940s, it had two evangelists in the diocese, one in Northcote and the other in Footscray. On the other hand, women of varying shades of churchmanship

were commissioned as deaconesses, and performed significant pastoral work in many parishes. And throughout the diocese, there was the ministry of lay readers. In the period when several isolated centres were connected to a larger church, their ministry was indeed essential. Before 1877, when the parish of Cheltenham was created, embracing Cheltenham, Mordialloc, Mentone, Beaumaris and Sandringham, lay readers from St Andrew's Brighton and St Mark's East Brighton visited these centres. Similarly, lay readers from St Peter's, Mornington, originally conducted services in centres extending from Frankston to Portsea. These readers functioned in an honorary capacity, and were often professional men. Stipendiary readers appeared at a much later date: in the parish of Fern Tree Gully, the first stipendiary lay readers were appointed at St Paul's Boronia, in 1945 and 1949, where their role coincided with the growing demands of the post Second World War population.

* * * * * * *

Contemporary Australian sociologists such as Hans Mol and Gary Bouma have pointed out that the affiliation of Anglicans, despite the non-attendance of many, is in keeping with Anglicanism's promotion

of the inclusive model of church as distinct from sect, promoted in both its official ecclesiology and as a result of its established status in England, and the attitudes inherited in the colonies from this. It is also possible that a concept of membership that was not exclusively defined by membership of a local congregation also helped worshipping Anglicans, and others, to move across the borders of geographical parish boundaries. And while this mobility has become increasingly common in the twentieth century, with the increasing private ownership of the motor car, it was not unknown in the nineteenth century, or in the earlier decades of this century when private ownership of a car was less common.

Certainly there could be a strong sense of regional identity. The most superficial reading of the Synod debates in 1877 concerning the site for the new cathedral reveals strong local loyalties at work amongst the supporters of East Melbourne, St Paul's and the pro-cathedral, with the supporters of St James eventually siding against the East Melbournians in favour of the St Paul's site. There was recognition of the equality of the legal claims of all denominations, coupled with the presence of strong Roman Catholic, Presbyterian and Methodist communities. Such a recognition made the parish church more attractive to those Anglicans who found this aspect of colonial life a new and threatening one. But while the most common basis of attachment to a church in the nineteenth century was geographical, there were exceptions to this rule from the very beginning. At Brighton, the burial register before 1870 records the names of those who came from outside, as well as within the parish boundaries, and amongst these, individuals from other already well established parishes such as St Kilda. At St Peter's Eastern Hill, the pew rent books of the 1850s record a handful of worshippers who resided in Richmond and South Yarra, who declined to worship regularly at churches closer to their homes. It was sentiment, the personality of the Vicar, liturgy, aesthetic or class factors and inertia, that created widening networks of affiliation, rather than any deep sense of the special holiness of a particular place. As the century drew to an end, it was possible for the decision-makers at St Peter's to consider selling the building and the site in order to make way for a series of doctors' rooms-in spite of the sentimental appeals that had appeared in previous decades, which played heavily on the image of the church as a survivor of the pre-gold rush days . Meanwhile, by the 1880s, its baptismal registers record the appearance of adults who had been baptised in the church during the goldrush. Now they were widely distributed, but were returning for the baptism of their children. They included James Grice, a son of Richard Grice, now resident at Robe in South Australia, and the station master at Bunyip in Gippsland, a Northcote bricklayer and a Prahran fruiterer. To these families, parish meant more than the church closest to their homes.

As the suburbs grew, one of the first attractions that caused worshippers to cross the borders created by parish boundaries was the aesthetic attraction of worshipping in buildings that were more sophisticated than the local church. Disputes over music took place in the 1850s and 1860s, following Bishop Perry's attempts to impose limits on this aspect of worship. This certainly reflected, amongst other things, the desire of some of the laity, and particularly the growing middle classes, to enjoy a repertoire and standard of performance that was not possible in a Melbourne church before the gold rush. It was the high choral standards achieved by Joseph Summers, director of music at St Peter's, East Melbourne, (1868 to 1879) and at All Saint's East Saint Kilda (1881 to 1883 and 1891 to 1896), that attracted a number of worshippers to those churches in the decades. The musical focus shifted elsewhere with the completion of St Paul's Cathedral. Other significant church musicians of this period include G. L. Allan and Philippa James.

The first Anglican congregations that were to become largely or strongly eclectic were those of the inner city churches. The principal factors in this change were shifts in population, technology, and churchmanship debates. *Melbourne Punch* commented that at St James, once 'a centre of aristocratic Melbourne', it was rare to find more than twenty worshippers on a Sunday; and the *Bulletin* described St John's LaTrobe Street as one of Anglicanism's 'most somnolent conventicles' before the First World War. At St Peter's, on the other hand, parish rolls indicate that in the first decade of the century, 111 worshippers out of a total of 434 lived at addresses some distance from the church itself. While one came from as far away as Geelong, and another from Queenscliff, several came from

Brunswick, Northcote, Albert Park, South Melbourne, Saint Kilda, Brighton, Kew and Camberwell. In the case of those worshippers from Saint Kilda, Albert Park and Brighton, it was far from a response to a particularly low churchmanship in the local parish church. It was the liturgy, with the full ceremonial of high mass, that was a drawcard, as well as the incumbent, the truly charismatic E.S. Hughes, champion rower and enthusiastic supporter of cricket. The Camberwell adherents doubtless sympathised with their own vicar, Charles Perry, a former curate of St Peter's, whose attempts to give a restrained expression to the principles of the Oxford Movement were strongly rejected by some of the local

The Laying of the Foundation Stone at St Mark's, Camberwell, by Archbishop Lees in 1927, with the existing church – now the parish hall – behind.

businessmen. The somnolence of St John's LaTrobe Street was equally broken with the appearance there of Cyril Barclay in 1915. His awkward handling of controversial issues alienated Archbishop Clarke, but it was not until the interregnum under A.G. Hindley that a *coup d'état* precipitated the closure and sale of the original property in 1921, amidst considerable bitterness. A pronounced churchmanship had proved to be a drawcard again, but with much less happy results.

Some degree of mobility was not a characteristic limited to the congregations of the city centre. In 1907, *Melbourne Punch* commented harshly on the residents of Toorak. Forty years before, St John's had been well attended by local residents, but not now: most worshippers in what the paper described as 'the most Godless, or rather, churchless, suburb' came from the 'Prahran valley'. Whether this represents an example of disappearance of the well-to-do from Anglican churches, a theme that recurs from time to time in the columns of this journal, is not so clear. Elsewhere, its church columnist noted that in its earlier days, St Matthew's Prahran had a restrained high church profile, due to the influence of J. H. Gregory, the long standing incumbent of

All Saints East Saint Kilda (1858-1893). Had an alteration of profile under the incumbency of one of the Langleys at St Matthew's led former parishioners to seek solace at St John's with C.E. Drought, whose appointment there had been attacked in the *Victorian Churchman* as part of the creeping growth of ritualism?

At the same time, the pro-cathedral was identified as the city's evangelical centre, and other centres with a markedly conservative presentation of doctrine and liturgy included St Columb's Hawthorn, Holy Trinity East Melbourne, and Christ Church St Kilda. It was evidence of the compexity and diversity of Anglicanism that each of these churches had a nearby neighbour that offered a marginally or markedly different shade of churchmanship: Christ Church, Hawthorn, provided a marginally more central profile than St Columbs; Holy Trinity had always been a foil of some sort to St Peter's; and All Saints' East St Kilda, provided an adequate alternative for those who were dissatisfied with Christ Church. From the point of view of the bishops, Bishop Moorhouse and all of his successors acknowledged the need to allow for expression of diversity, while they also sought to prescribe limits within which

variations could be permitted. While Archbishop Clarke asked Hughes to refrain from using incense, he would not forbid the use of vestments; and it was the evangelical Bishop Goe who asked Digby Berry, of Holy Trinity East Melbourne, to resign his canonry and his chaplaincy to the bishop because of his repeated involvement in nonconformist liturgies. And while the bishops acted as conciliators and arbitrators in trying to hold diverse expressions of Anglicanism together under the one umbrella, the new cathedral was subject from time to time to the criticisms of both Anglo-Catholics and the more extreme evangelicals for failing to deliver a package that conformed sufficiently with their predilictions.

The development of these first eclectic congregations is also one of the most obvious signs of the increasing impact of technology, but it was an impact that was already at work in the nineteenth century, even if its fruits were more obvious in the twentieth. In the debates in 1877 concerning the site for the new cathedral, it was pointed out that most worshippers in the city churches came from the suburbs, and that one factor in favour of the St James' site was that it was closer to a railway station than was

St Peter's. But to the modern reader, the most amusing reference to modern technology in this whole debate was the possibility that a spire might attract bombardment in the case of war - the speaker who voiced this fear reflected on the recent experience of Paris in the Franco-Prussian war. The burgeoning suburban railway system had an impact. In 1906, *Melbourne Punch* commented on the importance of the suburban trains for worshippers at the cathedral, and in 1921, the effect of a shipping strike on both trains and trams was described as 'diasastrous' for St Peter's congregations, while the parish paper of that church made ongoing references to the railway network as the major transport system for many of its worshippers.

If technology, particularly as it enabled an increasing degree of mobility, was making it possible for new attendance patterns to emerge, it was already being blamed for any perceptible declines. In 1907, *Melbourne Punch* claimed that while Toorak's Presbyterians were regular in attending their local church, that suburb's 'worthy Anglicans, or those who used to be such, must be motoring, golfing, yachting, reading, idling or something'. The young were already being castigated

for enjoying the leisure made available to them through technological advances: only a decade before this, C.O.L. Riley, Anglican Archbishop of Perth, had presided over a conference of Synod representatives at which speakers fulminated over the 'drift of our young', lured by pleasure boats on the river and by picnic spots made accessible by train.

The development of the urban rail system may well be regarded as one of the most significant technological influences in parish development, even if its impact was often indirect. In a parish in a comparatively isolated area such as Fern Tree Gully, the closeness of railway startions was important in the inter-war years for centres such as St Paul's Boronia, as well as St Bartholomew's Fern Tree Gully. And in Boronia in the years following the Second World War, it was in an area within a mile radius of the railway station that trebled between 1945 and 1957, with the results that have been referred to already. And such growth in this period was representative of what was happening in parish churches in many other arterial suburbs. The ubiquitous motor car, supposedly abused by Toorak's Anglicans, was equally an instrument of mobility that brought growth. To the parishes stretching

around the southern fringe of Port Phillip, such as St Mark's Dromana and All Saints' Rosebud, it was the motor car and the expanding network of roads, rather than the railway system, that brought new population and growth in the 1960s and 1970s. Workers could commute with greater ease to Frankston and Dandenong, and the distance from the city seemed to disappear. Similarly, the slow growth of parishes located in the Dandenongs reflected the comparative isolation of these areas, which retained a completely rural character with village centres for whom tourists and holiday makers were a significant source of income until after the Second World War. The parish of St Michael's, Mount Dandenong, gained an eclectic element in its congregation, when the combined influences of the Parish and People Movement, and the changes promoted through the liturgical experimentation that produced *An Australian Prayer Book*, marked it out as one of the few parishes that retained the regular use of Matins from the *Book of Common Prayer*.

A similar attraction for those dissatisfied with liturgical experiment was provided by other parishes that retained different *Book of Common Prayer* liturgies, whether

top: Church of the Resurrection, Macedon Ranges, dedicated 1986.

above: St Paul's, Gisborne, prefabricated church 1855-1960.

St Mark's, Templestowe, dedicated 1974.

Evensong or the Holy Communion, as well as the smaller number of parishes that retained what were originally revised rites, such as the 1928 rite or the interim rite. At the other end of the spectrum, there was the occasional parish such as St Mark's Fitzroy, that offered the solace of the Roman canon to those who felt that *An Australian Prayer Book* did not go far enough in a particular direction.

And to all of these centres, a high proportion of worshippers came by car, less often by public transport, from outside the geographical parish boundaries.

The 1970s saw the appearance of the charismatic movement, which expressed itself through a definite liturgical style, as well as having particular theological emphases. It had its greatest impact on a number of suburban churches, while finding almost no expression in the major city congregations. It sometimes brought worshippers together across the older churchmanship divisions, but created new ones of its own. One of its earliest centres was St Paul's Malvern. At St Paul's Boronia, most of its earliest adherents were not 'new Christians' but the already churched. Total attendance figures dropped, as some regular worshippers felt that they were regarded as second class Christians; the parish ran at a financial loss during the decade, and by 1977, what had been thriving tennis, netball and sports clubs had ceased to exist. While others became more deeply involved–the vestry membership in the middle of this decade recorded a particularly high proportion of new vestry members–the movement's exclusive understanding of the meaning of church membership was

accompanied by a narrowing range of contact between the worshipping community and the rest of the those who lived around it.

If there was further crossing of geographical borders with the appearance of the charismatic movement, strong eclectic or gathered congregations expressing variations within the evangelical tradition were developing in the same

period at centres such as St Jude's Carlton, and St Hilary's Kew. In the case of St Jude's, at the same time that age took its toll on a declining local congregation, so a new congregation was drawn from amongst the student population that rented accommodation in the area. As many members of that group moved to Fitzroy or Brunswick, their links with the parish were maintained, making it into a

St Mark's, Camberwell. Architect: Rodney Alsop, 1927.

congregation that was gathered, though substantially from nearby suburbs. And while the influence of the church growth movement, originally American in origin, may be detected in many elements of the life of St Hilary's Kew, the British evangelical tradition of expository preaching has more recently distinguished St Judes', while influences from the British evangelical and charismatic tradition, and particularly from St John's College Nottingham, have distinguished Christ Church Dingley. The influence of the charismatic movement can be detected in other ways in parishes such as St Alfred's Blackburn and St Luke's Vermont. And while the casual observer might understandably assume that a particular kind of large parish was evidence of the impact of the church growth movement, the proposed creation of a 'mega-parish' in Waverley owes more to the strength of the local communities; indeed, the South American experience of one of its prime movers created an awareness of the danger of an uncritical application of American models in a culture that only bore a superficial resemblance.

* * * * * * *

As yet, there is no comprehensive and detailed study which documents and analyses the changes in the socio-economic groups from which Anglican parishioners have come. The mythological image of Anglicanism presents it as a middle-class religion of formalism. A representative Australian expression of this image appears in Barry Humprhries' recently published autobiography, *More Please*, as the author recalls his enjoyment of the music, along with 'the smell of everybody's "Sunday Best"'; the camphor, the talcum, hair oil and the toilet water', and his mother's reluctance to attend, which he attributes to the 'sanctimoniousness' of the vicar, whose sermons focussed on the danger posed to members of the royal family by the Second World War. Ultimately, a well-documented overall study would also depend on the kind of detailed studies of individual parishes or localities that have yet (in most cases) to be written. However, there are pointers that suggest that some common assumptions need challenging. While it is generally true that by comparison with Roman Catholicism, nineteenth century Anglicanism drew a smaller proportion of its worshipping members from amongst the working classes, what is to be made of Richard Twopeny's comment that Anglican clergy seemed to be 'chaplains' to the upper and lower classes, rather than to those in the middle? And if early Melbourne Anglicanism enjoyed substantial support from some members of the merchant class, such as Richard Grice, overhasty assumptions about patronage by the well-to-do must be balanced against other comments in many 19th century sources that suggest a large degree of indifference in that very group. Twopeny's reflection on the lack of a sense of social obligation on the part of 'the plutocracy'-in other words, generous patronage of public institutions-is representative. The asides in *Melbourne Punch* concerning the decline in attendance at St John's by Toorak's well-to-do, and the large number of worshippers from amongst Prahran's small business owners, likewise raise similar questions. *Melbourne Punch* also commented on the 'democratisation of the pews', to quote its own term, in a number of Melbourne churches in the first decade of this century, claiming that by comparison, it was only Presbyterian churches such as those of Malvern, Toorak and Camberwell that remained 'aristocratic'. But it also claimed that by comparison with its English counterparts, the Melbourne diocese was 'Tory' when it came to social outreach especially amongst the working classes. On the other hand, individuals with a strong sense of mission in precisely that direction were not lacking: obvious examples are Mother Esther and the first members of the Community of the Holy Name, and, in the next generation, George Lamble, 'Brother Bill' Nicholls and G. K. Tucker. After the Second World War, it was a combination of the inspiration afforded by such individuals, and the embracing of the myth of the Anglo-Catholic slum mission priest, that moved a number of clergy to accept parishes in the growing area on the fringes of the western suburbs, which for a short time was identified as a kind of 'biretta belt'. But there, a tenuous relationship with a socio-economic group to which Anglicanism had never had a strong appeal became complicated by new factors in a rapidly changing society, including the growth of a number of strong ethnic communities. Amongst the first of Melbourne's ethnic Anglican congregations were the Chinese community at St Matthew's Prahran and the Persian community at St Jude's Alphington. The latter was ultimately a descendant of the Archbishop of Canterbury's mission to Urmiah in the previous century. Amongst

the Spanish-speaking community, a remarkable ministry, including a Spanish liturgy in the parish church, was conducted from St Peter and St Andrew Braybrook by Peter White. At the same time, it illustrated the weakness of all such ministry in this situation-its dependence on a strong individual. With White's acceptance of a SAMS appointment in 1987, this ministry ceased. Closer to the inner city, St Jude's Carlton has extended a more recent ministry of this kind amongst the Vietnamese, and St George's West Footscray amongst the Sudanese.

* * * * * * *

This returns the reader to the period with which this essay began: the boom of the 1950s and 1960s, and the subsequent and apparent decline. Decline or change? The overall pattern of parish life in the 1980s and 1990s shows the emergence of a small number of strong centres, an increase in the number of centres with small numbers and few organisations, and a consequent decrease in the number of parishes in a mid-range that appear to have real viability. Sociologists such as Hugh McKay suggest that the decline in involvement in institutionalised religion and in structured organisations must not be interpreted as indifference or hostility

to spiritual values. Though, as I have already hinted, an organisation such as CEMS was not entirely secure in the inter-war years, the much more open and consistent questioning of institutions and values that emerged in the 60s and 70s, contrasting with the seemingly greater acceptance of a variety of traditional institutions in the immediate post war decade, cannot be lightly swept aside in accounting for the decline of the parish organisations that once had some apparent strength.

A complex of factors brought about a marked change in worship patterns. Within the church itself, the recovery of the significance of the Eucharist, stimulated by both the evangelical and Oxford Movements, has been followed by unforseen consequences. Stress on the centrality of the Eucharist as a family liturgy in the Parish and People movement coincided with the growth in a wide variety of Sunday entertainments and increased mobility through private ownership of motor cars. Forces thus existed both within and outside the church, that reduced Sunday worship to a matter of a single act of worship, and a morning service at that, for most parishioners. Not even the maintenance of a good choral tradition

In the stained glass window:

I WILL FILL THIS HOUSE
WITH GLORY SAITH THE LORD
OF HOSTS

ST JAMES'
OLD CATHEDRAL
MELBOURNE

CHURCH OF THE
GOOD SHEPHERD
MT MACEDON
FOUNDED 1887

ST JOHN'S
RIDDELL'S CREEK
FOUNDED 1864

HOLY TRINITY
MACEDON
FOUNDED 1867

CHARLES STUART PERRY DD
BISHOP OF MELBOURNE

ST PAUL'S
GISBORNE
DEDICATED 1858

OLD ST PAUL'S
GISBORNE
FOUNDED 1858

above: St Mark's, Fitzroy.
Architect: James Blackburn,
1853.

inset: Stained glass window of
Bishop Perry, St Paul's,
Gisborne.

would ensure an evening congregation, in churches that once commanded respectable numbers, or were nearly filled for evensong.

The questioning of institutions and traditional values impacted on Christian education, but was not the sole factor at work. The decline of the Sunday school occurred at the same time that there was much questioning of attitudes towards education and educational institutions in general. However, it seems unfortunate that at the same time that an institution such as Sunday school was in decline, an outsider could find a bewildering array of attitudes towards baptism, confirmation and first communion across the diocese, and sometimes from parish to parish. And while the rise and fall of confirmation can be documented through diocesan records, the confused and haphazard statistics in diocesan records concerning admission to communion almost encourages a serious analyst or historian to invoke that highly dubious category, the conspiracy theory, as a way of explaining the hiatus. Though this is in reality highly unlikely, the figures, as presented, suggest that parish-based initiatives to form a regular sacramental life in the young have almost completely foundered.

Finally, attitudes towards community and local community have undergone new developments. Though many areas have seen the emergence of new expressions of community, ranging from local historical conservation groups to progress organisations, the post-war urban sprawl has also created a larger commuter belt from which much of the population is absent during working hours. The more recent stress on cultural diversity has encouraged the growth of many special interest groups that transcend local boundaries of various kinds. A cynical sociologist might well say that the all of the Christian churches are no more than special interest groups. As we have seen, what might well be called special interests - particular theologies or liturgical styles - have drawn people beyond identification with a local parish into worshipping in a gathered or eclectic congregation. But while some consider the only viable parish churches of the future to be large gathered congregations that cater to a clearly defined and identifiable taste - a 'niche market' - others still feel confident that many parishes whose worshippers are drawn from the locality will also survive, and that the forces that have weakened the ties that previously bound many local communities are already being balanced by others that are creating new expressions of regional community.

Further Reading

The quality of writing in publications on the history of various Melbourne parishes varies considerably. Some are chronicles, lacking analytical insight, and treating their subject as a self-contained social unit, without relating it to its wider local setting. A careful examination of a recent general local history will sometimes raise and answer questions that are important in understanding aspects of the history of a parish. The following histories of Melbourne parishes were particularly helpful in the preparation of this chapter:

* M.A. Hookey, *St Mark's Camberwell, The First Seventy Five Years*, Melbourne, 1988

* R. Kerr, *St Mark's in Time*, Red Hill Press, Melbourne, 1982

* A. de Q Robin, *Holy Trinity Kew, 1863-1988, A Historical Record*, Holy Trinity, Kew, 1988.

* H.L. Speagle, *A Light in the Hills, A History of St Michael and All Angels, Mount Dandenong*, St Michael and All Angels, Mt Dandenong, 1990.

* G Walker, *It Seemed Good, A History of St Pauls Anglican Church,* St Paul's Anglican Church, Boronia, Melbourne 1984.

The attention of readers should also be drawn to other recent histories not consulted in the preparation of this essay, particularly Jane Carolan's *St Columb's Hawthorn 1883-1983: A History*, St Columb's, Hawthorn, 1980; Sue Carcutt and Teresa Cirtue's *All Seats Free*, St Andrew's Clifton Hill, 1980; and Morna Sturrock's *Fruitful Mother: St Stephen's Richmond Parish History, 1851-1991*, St Stephen's Parish Publishing Committee, Melbourne, 1993.

This general overview would not have been possible without my own work on St Peter's Eastern Hill, contained in *'Awful Happenings on the Hill'*, E S Hughes and Melbourne Anglo-Catholicism Before the War, Melbourne University Press, Melbourne 1992, and *From Tories at Prayer to Socialists at Mass, St Peter's Eastern Hill Melbourne, 1846-1990*, Melbourne 1996.

The following sociological studies should also be consulted:

* G. Bouma: 'Australian Religiosity: Some Trends since 1966', in *Studies in Society, Practice and Belief*, ed. A. Black, P. Glasner, Allen & Unwin, Sydney, 1983, pp. 15-24.

* G Bouma and M Mason: 'Baby Boomers Downunder', in *The Post-War Generation and Establishment Religion, Cross Cultural Perspectives*, ed. W. C. Roof, J. W. Carroll & D. A. Roozen, Boulder & San Francisco, 1995, pp. 27-58.

* H. Mol, *The Faith of Australians*, Allen & Unwin, Sydney, 1975.

Readers looking for an unecclesiastical perspective on Melbourne's churches at the end of last century and in the first years of this one, should consult *Melbourne Punch*, which included a monthly column on what was happening in Melbourne churches of many different denominations.

Lowther Hall Anglican Grammar School, Essendon. Architects: Lawson and Grey, 1890. Acquired by the school 1920

School Education

in the Diocese of Melbourne

I

Charles Perry arrived in Melbourne in 1848 and almost immediately registered his profound concern about the parochial schools in his diocese and the quality of education they were providing: perhaps the lack of quality would be more accurate, with most of these single schoolrooms operating in cottages in parishes throughout the Diocese. The only schoolroom as such which was in any respect the property of the Church and under its control was 'a miserable structure of wood next to St James' Church,' according to George Goodman, the Diocese's earliest historian. Perry became and remained throughout his episcopate a vociferous and not infrequently controversial participant in public debates concerning education. The lasting memorials of his determination to establish the sort of school which became a paradigm of Anglican education are in schools of his foundation: Melbourne and Geelong Grammar Schools.

All of this is by way of asserting that it is more precise to refer to 'Melbourne Anglicans and Schools' than the more self-congratulatory description of 'School Education in the Diocese of Melbourne'. There have been attempts during the past century and a half to put in place a structured diocesan policy and practice in regard to schools, but it is evident that these attempts were individualistic or the work of a committed few rather than an endorsed and resourced program with the enthusiastic and readily funded support of the decision making bodies in Diocesan Synod and the Council of the Diocese. Indeed there is enough evidence to suggest that the schools which today are listed in the Diocesan *Year Book* as 'Anglican Schools' - and those which were once there but are no longer - were generally founded, nurtured and sustained in spite of the institutionalised diocese and not because of it.

Of course there have been occasions of keen and positive interest and investment of Bishops and Archbishops of Melbourne: notably Perry, James Moorhouse, Henry Lowther Clarke and Frank Woods, yet what has evolved has been a loose federation of educational institutions with nothing of the systemic pattern of the Roman Catholic Archdiocese nor even the interventionist supervision which has been seen in the Methodist and Presbyterian Churches in Victoria.

What the future of such an amorphous body and benign relationship will be in the next century is arguably a challenge to the Church at the present time. How this should or can be realised is unclear.

II

When we look at the schools which have come to be recognised as Anglican and, especially in the closing years of the nineteenth century and the early decades of this one and the conceptual parameters which were translated into practice, there was a conscious, albeit understandable, attempt to replicate British and especially English experience. In his Presidential Address to the Australian Church Congress held in Melbourne in 1925, Archbishop Harrington Clare Lees quoted - in translation - words of Horace in the century before the birth of Christ: 'Change of sky does not bring change of mentality'.

This is neither surprising nor to be deprecated. Our forebears needed their hidden baggage to survive as strangers in a strange land. If deprecation is ever to be justly laid at the door of the immigrants' successors, it would be if any institution, including the church itself, were to demonstrate itself as being quite incapable of changing and adapting to its environment with no apology felt necessary. This replication as the very purpose and style of the so-called 'Church Schools' was heard not infrequently. When Perry spoke at the formal opening of Geelong Grammar School in 1858, the frame of reference he used as his ideal for the new school was his own school days at Harrow, with comparative and approving references to Eton and Winchester Colleges.

Shortly after Henry Lowther Clarke arrived to become Melbourne's fourth Bishop (and subsequently first Archbishop), he addressed a 'lawn party' at Melbourne Grammar School. His approval was fulsome as he said of the school: '...my casual acquaintance with it today fills me with pride and satisfaction, because the buildings are so large and the grounds are so beautiful, and the whole thing looks like a delightful English public school'.

The speaker was an Old Boy of Sedbergh School in Yorkshire, and subsequently, in his retirement, the co-author of its history.

The inspiration behind the boys' schools especially was English - and both consciously and unconsciously so. The ideal of the 'Christian gentleman' - more Erastian than as a vital member of the Body of Christ - was exhorted and encouraged. The schools known as 'Anglican', whether for boys or girls, were necessarily founded as fee-paying schools with the abolition in the latter part of the nineteenth century of government grants. In spite of the laudable subsidies which schools have provided and continue to provide, they have been able to allocate most places only to the children of those parents who could meet the bill, and thus alienated from possible attendance, as they still do in most cases, the children of most Anglican parents.

The commercial hegemony which remains entrenched in Melbourne society has long been evident in the composition of the parent body in the Anglican schools. In 1912, Kathleen Gilman Jones, the Headmistress of the Church of England Girls' Grammar School (more latterly, Melbourne Girls' Grammar School) analysed the occupations of the fathers of girls attending her school of 282 girls. Seventeen occupations are represented in her list and included, using her categories: seventy-seven businessmen (insurance, accountants, agents, etc.); fifty-four merchants and manufacturers; thirty-four landowners; twenty-eight 'medical men'; eighteen clergy; thirteen architects; eleven bankers. Seven male parents were in trade, and five (only five?) in law. There was one artisan and one actor.

The composition of other Church Schools would have varied in the particular but not in the general, one suspects. Capacity to pay was not matched as an important criterion for entry by religious affiliation. Looking at Kathleen Gilman Jones' notes again we see that, although some seventy-two parents described themselves as 'Church of England', there were fifty Presbyterian and fifteen Jewish girls in her school. Amongst this last group were some of the most outstanding students, and subsequently alumni, of the school.

The fiscal factor had a profound effect on the schools as an inevitable and causal factor. In one of the many debates in the Church Assembly (later called Diocesan Synod) as to whether a Church of England Girls' Grammar School should be founded at all, there was one oft-repeated argument in opposition. The most tenacious of opponents was Judge Hickman Molesworth who repeatedly spoke against the proposed school as he felt that it was no business of the Church to sponsor in principle or funding 'a fashionable ladies' school'. The tone and history of the Church's schools may have had the public appearance of academies of the ladies and gentlemen of the elite, but in reality reflected necessarily the tone of the city in which they existed. In Melbourne's dominant years of the 1880s, the son of an Anglican priest, the journalist R.E.N. Twopeny, wrote that 'Australia is before everything a money-making place and anything like unremunerative expenditure with no possible chance of profit is considered foolish in all but a man who has made his fortune'.

The schools were dependent upon the middle class, successful or aspiring to be so, for enrolments. It was therefore the broader cultural nature of that particular class which exercised influence, rather than a specific desire for religious enlightenment through education. The governing bodies of the schools tended to reflect the parent body and the middle class mores, and thus influenced school policy and practice to be consistent with this.

During the years of Archbishop Clarke's episcopate there was a more concerted attempt than in years preceding or following to enunciate an Anglican policy for schools on a different level.

In June of 1912, the *Church of England Messenger* gave a detailed statement about education under the heading 'Anglicanism's Platform'. The first four points of the platform read:

1. It is the final duty of the State in modern communities to provide for and to control an effective national scheme of education.

2. In doing so the State should recognize the ability of private enterprise and denominational effort to realise within their schools an atmosphere peculiar to themselves, and making an invaluable contribution to the

educational machinery of the State.

3. The principle should be laid down that education without religion is morally, and therefore nationally, futile.

4. It is, therefore, the Church's duty and the responsibility of wealthy Churchmen to endow wherever possible Church schools, and Government subsidy of such educational efforts should be made to all or none at all.*

(The underlining is in the original.)

This statement has significance in understanding the Diocese and its schools, not only in the year in which it was written at a time when a number of Anglican schools came under the diocesan umbrella but also in any exploration of the ethos of Anglican schools generally in the sesquicentenary year.

Unlike the years when the Melbourne and Geelong Grammar Schools were established and later a number of secondary schools for both boys and girls, schools which were to become officially Anglican, in the year of the statement the fact of a new player on the field was accepted, as it had to be accepted, and that was the intervention of the State in controlling and providing secondary schools. The control by the State came about through the compulsory registration of schools and teachers, and the establishment of the Schools' Board, with responsibilities for curriculum. In more recent years the policies and practices of Commonwealth Governments affecting funding to independent schools has affected the autonomy of schools which are pleased to call themselves Anglican.

The 1912 statement asserts what the Anglican schools would continue to say and that there is a place for a dual system of education; in fact, there are in 1997 four 'systems' of schools: those of the State, the independent schools of which the Anglican schools are part, the systemic schools of the Roman Catholic Church and the recently established community schools. In the Diocese of Melbourne there is no system of schools as such. Each has a degree of autonomy: virtually all are incorporated companies with some nexus with the Anglican Church in their Articles of Association. Nevertheless, attempts have been made to have something in the Diocese of Melbourne more akin to a systemic structure than has existed for seventy years.

The most ambitious of these was in the establishment of the Diocesan Board of Education in 1905, largely at the instigation of the Archbishop of Melbourne, rather than the initiative of Synod or the Council of the Diocese. The Board had a number of designated duties. These included the promotion of education of girls and boys and the appointment of inspectors to report to the Archbishop in Council 'on all schools with special reference to religious instruction, general efficiency, financial condition and the state of buildings'. A special charge was

To determine the terms and conditions on which Schools may be established with the sanction of the Board and also on which the name 'Church of England' may be used by Schools which have been or may from time to time be established by parochial or other authorities or persons.

In this last respect there are schools which date their existence as Anglican Schools from the effective days of the Board of Education- Firbank Anglican School (purchased with funds which had been bequeathed to the Archbishop); the shorter-lived Adamsdown in Caulfield which was to be subsumed by Melbourne Girls Grammar School; Berwick Grammar

School for boys which was officially opened in 1918 but succumbed to the Depression of the 1930s; Tintern Anglican Girls' Grammar School; Korowa Anglican Girls' School; Lowther Hall Anglican Grammar School. Of contemporaneous foundation, but a school neither of the Board but – as its founder Sydney Buckley was wont to say – born *in spite of* the Diocese was Ivanhoe Grammar School. Established in 1915, within five years Ivanhoe became a company limited by guarantee and incorporated under the Companies Act – a forerunner for the present norm and worth referring to for that reason.

The aim of the *Act of Synod* establishing the Board to establish a network of Church Schools – owned by the Church and directed by diocesan policy – was never fulfilled as had been hoped. In a typescript Notes on Church Schools, the Reverend H.A. Brooksbank – a member of the Board and champion in Synod of its work – identified the major problems which inhibited the grand notions which had been held – the lack of funds and the tendency of Archbishop Clarke to act first and tell the Board afterwards. '...it might be the only way,' he wrote, 'but it is fatal to Board policy'. Clarke's vision was not shared by the Diocese as such. What success it had was the outcome of the commitment of individuals to the provision of Church-related schools.

Compared with the Roman Catholic Church, which saw a dramatic extension in the provision of secondary schools, independent schools had the inhibiting factor of finding salaries for its teachers. There were, in the early years of the Board of Education, hopes expressed that women might commit themselves to a teaching order for a time in order to contain costs. This was not to be, although there was an exemplar in St Michael's School, established, owned, and operated by the Community of the Sisters of the Church and in schooling for poorer children within the city conducted by the Sisters of the

above: Dr J.E. Bromby, Headmaster, Melbourne Grammar School, 1858-75

right: Sir James Darling, Headmaster, Geelong Grammar School, 1929-61.

Dr Alexander Leeper, Warden of Trinity College, University of Melbourne, 1876-1919 and ex-officio Council member, Melbourne Grammar School.

Community of the Holy Name. These were, and remained, the exception.

Without enthusiastic diocesan commitment or funds, by 1924 privatisation was the stated policy- a policy which, by and large, has continued. Addressing Diocesan Synod in that year Archbishop Lees spelt out what he called 'the only lines which he could in future recommend as part of our Educational Policy as a Church'. Those lines were the devolution of control from the Diocese to School Councils. He said: 'I ...believe that personal initiative, local enterprise, and all that goes with school esprit de corps need to be given a fuller opportunity than was perhaps possible in their earlier stages'.

Whilst retaining the right to grant or withhold a school's calling itself 'Church of England', though having representation on School Councils and through the potentially powerful position of the Archbishop as Visitor, the diocese nonetheless retreated from the dream of a system of schools.

The question needs to be considered as to whether there is anything 'Anglican' at all about Anglican Schools. Archbishop Frank Woods was a strong supporter of the schools, influential in discussions about the recognition of existing schools as Anglican and a participant in moves for the establishment of at least one new school to be an Anglican School. As President of its School Council he found himself in the early years of his episcopate closely and centrally involved in the turmoil at Melbourne Church of England Girls' Grammar School. The schools of the Diocese received frequent attention in his Charges to Synod. Addressing his final Synod, he identified ways in which he saw the schools furthering the Kingdom of God and thus playing an integral part in the Church's mission:

> ...first and perhaps the least important is that every school has a constitutional connection with the Diocese of Melbourne. But secondly, and far more important, every one of the headmasters and headmistresses is a dedicated Christian...And, thirdly, their chief aid in this purpose is the presence of a Chaplain, or a whole-time director of Religious Education who is a full member of the staff.

III

For the vast majority of those who call themselves Anglican, and indeed those who are active in the life of the Church, any thought of school is in the State and not the independent sector. To recall the platform of 1912:

> The principle should be laid down that education without religion is morally, and therefore nationally, futile.

From the passing of the *Education Act* in 1872 establishing State education as free, compulsory and secular, the means by which the Church might have access to Government schools for any form of religious or scriptural instruction has exercised not a little energy - including involvement in the political arena and public controversy.

Apart from the educational question as to the place, if any, of a study of religion in the curriculum for education to create an awareness of the wholeness of the individual, in the history of the Diocese the debate has centred on the word 'secular' in education legislation, as it has been interpreted and as it was intended. In 1883 Bishop Moorhouse addressed the Bible in State Schools League which, he was reported as saying:

...asks that the word 'secular' shall have such a meaning given to it as may leave it possible for the state school teachers to give undenominational Bible instruction in school hours. This it believes to be possible with the understanding between politicians when the present act (1872) was passed, and necessary for the public welfare.

Bishop Field Flowers Goe called for an amendment to the *Education Act* in 1889 to permit religious instruction in State schools. The Church Assembly again and again returned to the issue, passing, in 1896, a resolution

That this Assembly respectfully request the Bishop to continue his efforts to obtain such an amendment in the existing law as shall allow of religious instruction being effectively given in State schools.

In an attempt to resolve the issue which had been in the public arena for what was probably too long, the Victorian government in 1904 passed legislation to bring before the people a referendum on Scriptural instruction in the government schools. The referendum put three questions to the people:

1. Are you in favour of the Education Acts remaining secular as at present?
2. Are you in favour of such Legislation as shall cause the scheme of Scripture lessons recommended by the Royal Commission on Religious Instruction (*) to be taught in State Schools during school hours to children whose parents desire the teaching?
3. Are you in favour of the Prayers and Hymns selected by the Royal Commission being used?

(* *The Royal Commission referred to reported in 1900. Working under the chairmanship of Archdeacon H.A. Langley, subsequently first Bishop of Bendigo, the commission consisting of representatives of the Anglican and Protestant churches drew up a series of Scriptural lessons for both senior and junior levels together with a selection of prayers and an appendix of hymns for senior and junior divisions.)*

The referendum produced a contradictory result. The Archbishop and others believed that the questions themselves were confusing and unclear, as indeed they were. In fine, a majority of those who gave their opinion believed that there should be no change in the Act, and a majority stated that they were in favour of the lessons, hymns and prayers proposed by the Royal Commission of 1900. An impasse.

Nonetheless, a *Scripture Lessons Referendum Bill* was brought to the legislature in 1907 with a possible view of putting the issue again, but this time in a manner that might be understood by the people. The Bill was unsuccessful with two arguments dominating. The first was in the interpretation of the word 'secular' as meaning the exclusion of the religious. The second addressed the 'sectarian' issue noting that the Roman Catholic Church was not prepared to be party to any joint syllabus. Some argued that it was possible to provide 'unsectarian Scripture lessons'. The Premier of the day - the legendary Thomas Bent - replied to those who asked him what such a thing might be, 'You can just put on it whatever you like, my pretty dears'. The flippant dismissiveness was indicator enough that the parliament was wiser than it may have realised in defeating the Bill. The practice of permitting clergy access to the State schools *before* or *after* the normal school sessions which had been allowed under the Act continued.

The opportunity was not taken up with any enthusiasm according to many comments and reports. In 1919 a conference was held in the Diocese for clergy and laity to come together and discuss with the Archbishop ways to overcome the apathy of many parish clergy and to look at ways in which religious instruction in State schools might be more effective. Seventeen people attended the meeting. This was at a time when there were some 225 licensed clergy in the Diocese and more than thirty thousand communicant Anglicans.

The most significant development in Church involvement in State schools came with a group of representatives of Anglican and Protestant churches working together to frame an agreed syllabus. From that the Council for Christian Education in Schools evolved, with H.T. Langley, sometime Dean of Melbourne and who, to use his own words, 'had a hand in founding two girls' schools'- St Catherine's in Toorak, and Shelford as the Parish School of St Mary's Caulfield where he was Vicar. The Council for Christian Education in Schools, in association with the World Council of Churches and with the public support of Archbishop Joseph Booth, achieved in 1950 amendments to the *Education Act* which gave approved instructors access to schools during the normal school day. The provision for those parents who wished to do so to withdraw their children from Religious Instruction classes remained, as it had from the days of the original act; however, the relegation of R.I. to what was in effect the beginning or ending of the school day made a different statement. The Council further extended the involvement of the churches in the State's schools with the appointment of chaplains to secondary schools. These developments could only come about if churches were (and are) willing to perceive religious education in terms other than doctrinal instruction and chaplaincy in terms other than proselytising. The work of the Council for Christian Education in Schools and the material produced has also affected the Anglican schools as such who took on board what came to be known in the 1960s as a 'revolution in religious education', explicated by such English writers as Harold Loukes, Ronald Goldman and the Australian expatriate John Hulls. In this respect the Council as an ecumenical body - with a strong Anglican presence in its directors and Dean Tom Thomas as its long-serving chairman at this critical time - did what the Anglican Church by itself was unable and often unwilling to do. It also started to put paid to the charge of sectarianism which was a potent factor in aborting the goals of the 1900 Royal Commission and those who approved of its recommendations.

IV

Most Anglican children were and are not in Anglican schools where in past years Anglican doctrinal instruction was often given. Those children in the State schools, if they received any religious instruction at all, would not be learning their catechism or such important things as why liturgical colours change or why a bishop carries a strange stick. It was in the Sunday schools that Anglican religious education - or instruction to be more accurate - was given. Bishop Moorhouse founded the Sunday School Association in 1880 'to increase the efficiency of Sunday-schools belonging to the Church of England within the Diocese of Melbourne and to promote the establishment thereof'. The Association for the first half of the twentieth century concentrated upon the preparation of teaching material and the training of teachers. Many of these were assessed and, if successful, received their 'Commission to Teach'. The writer clearly remembers large congregations in St Paul's Cathedral in the mid-1950s when Archbishop Booth presented certificated commissions to those who had qualified.

The role and influence of Sunday schools as schooling experiences in the Christian faith cannot be underestimated in the story of the Diocese. But things have changed! In 1913 there were some 2 48 Sunday schools in the Diocese of Melbourne where twenty-one thousand children were instructed by nearly two and a half thousand teachers. The 1996-7 *Year Book of the Diocese of Melbourne* records an average attendance of three-and-a-half thousand children instructed by a little more than one thousand teachers. At least the pupil-teacher ratio has improved.

It is right to include this brief discussion of Sunday schools in an essay dealing with Anglicans and schools, for schools they were as places of both instruction and socialisation. The commitment to Sunday schools was clearly asserted in Presidential Charges to Synods and through the Diocese's official organ, the *Church of England Messenger*. Amongst the former we read such statements as describing Sunday schools as 'our church nurseries, and our most efficient way of bringing up our children in the rules of faith and conduct'. Roscoe Wilson was Director of Sunday schools from 1914 to 1916. In that brief time, he published a series entitled *Pamphlets for the People* and wrote frequently in the *Messenger*. 'The Sunday School,' he wrote on one occasion, 'is to train the future membership of the Church' and exhorted that 'Every member of the Church should be on the alert to get children into the training-school of the Church'. It is a matter for thought that with the demise of many Sunday schools and the reliance upon effective education through the experience of worship (something not to be dismissed out of hand), programs for religious education and the nature of liturgy within the parish need to receive perhaps more attention than they do in some places.

V

The Church, broadly defined perhaps, has had and maintains some involvement with educational institutions at the tertiary, secondary and primary levels and within the parish structure. Not recognised as much as it should have been is the involvement of the diocese in pre-school education or kindergartens. This deserves mention both because of the need to stress the importance of education in those early years and of the pioneering work of the church in this area.

The *Church of England Messenger* for June 1913 carried photographs of the first of a number of free kindergartens established the preceding year at St James' Old Cathedral 'for city children'. Later, in other suburbs which could not be described as affluent by that stage of their history, kindergartens were opened at Collingwood, Carlton and North Melbourne. When the 'Alice Lovell Clarke Kindergarten' - named in memory of the Archbishop's late wife - was opened in Fitzroy, a network of free kindergartens of inner-suburban pre-school centres was completed.

The Anglican Council for Early Childhood Services now lists more than thirty affiliated centres (more than the number of schools listed as being Anglican). The activities of early childhood centres are indeed educational and they deserve to be considered with the Diocese's involvement with schools. The Church's innovative work in this area can be lauded, but so must be the continuing work in early childhood education which has never received the attention which its impact and influence on young lives merits.

VI

A review of the past is important insofar as it may give insight into the ethos and culture of a group, both for those inside who take their mental set for granted as well as those outside who seek to crack the code. A review of the past, even with broad strokes, can enrich our appreciation of the capacity of human beings to dream, to strive and to persevere to achieve a vision; however, the past should not be the manipulative and formative influence for the present, and certainly not for the future. Any retrospective study cannot but reveal a process of change and adaptation. It is therefore both apt and probably responsible to reflect upon the process observed and conjecture on its manifestation in the present and its progress to the future.

The 1912 'Anglicanism's Platform' for education referred to earlier included a stunning expression of hope when it said that it is 'the responsibility of wealthy Churchmen to form and endow wherever possible Church schools'. Would that they had, a number would say. The role of Anglicans as individuals or in small groups in the activities of the Church in relation to education cannot be underestimated. As has been said earlier, and more than once or twice in this essay, it was not the enthusiasm of the decision-making bodies which established the schools. It was the Sydney Leonard Buckleys who battled to get any affirmation and even support in principle. At the meeting of the Diocesan Board of Education, chaired by the Archbishop, which met to discuss endorsement and recognition of Buckley's proposed school, later to become Ivanhoe Grammar School, the powerful Archdeacon of Melbourne, W.G. Hindley, described Buckley's thought to the archiepiscopal chairman as a 'mad venture'. Buckley countered, 'But a splendid one, Your Grace'.

The initiative of those outside the diocesan structures in establishing schools which were to come to be recognised as Anglican was determinative in years long after Buckley's founding The Ivanhoe Grammar School. Reflecting on the years of his episcopate in his final Charge he gave to Diocesan Synod, Archbishop Sir Frank Woods recorded: 'In 1961 a group of determined and far seeing lay people, amongst whom was Sir Reginald Ansett, brought the Peninsula Grammar School into being, a similar group of lay people founded the Yarra Valley Church of England School'.

It could be said that any institution, or parish for that matter, which grows from the committed involvement of local people rather than as a result of some fiat from on high has a strength in its foundation, even something very Anglican about it. Comments such as Buckley's are indicative of this and the enthusiasm underlying them integral to success, especially where the undertaking has a community base.

Memorable as such statements as Buckley's are and typical of the need for a champion to ride into the lists if things are to be achieved, the complexities of the foundation and operation of independent schools as a price to be paid for Government assistance require more than the enthusiasm of an individual or of a few. Together with this consideration is the possibility of Church schools addressing the greatest criticism levelled at them, namely, their exclusiveness

Geelong Grammar School, 1960.

resulting from fee structures which place enrolment of their children well beyond the circumstances of most Anglican parents, no matter how much they may desire an Anglican education for their children. The establishment of lower fee, that is more highly subsidised, schools can be a realistic

activity for the Church. The Dioceses of Brisbane and Perth, in particular, have achieved in this respect by setting in place some centralised structure while still supporting the schools already in existence which seek to serve their Anglican heritage. The Diocese of Melbourne might well

emulate them. The existing schools may need to examine themselves and come to terms with any disquietude they may have, if even the most kindly as well as efficient of diocesan structures is put in place. Perhaps each school needs to ask itself from time to time whether the independence

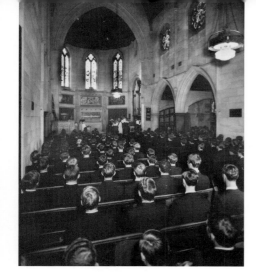

The Chapel of St Peter, Melbourne Grammar School, 1964.

and autonomy it believes it enjoys means more to it than its Anglicanism. In 1991, the Diocesan Committee on Education in the Diocese of Melbourne organised a conference under the title 'Being an Anglican School'. The keynote speaker was the Reverend Dr Bruce Kaye, at that time Master of New College, University of New South Wales. In his address on the conference theme Dr Kaye commented on 'the nature of the Anglican ethos, about the way in which human identity is formed in a plural society such as Australia and the character of the school as an institution'. He then went on to draw those points together, to use his words, and see them in the context of that which is an Anglican School. The identifying marks he discussed were the place of reason and understanding, tradition, the focus on the Incarnation, worship, and social interaction.

There has been a significant shift if Dr Kaye's approach to his allotted theme is accepted as valid. Some fourteen years before that address was given, a conference sponsored by the Archbishop-in-Council was held for 'clergy and educators'.

In passing, it is worth recording and to leave for contemplation the fact that, although the Heads of Anglican Schools had continued to meet annually with the Archbishop as a group, the 1977 conference had no successor addressing the broad issue of diocese and school until the 1991 gathering.

The 1977 conference title was 'Church and School; Partners in Education'. Episcopal utterances on that occasion are recalled by participants as being far less affirming of the independent Anglican schools and perhaps less informed than those of the later conference. Herein lies the shift- and a dramatic one at that. The 1977 conference's preoccupation with the structural had far more in common with the sorts of comments being made in the *Church of England Messenger* fifty-five years earlier than it had with the conference less than twenty years later. The integrity of the Diocese may demand its taking more seriously the appointment of representatives to Boards of Governors and Councils of Anglican Schools. Nevertheless, it may be that the future ministry of the diocesan structures to the schools within it which bear its name will be more in terms of support and resource to Heads, Councils, and chaplains in particular, to enable them to express an Anglican ethos in ways and through structures best suited to them, rather than being imposed by any centralised bureaucracy.

The genius of Anglicanism may well be to maintain in a creative tension different emphases and even statements which are contradictory to some but 'Anglicanly paradoxical' to others. With the realities of government funding for independent schools (so strongly resisted by Anglican voices for decades), there may be advantages for some schools, especially co-operative community schools and those for whom higher subsidy enables a broader and more representative socio-economic enrolment.

At the 1977 conference Bishop Ged Muston (at that time a Regional Bishop within the Diocese) spoke some uncomfortable words when he said:

I have no doubt that some Church Schools are genuinely trying to provide a truly Christian education: but there can be little doubt that we appear to be interested in giving this great privilege only to a limited and privileged section of the community. I believe this to be a major deficiency in our Church School system in this Diocese and a critical hindrance in the Church's wider preaching of the Gospel.

If this was true and still is, it is impractical to expect existing schools to set their sights principally on addressing this problem or perhaps to perceive that this is a major problem when many are facing problems with sustaining the enrolments they have. Nonetheless, there may be something here for a quasi-systemic approach initiated through the Diocese which might address what Bishop Muston was saying.

There are schools with a special relationship with the Anglican Diocese of Melbourne and there are schools in the Diocese attended by more Anglican children than are in independent schools. Again at the 1977 conference there were disturbing words, in this case spoken by the Right Reverend Robert Dann following his election and prior to his enthronement as Archbishop. The Conference Report records him as noting that '6% of Anglican children attend Anglican schools, 3% attend other independent schools and 91% attend other State schools'. The report continues:

> On the basis of these figures, the Bishop asked, as Archbishop-elect of the diocese, where his energies, cares and responsibilities were to be given in relation to the education of the membership of the Anglican Church alone.

If the Archbishop is seen as a representative person of the Church, then this quotation can be interpreted broadly. The work of the Council for Christian Education in Schools, through its religious education program and personnel and through chaplaincy, has been acknowledged. Anglicans can feel gratification in the determinative influence of a number of its clergy and lay people in the administration of that Council and as those working under its aegis. Again there has been a shift which may have more impact on the relationship of this church (and other churches) than is realised or being addressed.

Recent changes to the unit offered for the Victorian Certificate of Education have seen the introduction of the study of ethics, including the approaches of various religions to moral and ethical questions, and the study of religious texts and traditions. Although it has been the independent school sector which has included these studies in its curriculum, the possibility is there for State schools to extend their offerings to students by including such studies. There is a place for some Church support for such a move and encouragement of those of its own membership working in State schools to agitate towards this end. That may require an even more dramatic shift!

VII

From the days of its foundation one hundred and fifty years ago, the Diocese of Melbourne has been involved with education. This has not always been seen as a vital part of the Church's mission and ministry if those matters which diocesan Synods have addressed are taken as any guide. Perhaps the time is ripe for the Church to evaluate its place in education at all levels and across all sectors in the educational spectrum. If there is something to be done there, should it not be done well? If we cannot commit ourselves to a lively involvement in the educational enterprises of the community with which we have constitutional links, should we be there at all?

CHAPTER SIX

SHURLEE SWAIN

6

Canon Neale Molloy at St John's Home,
Canterbury.

Philanthropy and Welfare
in the Diocese of Melbourne

Here you see Jack is the master, not the man, and that is very difficult for us in doing the work...The people seem to consider it is our duty to do everything we can for them and they are not at all grateful.[1]

Deaconess Emma Silcock, addressing the Victorian Royal Commission on Charitable Institutions in 1891, expressed a confusion shared by many of her fellow Anglicans who set out to relieve the poor. Coming from an England in which the established church both administered and augmented the national *Poor Law* they found themselves amongst a people who had turned their back on that system and all that it implied. In a new colony, named after the new queen, such poverty as did arise would be relieved by voluntary effort, with citizens of substance donating a part of their new-found wealth to assist those who had fallen on hard times.

The affluence of the gold rush years ensured the early success of this voluntary scheme. Building on what had been established in the 1840s, large institutions were begun both in Melbourne and in the major provincial centres, each devoted to a specific category of need. Financed by a mix of voluntary contributions and government grants, they were managed by a committee elected by the subscribers. Augmenting such institutional solutions was a chain of ladies' benevolent societies which provided outdoor relief in their local area and, through regular visiting, supervised the use to which such relief was put.

Whatever their origins, both institutional and outdoor relief organisations claimed to be above denominationalism. Where Christianity was acknowledged, it was as part of a broad belief system common to the colonial elite, described at its most specific as Protestant and evangelical but never seen as excluding anyone with a responsibility to benevolence. In the early years there were few Roman Catholics wealthy enough to demand entry to what were essentially upper class organisations, although the local priest was occasionally invited to join the hospital committee in order to represent his flock. In later years, as individual Catholics became wealthy, they were more likely to donate to specifically Catholic organisations than

to attempt to assault what had become a Protestant enclave. Increasingly, the nondenominational institutions came to be seen as sites of proselytism from which the faithful needed urgent rescue.

Anglicans, initially, had no such fears. As a denomination they were over-represented amongst those who administered the charitable organisations of the colony and under-represented amongst those who had need to call upon their services. Individual clergy did distribute relief in their parishes but they did so with far less authority than they would have had at 'home'. As one clergyman's wife, Ada Cambridge, commented:

> There was none with whom a clergyman or his wife could safely take the liberties so customary at home. When a sister-in-law, once my fellow district visitor, came out to be our guest for a while and started to make herself useful by teaching our parishioners their duty on the traditional lines and by bestowing doles of old clothes and kitchen scraps upon them, she got some tremendous surprises – 'insolence' that simply staggered her.[2]

Despite such difficulties individual parishes did establish visiting or Dorcas

societies to distribute relief in their immediate area. While some of the larger charitable organisations trace their origins to such societies, it was their ability to represent themselves as non-denominational which gave them legitimacy and access to much-needed financial support.[3]

The participation of Anglicans in such organisations mirrored their position in the colonial elite. The most prestigious colonists sat on the committees of the most prestigious institutions, almost exclusively male committees managing hospitals and similarly large budget institutions. The Bishop of Melbourne was usually among their number. His wife sat alongside the wives of other prominent Anglicans on the committees of the slightly lower ranking organisations devoted specifically to the welfare of women and children.[4] Further down the scale came the local benevolent societies which had female committees of lower status advised by a committee of gentlemen, amongst whom clergy played a prominent role. Their wives, as women of education and breeding, were often called upon to take office in such societies, bringing with them female parishioners prepared to take on the arduous responsibilities which district visiting involved.

The only specifically Anglican welfare organisation to be established in the first fifty years of European settlement stood apart from the local charity network. The Mission to Seamen was the local branch of an English organisation founded in Bristol in 1837 which aimed to evangelise sailors at ports around the world.[5] The Melbourne station commenced operation at the peak of the goldrush with the arrival, in 1853, of the Reverend Kerr Johnston and his family. They established themselves in a Government-donated American hulk which they renamed the Bethel Sailor's Church.[6] Later, the Mission moved its operations ashore, establishing stations in the major ports which became centres from which the church could show its concern for visiting sailors. Although it attracted support from within the Diocese its focus was essentially outward. Staffed and directed from London, it was more an instance of

Archdeacon Charles Bailey, Director of Chaplaincy, 1978-88.

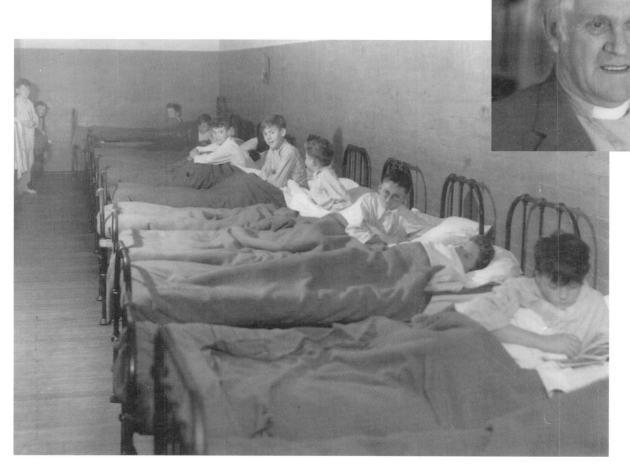

Dormitory at St John's Home for Boys, Canterbury, 1941.

missionary outreach to the colony than a part of the diocesan welfare effort.

It did not, however, exist in isolation for, in the docklands area, other Protestant missions had entered the fray. Competition was increasingly evident at the parish level as well. 'Sometimes,' Ada Cambridge recalled, 'an unfriendly competition...smart dodges to take the wind out of a rival's sails; more often...a tacit fraternal arrangement to aid each other, or at anyrate not get into each other's way.'[7] In the crowded residential districts of the inner city, such competition became intense with the opening of numerous mission halls intent on evangelising the local population. These were not subscriber charities, but private organisations completely under the control of the sponsoring denomination or alliance determined on spreading its particular views. The Church of England with its parish churches of St James and St John in the western end of the city and St Peter's Eastern Hill situated between the crowded areas in the north-east, and the emerging working class district of Fitzroy, faced the risk of losing members of its flock to these more aggressive intruders.

That the Church found itself in this position is indicative of the degree to which the redistribution of wealth through the processes of gold and migration had upset the class system in the new colony. As Bishop Moorhouse observed in 1885,

People at home sometimes forget that there have been no endowments here and that thus in a new country we are much poorer than the poorest Diocese in England...I dare say you hear that Melbourne is a rich city, but you must remember that the rule of the old country no longer obtains here. Our richest men are Presbyterians. Again most of our Cornish and Welsh miners are Wesleyans. The Church of England lives here in the fierce light and constant strain of keen competition.[8]

This sense of competition was felt more strongly in the increasingly influential Anglo-Catholic wing of the Church, which was uncomfortable with the evangelical tone of the interdenominational charities.

The first specifically Anglican welfare organisation in the Diocese of Melbourne arose out of this tension. The Diocesan Mission to the Streets and Lanes has its origins in a meeting of clergy of the parishes of St Paul's, St Peter's and St John's called by Bishop Moorhouse in March 1885. His intention was to develop a 'women's agency' to work in the 'lower parts of the city', establishing an Anglican presence amongst people who had long since lost contact with the church. The Mission which was established as a result of this meeting set out to recruit

Ladies duly qualified, and with the commission of the Bishop...[to] visit in the lanes and courts and bring the message of the Gospel to the poor and fallen, and by the force of their Sisterly example 'compel' the outcast to 'come in' to the house of their Father...The object is to have the presence of good women near where the sadness prevails. The hope is that such a presence will be a leaven for good.[9]

Essentially a high church foundation masquerading under an evangelical cover, the new mission had to tread cautiously in order to avoid alienating those within the Diocese who were concerned about the 'Romanising' aspects of such a proposal. While in its regular routines of mother's meetings, boys' and girls' clubs, factory, court, prison and hospital visiting and the distribution of material and medical relief the Mission hall in Little Lonsdale street differed little from its Protestant neighbours, its mode of organisation was increasingly distinctive. With Canon Handfield, Vicar of

St Peter's, Eastern Hill, as its chaplain and Sr Esther (Emma Silcock), previously a novice at the Community of St Mary the Virgin at Wantage, England, as the Sister-in-charge, the new Mission aroused increasing suspicion within the Diocese. Evangelical forces who believed they had approved the revival of the 'primitive' order of deaconesses 'serving under the authority of pastor and bishop' saw instead an independent group of women, living as a community, and carrying out their daily activity without apparent masculine control.[10]

The new mission was quickly drawn into institutional as well as outdoor relief. Living in the centre of Melbourne's red light district, the sisters formed strong views about the dangers of prostitution. However, they had difficulty finding suitable places to shelter women who were willing to leave the trade. Their first institution, the House of Mercy at Cheltenham, was designed to meet this need. Opened in 1892, it provided accommodation for two sisters and, initially, twelve women who, through a strict regime of prayer and hard work, were to be persuaded to turn aside from their lives of sin. It was not the first female refuge established in the colony but it was the first with a specifically Anglican orientation, reflecting the growing denominationalism of Victorian charity.

The second institution, the Church of England Home for Neglected Children opened at Brighton in 1894, sprang from similar roots. The *Neglected Children's Act* of 1887 which licensed private individuals to 'rescue' children at risk had exacerbated existing denominational rivalries, encouraging the growth of a parallel, and denominationally based, child welfare system alongside the existing Neglected Children's Department. Where the old system had rigidly preserved a child's religious affiliation, the 'child savers' licensed under the new legislation openly used their positions to increase church membership. 'The Church of England', the Inspector of Charities warned, 'would soon cease to have any members among the poorer classes if it allowed the neglected children to pass out of its hands.'[11] Sr Esther had been registered under the Act and the opening of the Children's Home enabled the sisters to extend their work in this area, later acquiring a second property in order to be able to accommodate babies as well as school-age children.

In the early years of the twentieth century the mission expanded its work further, taking responsibility for two former charity schools in the Lonsdale street area[12] and founding and managing two hospitals,[13] stretching its resources to the full. However, with a committee of ladies as its governing body, the mission lacked access to the decision-making structures of the Diocese. When the Warden presented its annual report to Synod, he was received with polite applause but no offers of direct assistance or support. In establishing its first distinctively Anglican welfare organisation, the Diocese of Melbourne had set the pattern for all which were to follow. Groups or individuals with plans for outreach amongst the poor were to be encouraged, but they had to be able to pay their own way.

Several such projects were attempted around the turn of the century but most were short lived. The reformatory at Apollo Bay had its origin in similar legislation to that which facilitated the development of the Mission to Streets and Lanes' Children's Home. While the Roman Catholics and the rapidly expanding Salvation Army were quick to establish private institutions for juvenile offenders the Anglicans were once again slow to respond. Fears that the church was losing potential recruits led a group of gentlemen to establish and attempt to administer a similar home at Apollo Bay, but distance and isolation brought continuing difficulties and the reformatory was closed

model to revitalise its presence in the inner city, preaching social reform from the pulpit while offering practical services from the mission hall, the Church of England was ineffectual, bewailing the shrinking congregations of its city churches but unable to agree as to an appropriate response.[16]

It was the Methodist model which evangelicals had in mind when they sought to revive the church in such working class districts. Reporting on their efforts in 1906, the *Church of England Messenger* declared that:

> What is wanted is the formation of Mission districts worked by bands of clergy living in community life. For a city church, in the midst of poor lanes and mean streets, to be the focus of suburban worshippers who journeyed there on Sundays only from motives of old associations, is a mistake. The endowments are meant for the upraising of those who need it most.[17]

It was a further six years before a more concrete form of this proposal, focussed on the western city parishes of St James and St John, reached a cautious Synod which only agreed to the proposal on the condition that the rights of the present incumbents not be encroached upon. War

in 1910, after only five years of operation.

Individual churches, of both evangelical and high church inclination, established mission halls in the poorer parts of their parishes offering the 'unchurched' a range of welfare and spiritual services. Most were shortlived, dependent for their survival on the enthusiasm of an individual priest or layworker and insufficiently resourced to meet the needs which their presence generated.[14] Only in the large kindergartens attached to several of the inner city parishes was there evidence of the church's concern for anyone other than those who occupied the pews of a Sunday.[15] While the Methodist Church was able to use the central mission intervened and it was 1917 before the issue was raised again. Even then, entrenched interests in the two parishes were able to ensure that the proposal was referred to a committee to report delaying its implementation for a further two years.

This was, however, only a temporary reprieve. Reporting to the 1919 Synod the committee concluded:

The need which made them act in 1912 still existed. They should have a mission not only ministering to the wants of the people by the methods of a parish Church, but with the larger idea of carrying on definite mission work by evangelistic effort...They were not degrading the parishes, but calling upon two old parishes to begin a Forward Movement.[18]

The *Mission District Act* of 1919 constituted the parishes of St James and St John as a 'special Mission District...to make provision for facilitating the regular and systematic propagation of the Gospel...[and] to establish and maintain or assist in establishing and maintaining homes for the homeless and intermediate hospitals to provide means for the reclamation of the fallen'.[19] The new venture was not to receive direct diocesan grants, but had control of the funds of the old Metropolitan

Mission, the capital and income of St James Old Cathedral and St John's and St Matthew's lands. Compared with the assistance offered to the Mission to the Streets and Lanes, it was a substantial endowment.

The Archdeacon of Melbourne,

Archdeacon Hindley, was appointed missioner but, having established the basic administrative structure of the new mission, he quickly relinquished his role. His replacement, the Reverend Ainsley Yeates, was recruited from the Diocese of

Sydney, where he had had considerable experience of Home Mission work. In a letter written as he left Sydney to take up his new position, Yeates outlined his plans:

I am assured that there are endowments large enough to provide me with another three or four curates as well as deaconesses...In my vision of the work I can foresee Refuges for men and women in distress, Rescue Homes and like agencies, as well as clubs for men, where the manual labourer will be free to come and enjoy himself. [20]

In his four years at the helm, however, Yeates carried out a very traditional missioner role, organising clubs and activities at the mission hall, visiting in the homes, parks and institutions in the immediate neighbourhood and distributing relief as required. In contrast with its sister mission at the other end of the city, the Mission of St James and St John presented a very masculine face with the problems of homeless men and delinquent youth featuring frequently in its publicity. Its existence, the Archbishop declared, 'was a standing monument to that dastardly untruth...that the Church has no interest in the poor'. [21]

Canon (later Archdeacon) Lamble, who,

in 1925, succeeded Yeates as Missioner, was to transform the mission into a chain of 'standing monuments' to the church's concerns for the poor. Although relief continued to be distributed from the mission hall, Lamble looked towards longer-term solutions, putting forward an ambitious plan to establish

a chain of related institutions...to meet the needs of the unwanted babe, the deserted child, the wayward youth or girl, and the handicapped adult...to claim life at the beginning for the highest and the best, and to reclaim it at various stages when broken and battered by storms and temptations... Homes... conducted on modern scientific lines and under the most salutary and inspiring religious influence...will thus in the most efficient way mould human character and save human wastage. [22]

The institutional solution was a popular one at the time but the speed with which the mission implemented its plan is still remarkable. [23] The Arms of Jesus Babies' Home, opened in East Melbourne in 1925, was the first of eight institutions opened during Lamble's first three years as missioner. [24] This expansion transformed the mission from a local relief agency into

a state-wide service provider. With homes for babies, toddlers, girls and boys, single mothers, women with venereal disease and delinquent boys, it was a public face of the Church of England's concern for at least these categories of the poor and the suffering.

It was not, however, the only public face, for in almost every area into which the Mission had expanded, there were rival agencies also calling on the church for support. The reformatory institutions for women duplicated, at least in part, the work carried out by the Mission to Streets and Lanes at its House of Mercy in Cheltenham, and St Agnes' Home for Girls provided a similar service to that offered by the sisters at Brighton. The sisters had also accommodated babies and toddlers, although in conditions which, admittedly, were less than ideal. Their appeals for help in establishing a new home in the 'healthier' suburb of Darling ran alongside Lamble's appeals in both the Anglican and the secular press, leaving the Church of England as custodian of three such institutions by the end of 1927. [25]

Even the St Nicholas and St Paul's Homes for Boys could not be said to be without Anglican equivalents. Although the sisters had reluctantly decided to exclude boys from their Brighton Home in 1901, in the aftermath of the First World War the Diocese had become responsible for the Andrew Kerr Memorial Home, established in a Mornington property bequeathed for the purpose in 1921.[26] In the same year a home specifically for boys opened in Auburn, under the control of the Reverend Eric Thornton, who had co-ordinated the diocesan appeal through which it was funded. Although the Synod of 1919, which had given its approval to this appeal, had anticipated that the new home would come under the management of the sisters, a disagreement as to lines of accountability led Sister Esther to withdraw her support, leaving Thornton in complete control. Thornton, who drew his support primarily from high church sources, saw St Martin's as the first of a series of Anglican homes for boys, a dream which seemed to be coming true when he was offered tenancy of the Shrublands mansion in Canterbury, bequeathed to the Diocese by the Hindson family. The second home, St John Evangelist's, opened in 1924 but, two years later, difficulties in funding and administering the two institutions led Thornton to consolidate the two homes on the Canterbury site, bringing his hopes of a chain of institutions to an end.

The expansion of both the boys' homes project and the Mission of St James and St John was thwarted by the onset of the Depression, which severely reduced the fund-raising capacities of even the most enthusiastic supporters, while simultaneously increasing the calls for relief. It was a crisis which the Anglican Church, with no centralised welfare organisation, was ill-equipped to meet. Barbara Darling, whose thesis examines the response of the Church during this period, concludes:

Most churches did not reach out beyond themselves and become highly involved in relief work to those outside the church…Parish churches supported the church social welfare institutions where possible and were involved in some cases of provision of relief for needy parishioners, but were primarily concerned with self preservation and giving spiritual guidance…[The Church] saw itself as fulfilling an ambulance role of patching up the weak and injured…[but] it failed to respond to its few prophetic voices…who were proclaiming the need for justice for the oppressed.[27]

One of these prophetic voices was that of Father Gerard Tucker who, in 1933, was invited by Father Maynard of St Peter's Eastern Hill to bring his newly formed Brotherhood of St Laurence to take charge of St Mary's mission church in Fitzroy.[28] Although his vision of establishing an order of young ordained men, living in celibate communities and devoting their time and resources to the poor, did not survive beyond the Second World War, the distinctive philosophy which he developed did. The Brotherhood of St Laurence believed in standing alongside the poor and although this did not protect the new organisation from, on occasions, resorting to institutional solutions, it did require it to engage in social action, denouncing injustice rather than simply relieving its victims. The Brotherhood became involved in outdoor relief, the provision of hostels and a village settlement for the unemployed, and later, accommodation for the aged, but it attracted headlines for its more direct action, beginning with the famous 'verandah sitting' of 1944. To Tucker's nephew and successor, David Scott, this was

an outstanding instance of direct social action by an ardent member of the Church of England. Having exhausted all avenues of redress to enable a sick and elderly woman to return to her home, Father Tucker, Frank Coaldrake and Tony Bishop sat on the verandah of the house for five weeks as a protest against unjust housing conditions...The media were attracted...because of the apparent contradiction of a mild-mannered, respectable Anglican cleric who was prepared to take on government and ministers, and challenge 'holy cows'.[29]

The high profile which the Brotherhood was ultimately to acquire came gradually.

Based at St Mark's, Fitzroy, the Reverend R.G. Nichols, known through the media as Brother Bill, gave a far more prominent face to Anglican relief, establishing his Social Settlement in 1927 and distributing relief continuously until 1942. The settlement was an attempt to apply an idea which had had great success in both England and the United States to the Australian context.

A venture to bring men and women of education, ideas and refinement into living and vital touch with the workers, and particularly the young people in our industrial neighbourhood...Friendship is the basis of the Settlement. Service is its watchword...We hope to make the Settlement a kind of sociological clinic. Eventually our ambitions is to make it a training centre for social workers.[30]

Although there is little evidence that any of these grand aims were ever realised, the settlement performed a valued role in its local community.[31] At the peak of the Depression, it was feeding up to six hundred children per day in the Fitzroy/Collingwood area. In 1935, Nichols established a farm at Lysterfield for unemployed boys whom he hoped to be able to train for work on the land. The

farm survived longer than Brother Bill's mission. In 1943 it was taken over by the Church of England Boys' Society and was later used as part of that society's involvement in the post-war child migration program.[32]

Such a proliferation of church-based welfare agencies led to accusations from some quarters that the Church was divided against itself. These, Archbishop Lees was anxious to deny.[33] 'Individual enterprise and individual generosity,' he declared in 1926, '[were] two essential factors of Church life...Nearly all the great philanthropic work of recent times centred round a personality and the Church was glad to encourage such individual development'.[34]

These new organisations reflected the differences of churchmanship which co-existed within the Diocese. They drew the bulk of their support from parishes of like mind, with only the tendency of individual churches to support institutions in their immediate vicinity preventing a complete polarisation.[35] Although there were individual voices calling for a unified approach,[36] most members of Synod were content to receive each annual report, pass a congratulatory motion and let sleeping dogs lie.

The individual organisations were less

willing to co-exist. The rapid expansion of the Mission of St James and St John under Lamble brought a hostile response from the other child welfare agencies. It was irresponsible, Thornton argued, for the Mission to use its endowment to fund buildings and equipment. It was a theme he was to return to frequently during the Depression years as he struggled to raise funds for the unendowed high church agencies.[37] Lamble countered such attacks for calling for a united effort, emphasising the areas of need which demanded church attention. He had been a member of a sub-committee which met during 1924 to investigate the church's work amongst children, but the gaps which it identified remained unaddressed.[38]

The call for greater coordination was revived in 1931 in response to concern over the Mission's growing deficit. Lamble and Thornton were given the task of developing a scheme for improving cooperation between 'existing agencies for social work in the Diocese' but their call for the Council's finance committee to assume supervisory powers 'without interfering with the work of the various bodies or limiting their usefulness' was rejected as unsatisfactory.[39] Thornton's sudden resignation at the end of 1936 offered a further opportunity for change. With St Martin's leaderless and its committee weakened by public scandal, Archbishop Head acted to bring the boys' home under Mission control. However this plan faltered when Lamble died unexpectedly in 1939, plunging the Mission into crisis. Although the Archbishop clearly hoped that the amalgamation would proceed, the two organisations used the opportunity to move further apart. A special edition of the *Church of England Messenger* produced in 1940 to publicise the Diocese's welfare work, was once again called upon to justify a divided effort:

> Our Church is working through many agencies to alleviate the effects of poverty, unemployment and sin on human personality. Viewed sectionally each effort appears to be separate and self-contained, engaged only in its own particular sphere, appealing only for its own support. Taking a larger view it is seen that each is just an arm of the whole; the Church is engaged in this war against the evil effects of sin and bad economic conditions; she is concerned with distress suffered by human beings, and by all means within her power is out to combat it.[40]

In the post-war world, church-based welfare agencies faced new opportunities and challenges. The expansion of the welfare state promised long-term relief to many of the problems which church workers had addressed in the past. But when specialised programs and structures were required, Governments continued to look to churches for support and for the first time, it was a support for which they were willing to pay. In the emergency housing area of Camp Pell, Brotherhood of St Laurence social workers became involved in an innovative program 'to bring so-called multi-problem families up to Housing Commission standards of acceptability'. It was a program which focused not only on changing behaviour within poor families but on challenging the ways in which the community at large defined the causes of poverty.[41] On a larger scale, the availability of Commonwealth Government funding enabled the church to add a further branch to its institutional work with the development of homes for the elderly.

Asked in a 1947 Department of Social Services survey what provision the Anglican Church in Melbourne made for elderly people the Registrar offered more promise than reality:

> Apart from Lovell House, a small institution providing a Home for about twenty aged women, the Church of England has no Homes for the aged. It is, however, as soon as the building regulations permit proposed to establish Homes for old people of both sexes. The Reverend Canon J.L.Watt, of the Mission of St James and St John, will give you further details of what the Church proposes to do in this matter in the future.[42]

It would appear unlikely that Canon Watt ever carried out this task for although there were plans afoot for expansion in this area, the Mission of St James and St John was certainly not involved.

Several of the other church agencies, however, were, ensuring that once again the church's response would be a divided one. Lovell House, which had come loosely under church control in 1927, had been established many years earlier by the committee of the Governesses' Institute as a retirement home for women who had spent their lives as teachers. It had retained its own committee and had no association with any of the other church welfare organisations. After the war the Brotherhood of St Laurence had also moved into this area, accommodating homeless elderly people from the inner city in the cottages at the Carrum Downs settlement which was no longer needed for the unemployed.[43] Despite a Synod resolution in 1947 establishing a board to co-ordinate the church's response, the Sisters of the Holy Name also decided to proceed alone using the resources they had retrieved from the sale of St George's Hospital to establish Ellerslie, a home for elderly women, which opened in April 1950 and closed in 1981. A fourth home was announced in the following year after the Poolman family donated their South Yarra home to the Diocese, which appointed yet another committee to oversee its operations.

The 'official' response to the problem of the elderly was slower to get started. The Board appointed by Synod had purchased its first property in 1949 but it took a further two years of fundraising before the home, renamed Broughton Hall, was ready for occupation. It was the first of a series of properties in the Camberwell area which provided the nucleus for Church of England Homes for Elderly People offering accommodation ranging from independent units through to nursing home care. Later, the Board was to extend its work to auspice aged persons' accommodation on church land in the eastern and southern suburbs. With government funding freely available and many parishes keen to develop facilities in their own areas, the organisation grew quickly. However, this expansion was not without problems. With the initiative coming largely from individual parishes, there was a greater willingness to provide for the affluent active elderly rather than the poor and non-ambulant. Local committees of management were unsure of their relationship to the Board and the older church-affiliated homes remained independent of its control, although they were reported to be liaising closely with the Warden.[44] With the opening of its second settlement at Lara, and the purchase of the Carinya Nursing Home in Box Hill, the Brotherhood of St Laurence confirmed its intention to continue to work independently.

Government funding in the post-war years also enabled the church's child welfare agencies to grow. Initially, this came in the form of building grants which, in conjunction with extensive fundraising, enabled all of the child welfare institutions to abandon their older institutional models in favour of small group cottage-style care. Later government support was important as agencies moved into the community where preventive services and foster care all but eliminated the need for even the smaller residential units. Church-based agencies increasingly came to be seen as an adjunct of the government, presenting alternative, and sometimes innovative programs aimed at the preservation of family life.

This public perception reflected a financial reality. Prior to the Second World War the church's child welfare organisations were self-funding, but they were able to be so because they were cheaply run. The mansions in which they operated had often been donated, as was much of the food and the clothing which the children required. More importantly, they were staffed by people who saw their work as Christian service with vocation their primary qualification. Parents' contributions, usually small and often irregular, supplemented by fund-raising, were sufficient to cover the rest. In the face of inflation and professionalisation in the post-war world, this was no longer the case. Very few of the people seeking to place children had the means to pay the real cost of their care. Increasingly the State came to fill the breach, either subsidising private placements or accepting full responsibility for children as State wards. Although the image was one of partnership, the church-based agencies were constantly aware that 'the man who pays the pipe calls the tune' and that that man was now quite definitely the State. [45]

Given the loose ties which existed between diocesan welfare agencies and the church, this growing dependence on the State posed a particularly strong threat to their Anglican identity. It seemed, St John's director, Canon Ian Ellis, suggested, 'that welfare agencies which were set up to orbit around the church have been pulled across into orbit around the government departments'. [46] The Government, having recognised its responsibility to provide for those in need, was there any reason for the Church to continue to be involved? If so, was this involvement best exercised at the local or the specialised agency level? The traditional justification for the specialised

agencies was that they gave 'public expression to the fact that the church has a welfare obligation which, among other qualities, also involves a well organised, high standard, professional commitment'. [47] Yet critics noted that these professional agencies were distant from individual churches and, often, no longer overtly Christian. What then was their value as the church's public face? [48]

Divisions within the church left it ill-equipped to provide an answer to these questions. Calls for greater co-operation between the various agencies echoed throughout the post-war years but, what Archbishop Booth liked to describe as 'certain difficulties' led him to believe 'it wiser to carry on with the voluntary co-operation now in vogue'. [49] The Church of England Social Services Advisory Committee, which operated throughout the 1960s as an attempt to overcome the gap between the agencies and the parishes, floundered when it tried to bring the agencies themselves closer together. Individuals working within the agencies, whether or not they were members of the Anglican Church, found they had more in common with other professionals in the field than with fellow workers in Anglican charities. Parish clergy, faced with social problems,

found it was more appropriate to refer to a local professional agency rather than to one associated with the church. [50] As Anglican agencies diversified, they increasingly saw themselves as providing a service to the regional area in which they were located, rather than to the Anglican church as a whole.

One of the questions facing the steering committee appointed by the 1976 Synod to develop a diocesan policy on welfare was to develop a justification for such agencies to continue to operate under church auspices. The role of the church in an imperfect world, the steering committee concluded, was fourfold: to pray, to care, to stand alongside the oppressed and to strive for a better world. Where, in the past, the church had sought to meet these obligations through developing its own organisations, it now had to acknowledge 'that God is already in the world working through all people of goodwill, in a variety of different agencies, whether government or non-government, religious or secular' and to relate to such agencies 'as co-workers in a common cause of social justice and development'. There was, the committee argued, still a case for a distinctive Christian voice:

So long as the welfare services of

Church and State work hand in hand, the theological basis of involvement by Christians in community welfare can remain unstated. But when community standards and practice diverge from or conflict with those Christians, then the prophetic voice of the individual Christian and of the Church may need to be sounded...It is never enough for Christians merely to cast a critical eye on all imperfect human endeavour; nor is it enough to serve uncritically in an imperfect world. As Spirit-led people, moving towards but already experiencing the Kingdom of God, they also have a responsibility to work for a society reflecting this character.[51]

It was left to the individual agencies to decide how best to incorporate this vision into their practice. Gone were the compulsory religious observances of the past, replaced by an intent to model Christ in the services which they offer. More challenging was the call to adopt a prophetic voice where the actions of government appear to diverge from Christian goals. While the Brotherhood of St Laurence defended its decision to incorporate through an act of Parliament rather than an act of Synod as giving it the ability to 'express itself more dangerously than can the official Church' no other Anglican agency has been prepared to follow this lead.[52]

The challenge was more forcefully heard back in the parishes. The Steering Committee had found few parish-based welfare programs, and a general impression amongst community workers that 'Anglicans keep to themselves'[53]. Its recommendation to Synod made special mention of the need to encourage programs at this level. One of the first parishes to respond was St Mark's, Fitzroy, which in September 1980 set up a committee to formalise its emerging welfare program as the St Mark's Community Centre. Other parishes followed on a smaller scale, identifying particular needs in their local areas and developing their own solutions. It was a development encouraged and resourced by the Diocesan Division of Community Care but never directly under its control, a further diversification of the Anglican response to people in need.

While such a diversified response did not directly challenge the established Anglican welfare agencies, it did have the potential to impact upon their fundraising at the parish level. It also acted further to limit any possibility of the Church taking on its prophetic role to speak out against injustices wherever they occurred. In a declining economy, the consensus on which the post-war welfare state had been constructed was under challenge, threatening the alliance between the church's welfare agencies and the Government, their principal benefactor. In such a climate of change, calls for amalgamation have arisen once again.

The call is most pressing in the area of children's services, where the three agencies are doing substantially similar work. While an agreement dating back to the 1970s has, until recently, ensured that they do not directly compete with each other in service provision, in an era of competitive tendering for government contracts there is still the potential for their being placed in competition with each other for such funding. Although the differences in churchmanship which marked the origins of these agencies have greatly diminished, each still approaches the parishes on their own behalf and retains a substantial public relations department to appeal for support to the wider public. More importantly, perhaps, there is no mechanism through which the considerable expertise that has been built up over the years can be shared and nothing on which to base coordinated research.

The current call for amalgamation of the three agencies traces its origins to the Steering Committee investigations of the 1970s, but residual antagonisms and the conservatism of governing bodies, anxious to maintain the loyalty of existing donors, have meant that progress has been slow. Such concerns have been of less importance to the wider church, which is confused as to the identity of the individual agencies and anxious to see the Diocese speak with a united voice.

In April 1994, in response to such calls, Archbishop Rayner appointed a working party to reconsider the issue. Its report re-affirmed the centrality of the church welfare agencies to the mission of the church, but argued that they would fulfil this most successfully if they worked as one organisation and spoke with one voice, deriving most of their funding from government but 'being alert to emerging need and being prepared to break new ground'. While all of the report urged all Anglican agencies to look towards greater cooperation, the initial emphasis was on bringing about the amalgamation of the three child and family welfare services, the Mission of St James and St John, the Mission to Streets and Lanes and St John's Homes. Agreement was reached in discussions during 1996, with the three organisations coming together as one on the first of July of the following year.[54]

This recommendation marks a dramatic reversal of the individual effort which has marked welfare activity in the Diocese of Melbourne over the last 150 years. Such individual effort produced a remarkable range of activities, but their lack of coordination ensured that the Anglican Church has never had the profile in this area that more unified religious organisations have had, confusing even committed Anglicans and limiting the Church's ability to speak out on behalf of the poor. Commending the amalgamation plan to the boards of the three agencies involved, Archbishop Keith Rayner admitted that Anglican welfare agencies did have much in common with similar organisations without a religious base, yet he argued that they should 'seek to have a distinctively Christian character. Their primary motivation will be to express the love of God towards his creation'.[55]

Finding a way to do this as agents of Government in an increasingly secular world is the challenge facing all Anglican agencies today.

1   Royal Commission on Charitable Institutions, 1890-91, *Votes and Proceedings of the Victorian Legislative Assembly*, 1892-93, vol.iv, p.622.

2   A. Cambridge, *Thirty Years in Australia*, Kensington, 1989, p.36.

3   The Melbourne Orphanage (the antecedent of the organisations now known as Oz Child) traced its origins to the St James' Dorcas Society founded in 1845. From its foundation the society accepted applications irrespective of denomination, but the denominational base was not shed until 1853 when, the work of running the asylum having become so great, it was considered appropriate that its committee separate from that of administering outdoor relief. D.Jaggs, *Asylum to Action: Family Action 1851-1991*, Oakleigh, 1991, pp.4-9.

4   The first three presidents of the Children's Hospital, for example, were Anglicans. The founding president, Frances Perry, who had also served as president of the Women's Hospital, was succeeded by Mrs J.E. Bromby, wife of the headmaster of Melbourne Grammar, and Mrs Wilberforce Stephen, wife of the Chancellor of the Diocese. Fellow committee members included Mrs Leeper, wife of the Warden of Trinity College, and Janet, Lady Clarke, wife of one of the Diocese's wealthiest laymen. L.Gardiner, *Royal Children's Hospital, Melbourne, 1870-1970*, Melbourne, 1970, pp.31, 227.

5   The history of the Missions to Seamen is told in L.Strong, *Flying Angel: The Story of the Missions to Seamen*, London, 1956.

6   *Church of England Messenger*, 3 May 1940.

7   Cambridge, p.103.

8   Quoted in L.Strahan, *Out of the Silence: A Study of a Religious Community for Women*, Melbourne, 1988, p.23.

9   1885 public appeal document quoted in Sr. Elizabeth, *Esther, Mother Foundress*, Melbourne, 1948, p.12-3.

10 P.Grimshaw, 'In Pursuit of True Anglican Womanhood in Victoria, 1880-1914', *Women's History Review*, vol 2, no 3, 1993, pp.340-1.

11 Quoted in Strahan, p.35.

12 St George's, previously the Hornbrook Ragged School and St John's, LaTrobe Street, both of which were transferred to Mission management in 1907. Strahan, pp.48-50.

13 St George's Intermediate Hospital in Kew, which opened in 1912, and St Ives Private Hospital in East Melbourne, which opened in 1917. Strahan, pp.50-3, 69-71.

14 The Mission of the Holy Redeemer, established at St Mark's Fitzroy in 1889, is the most prominent of these missions, but it appears not to have survived the pressures of the depression in the following decade.

15 A report of a visit of inspection to Church of England kindergartens in December 1920 lists five, including the Alice Lovell Clarke kindergarten in Fitzroy, which also incorporated a creche and was able to offer short-term residential care to children in distress. *Church of England Messenger*, 21 December 1920, 8 June 1922.

16 For a discussion of the Methodist Central Missions during this period see R. Howe and S. Swain, *The Challenge of the City: The Centenary History of Wesley Central Mission, 1893-1993*, Melbourne, 1993, ch.4.

17 Quoted in K.Cole, *Commissioned To Care: The Golden Jubilee History of The Mission of St James and St John, 1919-1969*, Melbourne, 1969, p.14.

18 *Church of England Messenger*, 17 October 1919. The Forward Movement was common to most Protestant denominations struggling to come to terms with providing effective Christian witness in the growing industrial cities. Its origins are discussed in K.S.Inglis, *Churches and the Working Classes in Victorian England*, London, 1961. In Melbourne, its principles were best encapsulated in the transformation of Wesley Church, Lonsdale Street, into the Central Methodist Mission in 1893, which is described in Howe and Swain, *Challenge of the City*, Ch.1.

19 Cole, pp.16-17.

20 *Church of England Messenger*, 22 July 1921.

21 *Church of England Messenger*, 13 March 1924.

22 Quoted in Cole, p.27.

23 Rev. Samuel Hoban, Superintendent of the Central Methodist Mission at Wesley Church, used the same 'chain of institutions' argument to justify the expansion of services during his term of office, but his 'chain' was completed with the addition of only three homes. Howe and Swain, *Challenge of the City*, p.89.

24 This expansion was greatly facilitated by the availability of women trained through the recently established St Hilda's Training Home to staff the new institutions. Cole, p.25.

25 ie. the Arms of Jesus (1925) and Ramoth Toddlers' Home (1927) under Lamble's control and the Darling Home for Little Children (1927) controlled by the Mission to Streets and Lanes.

26 The Andrew Kerr Memorial Home was initially conceived of as a temporary care home but increasingly became involved in long-term care as well. It was managed by a local committee with strong connections to key Diocesan administrators and was the only Anglican institution to receive financial grants from the Diocese in response to its regular financial crises. It was transferred to the control of the Mission of St James and St John in 1941.

27 B.Darling, The Church of England in Melbourne and the Great Depression, 1929-35 MA thesis, University of Melbourne, 1982, p.vi.

28 Fr Maynard's reasons for initiating this invitation are explored at much greater length in Colin Holden's *From Tories at prayer to Socialists at Mass*, Melborune, 1996; The story of the Brotherhood is partially told in two histories, I.Carter, *God and Three Shillings: The Story of the Brotherhood of St Laurence*, Melbourne, 1967 and J.Handfield, *Friends and Brothers: A Life of Gerard Kennedy Tucker, Founder of the Brotherhood of St Laurence and Community Aid Abroad*, Melbourne, 1980.

29 D.Scott, 'The Brotherhood of St Laurence's Evolving Attitudes to Poverty, Research and Social Action' Brotherhood of St Laurence, in *Looking Forward Looking Back: The Brotherhood's Role in Changing Views of Poverty*, Fitzroy, 1993, pp.10-11.

30 *Church of England Messenger*, 26 August 1926.

31 The settlement house model failed wherever it was tried in Melbourne. See R. Howe, The Response of the Protestant Churches to Urbanisation in Melbourne and Chicago, 1892-1914 Ph.D. thesis, University of Melbourne, 1972, Ch.4.

32 By the time the migrants arrived, the farm had been moved to Yering, the Lysterfield property having been resumed by the Melbourne and Metropolitan Board of Works.

33 *Church of England Messenger*, 23 September 1926.

34 *Church of England Messenger*, December, 1926.

35 Darling, pp.25-6.

36 See, for example, the article by the Rev Roscoe Wilson, 'The Church and Social Questions', *Church of England Messenger*, 20 August 1920.

37 See, for example, the interchange between Lamble and Thornton at the 1927 Synod, *Church of England Messenger*, 20 October 1927. In addition to his position at St Martin's and St John's, Thornton was appointed Warden of the Community of the Holy Name in 1934 and spoke on behalf of both organisations until his sudden resignation in December 1936.

38 The Committee reported back to the Archbishop-in-Council in February 1924 but no action was taken on its recommendations until after the report had passed through Synod in October of that year. There is no record of its recommendations ever being implemented.

39 Archbishop-in-Council minutes, 27 May 1932, 8 July 1932.

40 *Church of England Messenger*, 3 May 1940.

41 Brotherhood of St Laurence, *Looking Forward Looking Back: The Brotherhood Role in Changing Views of Poverty*, Fitzroy, 1993, p.5.

42 Registrar to J.L.Collopy, Deputy Director of Social Services, 21 April 1947, Church of England Homes for Elderly People File, Archives of the Diocese of Melbourne.

43 Appeal literature suggested a more ambitious plan retaining the family homes but adding cottage homes for children, small bungalows for old age pensioners, a poultry farm and market garden, kindergarten and social centre, but Brotherhood records would suggest that the settlement was providing only for the elderly from 1946. Brotherhood of St Laurence, *A Brief History*, Melbourne, 1993, p.6.

44 Church of England Homes for the Elderly, *Annual Report*, 1959.

45 This realisation was made the more complex by the fact that key leaders in the church-based welfare sector had actively courted this relationship in an attempt to bring what they saw as sub-standard child welfare organisations into line. R.Howe and S.Swain, *All God's Children: A Centenary History of the Methodist Homes for Children and The Orana Peace Memorial Homes*, Canberra, 1989, pp.152-7. Evidence of this disease within Anglican agencies can be seen in the undated letter (c.1959) from Reverend Donald Menzies to the Child Care Committee of the Church of England Social Services Advisory Committee, Church of England Social Services Advisory Committee file, Anglican Archives, and in the discussion paper 'A Summary of the Proposed Set Up of the Department of Social Welfare' included in the Board of Management Minutes of St John's Homes, 18 May 1959.

46 Background on Legal Incorporation for 1983 Synod, Incorporation of Anglican Welfare Agencies File, Archives of the Diocese of Melbourne.

47 Bishop Peter Hollingworth's note in response to Ellis in Background on legal Incorporation for 1983 Synod, Incorporation of Anglican Welfare Agencies File, Anglican Archives.

48 These criticisms are implicit in the report of the Diocesan Social Services Review Steering Committee in 1978.

49 *Church of England Messenger* reporting on Provincial Synod, 25 July 1952.

50 *Diocesan Social Services Review Steering Committee Working Papers*, Diocese of Melbourne Synod 1978, p.5. The failure of CESSAC is discussed in more detail in an account written by its executive officer, R. Catherine Smith, 3 January 1976. *Social Services Review: Historical Review File*, Archives of the Diocese of Melbourne.

51 *Steering Committee Working Papers*, pp.13-16, 19-20, 21-22.

52 Archdeacon G.T.Sambell to Archbishop Woods, 7 March 1960, Brotherhood of St Laurence File, Archives of the Diocese of Melbourne.

53 *Steering Committee Working Papers*, p.7.

54 Joint Anglican Child and Family Welfare Agencies Working Party, *New Directions for Challenging Times*, Melbourne, 1995, pp.4-5.

55 *New Directions for Challenging Times*, p.4.

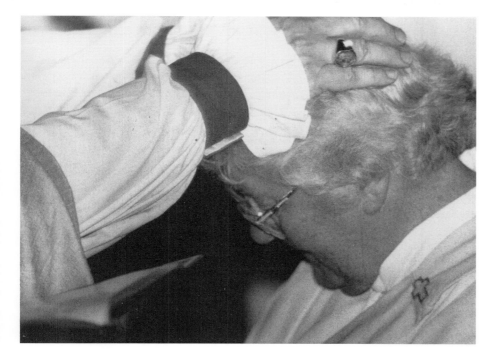

The Reverend Elizabeth Alfred, first woman to be ordained priest in the Diocese, 1992.

Women in the Diocese of Melbourne

Two steps forward, one step back

an ambiguous history

From the inception of the Anglican Diocese of Melbourne, the role of church women has been, to say the least, ambiguous. The Anglican Church could never have attained such a solid early footing in this colony without women's efforts, particularly in fund-raising, an essential factor in establishing and maintaining parish life. Yet their very indispensability intimidated the church's male leaders. Fearful that too predominant a female role would alienate even further the always-elusive male worshippers, they kept even laywomen 'in their place', effectively until the mid-1950s. Within just two decades of allowing women at long last to join Vestries (parish councils), however, this Diocese was a leader of the movement for women's ordination, and now boasts one of the finest records for women's affirmation in the country.

However, since the 1970s, the Anglican Church, along with other denominations, has lost the allegiance of the vast bulk of its laywomen. Older women, remnants of the housewife generation, are still in church. Middle-aged women and their younger sisters, the age-groups whose untiring efforts once kept the church viable financially and in every other way, are no longer present in the same proportion as they were in the past. The modern generations of career women have different priorities from those of their mothers and grandmothers. Did the churches try to keep women 'in their place' one generation too long? Are they now paying the price, not just in Melbourne, but throughout the Western world?

* * * * * * *

The early years

The first influential group of women in the Anglican Diocese of Melbourne were clergy wives. When the first bishop, Charles

Mrs Frances Perry, wife of Bishop Charles Perry.

PHOTO: COURTESY OF ROYAL WOMEN'S HOSPITAL.

Perry, arrived in the colony in 1848, there was just one clergy wife – Zelie Adelaide Thomson – resident in the village. With Perry and the clergy who came with him, came not just his redoubtable wife Frances, but four other women who, with her, would set the pattern for clergy wives in the early years of the new Diocese.

In those first years of the Colony of Victoria, in tough pioneering conditions, all the usual patterns of middle-class life in the vicarage these women had known at home had to be abandoned. Faced with the daunting task of building a Diocese from scratch with few of the resources they had been used to in England, these 'unpaid curates' were, quite literally, worked to death.

Research by Melbourne historian Peter Sherlock has uncovered an astonishing – and tragic – statistic.[1] Between 1848 and 1870, no fewer than 24 clergy wives died. In the same period, only seven clergymen died. The women's average age at their time of death was just 39.5 years. And this at a time when, in the dangerous world of the colonial frontier, in the general community, men generally died earlier than women.

Back in 1870, Melbourne's first Dean, Hussey Macartney, was bewildered by the rash of deaths among clergy wives. Mourning the death of Elizabeth MacCullagh, wife of the Vicar of Lancefield, at the tender age of 27, Dean Macartney wrote: 'We confess ourselves utterly unable to account for this strange reverse of the ordinary mortality – but three painful words will here inform us – toil, privation, anxiety.'

Without the benefit of modern medical knowledge, the colonial doctors ascribed the women's deaths to causes that are infuriatingly vague. While some died clearly as a result of childbirth, others are recorded as having died from a 'broken heart', 'colonial fever', or, in one case, from 'exhaustion' after three weeks of 'hysteria'. One was apparently left an invalid for 25 years after having 'thoughtlessly exposed herself to the sun not long after her arrival in the colony'!

But whatever the vague official causes, the general view in the colonial church was that overwork was the major reason for these untimely deaths. The high death rate continued well into the 1890s. Periodically, the diocesan paper, the *Messenger,* blamed the persistent deaths on overwork. In 1875, it said: 'It has been the incessant toil, the hidden racking care of this unequal struggle to make both ends meet, that has laid low before their time so many wives of our clergy.'

Sherlock's account of a number of these long-suffering women reveals the drudgery and difficulty of their lives. Far from home, in a new settlement on the edge of the known world, they battled intense loneliness first of all. The strange climate taxed their health to the limit, while housing in the early years was often rudimentary. Servants were hard to get and harder to keep, making the demands of home, family and parish work extremely demanding for the 'unpaid curate'. For parish work must have taken up an inordinate amount of time for these dedicated women.

In both city and country, they often did everything from visiting the sick and needy, teaching large classes in the Sunday school, playing the organ, conducting women's and children's groups, and of course that hardy perennial of parish life, fund-raising. Hospitality was, as today, an important part of their duties.

In the country, they often endured extreme isolation, while in the city, the clergy wives were in considerable demand in the establishment and running of benevolent societies. Frances Perry was a noted philanthropist, taking a leading role in the establishment of, among other things, the Women's Hospital.

All of this had to be managed on pitifully low incomes. In the 1890s, when Melbourne endured one of its worst financial depressions, stipends sank to an all-time low. This prompted an extraordinary rash of letters to the *Argus,* Melbourne's main newspaper at the time. An anonymous clergy wife, calling herself the 'poor parsoness', wrote to complain of the terrible poverty of country clergy families in particular. She complained that she and her seven children were forced to live in poverty because of her husband's meagre stipend. Their clothes were threadbare, their horse had died, and the parsonage was in disrepair.

Other clergy wives - most of them also anonymous - wrote to support the claims of the 'parsoness'. The heated correspondence at least ensured a healthy trickle of donations to the Bishop's country clergy fund.

But not everyone was sympathetic to the plight of the clergy wives. In 1860, the *Messenger* carried a comment that at least the deaths of the wives were not as great a hardship as the deaths of their husbands would be! Better the wives and children die than to have the family 'sorrow-stricken by the removal of their head, and Parishes left without a pastor. In God's mercy the father lives, the pastor survives'!

Wives were, after all, replaceable. More than half the grieving widowers remarried, most within a year or two. And in any case - in an age when there were no pensions and no superannuation schemes - the church had little financial provision for clergy widows.

The lives of the colonial clergy wives were, for all their difficulties, not as entirely circumscribed as those of women of the same social standing in the community. Their role as hostess, teacher, musician, society leader and even 'unpaid curate', provided greater scope than the mere domestic round ever could have. Though male church leaders expected them to 'keep their place', that place allowed more initiatives than were generally available to other women.

There can be no doubt that their efforts, combined with those of the other lay women they inspired and led, were crucial to the establishment of the Anglican Church in Victoria. Their work in fundraising was all-important for a church cut off from the patronage and endowment systems that funded it in England. Their work, however, was important for the wider mission of the church, that is, to the benefit of the general community. Clergy wives were often prominent leaders in the establishment of benevolent societies and organisations of many kinds.

In this area, the leader was undoubtedly Frances Perry.[2] She worked tirelessly beside her husband for the 26 years of his episcopate in Melbourne, carrying out most of the duties of any other clergy wife. Being childless, she was free to undertake even more duties than most, however, and spent a good deal of her time travelling with her husband as well as in her own philanthropic pursuits. Over the years, she was variously president of the Orphan Asylum Committee, president of the ladies' committee of the Carlton refuge for homeless women, founder of a home for governesses, and involved in the organisation of the Benevolent Asylum and a Church of England Mission to Aborigines. One of the major interests of this childless woman was the formation of the Lying-In Hospital, which later became the Royal Women's Hospital, and which has, to this day, a wing named after her. The aim of this hospital was to provide somewhere for respectable poor women to give birth, if they had nowhere suitable at home.

The key to admission to the new hospital was respectability. Only women who could produce their 'marriage lines' were admitted. Unmarried mothers, and certainly prostitutes, were barred in a society in which 'respectability' was the by-word. Any woman who turned up actually in labour was admitted, however.

In their benevolent work, some nineteenth century women came perilously close to stepping outside their 'place' in church and society. Some doctors - males only, at that time - resented their involvement in the running of public hospitals. The hard-working women discovered how ambiguous was the line that divided their 'proper' sphere from the world that belonged to men.

A range of historical studies[3] has revealed the way in which the 'proper' female role was constructed in the nineteenth century. Evangelicals, particularly of the Clapham Sect, in the aftermath of the Industrial Revolution, had developed the full-blown teaching of women's rightful sphere as being the home. The growth of the middle class had created a new group of married women who no longer had to work for a family trade or business, and who, because they had servants, had abundant leisure time. Good works, both within the home and outside, were the answer for the Evangelical leadership, fearful that such women would otherwise occupy their times in frivolities like aristocratic women who were their only alternative role models. Women needed to be useful and hard-working, not decorative. But useful and hard-working in a manner that conformed to their subordination. So a view of the proper role of women as angels of the home attained to almost mystical proportions. Women were to provide places of 'sanctuary' for their husbands, to refresh them from the rigours and evils of the working world. They were to make of their homes 'divine workshops from which characters are developed for eternity', so bringing up their children, and particularly their sons, in the ways of strict morality. Women were, therefore, the moral backbone of society, beacons of social and moral purity of a high order. This was the very essence of female respectability in a society obsessed with drawing demarcation lines between the respectable and the outcast. The Christian churches were at the forefront in promoting this view.

Women who accepted this role and the onerous, self-denying duties that went with it, were exalted as being on a higher spiritual plane to men. But only so long as they exercised this mystical influence within the home! If they attempted to do so outside their expected limitations, then they were quickly chastised.

The growing women's movement posed a threat to this convenient division between home and wider society. Originally a response to the growing need of education for those middle-class women who did not marry and needed to support themselves in 'respectable' and suitable careers, the women's movement actually had its political origins in the philanthropic efforts of Christian women.[4] Its strongest modern impetus had come from the United States, where Christian women concerned to combat the evils of slavery, found they needed first to defend their right to speak as women!

In the second half of the nineteenth century, radical ideas of female equality and female participation in all levels of society, were infiltrating the colonies from the old world. Moves were afoot to admit women to educational levels previously only available to men, though it took the Anglican Church longer than the other churches to found its first major girls' school in Melbourne (Melbourne Church of England Girls' Grammar School, founded in 1893). Melbourne University had already opened its doors to women in the 1880s. In the same decade, the cause of votes for women took root in the formation of the Woman's Suffrage League of Victoria, and the Woman's Christian Temperance Union, which had female suffrage high on its agenda. Property Acts, which at last gave legal rights to married women, and new divorce laws, signalled significant changes in the male/female relationship, and in conventional family values, in secular society.

Victoria's Anglican leaders, like their

peers in other States, were dismayed by these developments. Melbourne's second bishop, James Moorhouse, was quick to condemn them. Woman, 'the nurse, the comforter, the sanctifier', could only do her work if she kept out of the 'din of battle and the glare of publicity', he said. Woman's 'higher powers' were, he insisted, only effective in her proper sphere, the home. In their anxiety to keep women in their place, the leaders were only too glad to welcome the formation of the local branch of the Mothers' Union, a body formed in England in 1876 as a direct reaction to the growing influence of the women's movement. The Mothers' Union was explicitly created to combat these 'assaults' on the traditional family, and instead nurture and buttress woman's role in the home.

Though the Mothers' Union has, for some decades now, been a society thoroughly in tune with the role of modern women, both in Australia and abroad, it cannot be denied that it was founded to be reactionary. In its earliest years, it regarded the vote for women as an 'extra burden'; - 'as if wives and mothers had not quite enough to do'. And through its strict membership criteria, it drew a firm line between women deemed to be respectable and those who were not. Membership was limited to married women with or without children, or widows. Divorcees, as well as unmarried mothers, were out of the question until very recent times, causing great personal distress and division in many parishes.

In few places was the Mothers' Union more reactionary than in the Diocese of Melbourne, perhaps because of the influence of the conservative Evangelical third bishop of Melbourne, Field Flowers Goe, in whose term of office the Mothers' Union Melbourne branch began in 1895. At the time of MU's formation in Melbourne, the *Church Messenger* hailed it as a welcome response to the changing times: 'Among the various societies that have been organised in these latter days for the purpose of arousing women to a sense of their rights, we hail with satisfaction one that proposes for its aim to awaken women to a sense of their responsibilities'![5] The hallowing of a woman's 'duty' above all else, lay at the heart of the Mothers' Union credo, in Melbourne as elsewhere. The Mothers' Union mission was one of 'influence' - influencing women and girls to embrace a traditional, home-based role in the face of increasing society pressures; influencing the style of family life and the raising of children; and so influencing the moral fibre of the nation and Empire. From their essentially reactive outlook, they even encouraged society to reject or at least treat cautiously many modern developments, such as 'motion pictures' and motor-cars.

The Mothers' Union was neither a fund-raising body for the church, nor a highly active or outspoken body, let alone a body concerned with wider social welfare work. Rather, true to its aim to promote the traditional role of the woman as mother first and foremost, it preferred to operate internally, and always under the guidance, even direction, of male clergy (A branch could not be formed, or even continue, in a parish if the Vicar refused permission. The Vicar appointed the branch president, and admitted women to membership.).

Their reluctance to make decisions and take on change or expansion fitted with their identification of themselves as the last obedient women,' writes Ellen Warne. 'It was in the 1920s and 1930s, when society had changed enough for middle-class women to have to make some sort of decision whether or not to continue their education, work or remain at home that the 'silent mission' was changed from a primarily religious role to one of the necessity and virtue of the housewife and

her tasks of 'practical mothering'. They hankered after infant welfare centres, absorbed the advice of experts such as Truby King on breast-feeding, and Charlotte Mason on education. And the earlier emphasis on social morality and the fibre of the empire or nation was transferred to the quality of individual families and the success, or lack of it, that individual mothers had with their child's development and progress in physical, psychological and religious realms.'

The strong support the Mothers' Union gained from the church leadership, encouraged Anglican women to direct their energies to this cautious body, rather than to the more radical Protestant bodies such as the Woman's Christian Temperance

Mothers' Union Celebration: Eva Beck with Mrs Freda Kalini of Zaire.

Union, with its strong and overt feminist agenda. Consequently, local Anglican women were not highly represented in the wider women's movement in the latter years of the nineteenth century.

There can be no doubt that the Mothers' Union had a persistent and reactionary influence on the Church's understanding of the role of women in its first decades. And yet the same women who met at Mothers' Union meetings, were also members of the Ladies' Guild, and doubtless some of them were Sunday school teachers. In both those capacities, they had perhaps a stronger and more direct influence on the life of the parish.

For it was the ladies' guilds which organised most of the fundraising that kept parish life afloat, with their bazaars, cake-stalls, and the rest. When moves to allow women to serve on Vestries came to Synod in the first decades of the twentieth century, the most persistent argument used to advance their cause was the fact that they raised the parish money, and therefore should have a say in its distribution.

Their role as Sunday school teachers, enabling the very existence of parish-based religious education, nevertheless posed a real dilemma for church leaders between the 1880s and the First World War. Simply, there were too many women teachers, and this was a 'great weakness'. Successive meetings of the Sunday School Association deplored the preponderance of female teachers – double the number of male teachers. The enthusiasm of the women was preventing men from involvement in this useful area of church work, because their large numbers 'feminised' the Sunday School and so made it unattractive to men.

As Patricia Grimshaw has argued,[6] an overriding concern of the colonial church leadership had been how to attract more male worshippers.[7] The Anglican Church had the greatest difficulty of all the churches in attracting lay male involvement at anything more than a nominal level in the late nineteenth century. The 'Englishness' of the Anglican clergy, and in particular the perceived 'effeminacy' of some clergy of Tractarian views, with their ornate liturgical dress, was off-putting to many Australian males. Much as the clergy could not afford to alienate further the women who did all the work and raised all the money, they could even less afford to further alienate lay men by allowing women any positions of power or authority. Grimshaw writes: 'It was surely the very sense of holding, or of belonging to the sex which held, the reins of power that endowed Anglican men with spiritual virility, and with the strength to withstand the derision of males outside the fold. If women were allowed access to power structures in the Church, the result might be a feminisation of the hierarchy itself, and a resultant male exodus of unforeseen proportions.'

It was this fear of alienating lay men from parish work that was the overriding reason why the Diocese of Melbourne persistently refused to allow women to join parish Vestries, despite a long-running debate in Synod that began before the First World War and continued until 1956. Presumably, it was assumed that women would not be alienated by this treatment, and for most of this century that assumption was right. However, the later refusal, in a vastly different social climate, to advance women to the ranks of the clergy, without a long and bitter struggle, may have finally tipped the delicate balance.

A professional role at last

While the Mothers' Union kept married women 'in their place', single women who wanted to dedicate their lives to the church were, for the first time, offered two options in the closing years of the nineteenth century. Anglican religious orders, revived in England in 1841, and an order of deaconesses, revived in 1862, took several decades to be transplanted to the colonies. They nevertheless conveniently fitted the model of 'true Anglican womanhood' so dear to the hearts of Melbourne's bishops. The nuns, by the nature of their calling and lifestyle, were not aligned to the modern women's movement, while the deaconesses, who worked in subordination to male clergy and bishops, were assigned a backroom role as nurturer, carer, and supporter of the values of home and family.[8] Neither group, however, was self-serving. Both offered practical social welfare work in some of the toughest areas in Melbourne, and were at the forefront of carrying the Church's mission into the community at large. Their hidden service over many years deserves greater affirmation than it has so far received.

In 1885, the newly-formed Mission to the Streets and Lanes was struggling to establish its work in the worst slums in inner Melbourne. The aim was to have 'duly qualified' ladies visit in the 'lanes and courts', bringing the message of the Gospel to the 'poor and fallen', mainly the prostitutes who frequented this notorious part of the city. The object was to have 'the presence of good women near where the sadness prevails'. The hope was that these good women would be 'deaconesses', though at that stage in Australia no such order had been created. After a hesitant start, the situation was saved by the arrival in Australia of Miss Emma Silcock, who had formerly been a novice in an Anglican order, the Community of St Mary the Virgin at Wantage, near Oxford, where she had taken the religious name of Esther. In that order, she had already had some experience working in the slums.

Miss Silcock had the good sense, in evangelical Melbourne, to speak of 'deaconess work' rather than the religious life on which her heart was actually set, and was appointed to the mission as a 'deaconess'. Most of the funds to support her and the fledgling mission, it is worth noting, were raised by the women's guild at St Peter's, Eastern Hill, one of the three parishes which had founded the Mission. Her first assistants, Emma (later Sister Ellen) Okins and Christina Cameron, were appointed on a voluntary capacity, a foretaste of the general expectation that deaconesses would be middle-class women with private means.

They were, writes their historian, Morna Sturrock, 'genteel, educated and competent middle class young women anxious to be of some use to society, rather than to be decorative ornaments. They were among many women caught up in the social and religious activity following the Industrial Revolution, seeing the need for specialised and sympathetic ministry, woman to woman, particularly in the large towns'.

The early records of this beginning of formal women's ministry in Melbourne are shadowy and incomplete. As Sturrock points out, the secular press took more interest in this ministry than the official publications of the Anglican Church, which often simply omitted any reference to the women's work. Throughout nearly a century, the deaconess movement in Melbourne would receive scant attention from the Church at large.

Sister Ellen and Sister Christina, though regarding themselves as nuns rather than deaconesses, were solemnly set apart by Bishop Field Flowers Goe as deaconesses in a ceremony at St Peter's, Eastern Hill in 1890, some two years after commencing their work. Sister Ellen was, sadly, to suffer the fate of many of the first clergy wives. She literally worked herself to death

Melbourne's first women priests with Archbishop Rayner, 1992.

by 1902, in her case by running the Community's children's home in Brighton from 1894. Mother Esther, however, was not 'set apart' in the same way; four years later, she took her final vows as a nun in the more sympathetic Diocese of Ballarat. The religious community she had founded under the guise of a deaconess order, the Community of the Holy Name, was not

officially recognised as such until 1912, when Archbishop Henry Lowther Clarke finally gave it its first formal charter.

The next seven members of the Community were both nuns and deaconesses, though the dates of their profession as nuns (a private ceremony) and public licensing as deaconesses were often separated by many years. A small

biography of Mother Esther, written in about 1947, records that the dual process was the compromise she had reached with Bishop Goe. A conservative Evangelical, he wanted the women's work, but not a formal religious community in his Diocese. She wanted some episcopal recognition for her sisters. The compromise was to allow the sisters to be made deaconesses, but she would not submit to such ordination herself. No wonder the diocesan authorities kept the women's ministry determinedly in the shadows. As Sturrock says, 'one can only marvel at the reticence, loyalty and obedience' of the nuns/deaconesses in the face of such harsh treatment.

A quite separate order of deaconesses, unrelated to the Community of the Holy Name, was founded in Melbourne in 1924, in the wake of the 1920 Lambeth Conference (the worldwide conference of Anglican Bishops, generally held every 10 years). The 1920 conference tried to establish some uniform guidelines for Anglican deaconesses, about whose ministry there was considerable confusion. Until that point, there was, world-wide, no official recognition of the order, no authorised form of ordination, and no clear role for the deaconess, other than that of parish visitor and worker among women.

In 1920, with women now finally allowed to vote in Britain and the United States, the bishops were nervous of losing

invaluable female support. But they were still firmly wedded to the traditional female stereotype. The Church must not do anything that might obscure woman's central vocation of motherhood, they declared, even as they tried to establish some role for women as deaconesses. But were deaconesses the same as male deacons? Yes and no! Women were spiritually equal to men, but in the 'world of action…man has a priority, and in the last resort authority belongs to him'. Their order of deaconesses would follow the 'primitive' model. They were not to have the same liturgical role as the modern male deacon. The bishops did, however, allow the women a very limited liturgical role (leading some public prayers, and

occasionally 'instructing' the congregation) which they had not had previously.[9]

The bishops' cautious green light did, however, encourage formal deaconess training and recognition. In Melbourne, in 1924, St Hilda's College, till then a training college for women missionaries, also became a diocesan deaconess training institution. Deaconess Minna Johnson, a Melbourne woman who had been trained and ordained in Sydney, came back to establish deaconess training. Sister Minna, as she was called, was even given special permission to preach in parishes around the Diocese, encouraging particularly middle-class girls with 'some means' to volunteer for training. In her severe 'semi-clerical black and grey uniform' and veil, she must have modelled an image

First ordination of women deacons, February, 1986.

that was something between a nun and an army nurse![10]

The close connection with the staunchly evangelical Church Missionary Society, which ran St Hilda's, was a drawback for the women's ministry in many Anglo-Catholic parishes, which in the 1920s and 1930s were often at the forefront of charitable work among the poor. So in 1940, deaconess training was moved into its own independent institution, which continued to operate until 1978.

In general, their work was parish-based, and confined to the behind-the-scenes roles of pastoral assistant, religious education teacher, organiser of the Girls' Friendly Society branch, and the like. Some duties were even more mundane; they were often required to care for the parish linen and communion vessels, as well as the parish roll. Their leadership and liturgical roles were extremely limited, and they did not even have the right to sit in synod with the clergy. One attempt to have them admitted by right to Synod, promoted by an archdeacon in the Synod of 1933, was defeated in the House of Clergy. Though the House of Laity voted solidly in its favour, two of the three women members of Synod at that time actually voted against it.

Over the years, the number of deaconesses was low. In all there were only about 60 deaconesses who served in Melbourne Diocese. The distinctive deaconess uniform - severe long-sleeved grey dress with white starched collar, grey hat, black shoes and gloves - together with low pay, limited work opportunities and no recognised place in the official life of the Diocese, combined to make deaconess work unattractive to all but the most dedicated women. During World War II another category of professional women, Trained Women Workers, was introduced, though the demarcation lines between the role adopted by these women and their deaconess sisters, were almost non-existent. Many Trained Women Workers went on to become deaconesses.

After 1978, when the deaconess institute finally closed, both deaconesses and Trained Women Workers were trained beside male ordinands at both Trinity and Ridley Colleges. The dowdy uniforms were gone at last, as the modern women's movement began to have its impact. Already, though, the horizons were expanding for women who believed they had a vocation to serve the Church. The last deaconesses ordained in Melbourne - Carlie Hannah in 1983 and Kay

Goldsworthy in 1984 - already had their sights set on the priesthood.

Pioneering the ordination debate[11]

In 1968, the Lambeth Conference had at last agreed that deaconesses in fact belonged to the same order as male deacons. The following year, however, the Australian General Synod, in its wisdom, declared that deaconesses were not part of the historic three-fold Orders of the Church, and insisted on a form of 'ordination' that clearly distanced the women from true ordination. Many of the serving deaconesses at the time were devastated. It galvanised previously reticent women into action. Elizabeth Alfred, until the previous year Principal of the Melbourne Deaconess House, began actively to campaign for women to be accepted into the full ministry of the Church.

At the same time, the General Synod's newly-created Doctrine Commission had the task of examining the issue of the ordination of women into the three-fold order. The impetus had come from the 1968 Lambeth Conference, and initially there seemed no urgency. It presented a brief report to the 1973 meeting of General Synod, calling for more time to explore the deep issues involved. The majority

The Reverend Kate Prowd, Curate of St Stephen's, Mt Waverley, 1986-88.

(eight) of the Commission members, nevertheless, declared they saw no theological objection to the ordination of women to the priesthood, or to the episcopate. The minority report, from three members, opposed any moves on the basis of women's fundamental subordination to men in both the congregation and in marriage. If women were ordained, they said, it would lead to 'theological and practical confusion'. By the time of the 1973 report, Elizabeth Alfred was herself a member of General Synod, having overcome her reluctance to stand for election as a lay representative, for the greater cause of giving women a voice.

In Melbourne the same year, a separate commission was set up, ostensibly to review the recruitment, training and deployment of deaconesses and Trained Women Workers. But with women now ordained as priests in other parts of the Anglican Communion (in Hong Kong), and with vigorous debate in the United States in particular (the first women priests would be ordained there in 1974), it was impossible for the commission to keep to its limited 'status quo' brief. 'The major hindrance to the fostering of vocations in the Church for women is the Church's confusion and ambivalence about what ministries are open to women,' it said in its report. Almost all the women who had taken part in the Commission's public consultations claimed that the Church's attitude (allowing women only a subordinate ministry) was an 'immense barrier' to the realisation of true partnership in Christian ministry even in those areas of the Church's life where ordination was not a prerequisite.

The Commission's members – five of whom were women – said that they saw no conclusive theological reason why women could not be ordained to the priesthood, and they called on Melbourne Diocesan Synod to make a similar statement, and to push the national church to take action. It was, it concluded, 'to the great loss of the Church that the opportunities for real fulfilment in ministry are not freely available to women'. The report was released in time for the 1975 Synod, which passed a resolution calling for further discussion about the ministry of women around the Diocese so that the 1976 Synod, and the General Synod of 1977, could 'reach informed decisions concerning the ministries open to women, especially the question of admission to holy orders'.

A series of seminars, held at Christ Church, Brunswick in June and July 1976, brought together an array of Anglican opinion on the issue, and initiated the first major public controversy on women's ordination. The papers from those seminars, later published in a booklet, flagged the main lines of dispute. These same lines flared in the Synod debate that followed, when the late Dr John Gaden, one of Australia's finest theologians and a great advocate of the ordination of women, brought a resolution calling for the admission of women to the Church's three-fold order of ministry. The motion, which also called on the national church to authorise their admission, was carried by a two-thirds majority. On that day in 1976, Melbourne Synod became the first in Australia to call for women priests, signalling its strong and radical leadership in this cause for the crucial 16-year debate that lay ahead. Though there would be many minor retreats before the first women priests were ordained in Melbourne in December 1992, Melbourne Synod's strong stand never dropped below that significant two-thirds majority.

Though always in the minority in this Diocese, those opposed to the ordination of women maintained a committed position throughout the life of the debate. Until the latter years, the division between the two sides was not as bitter and acrimonious as it was in certain other Australian Dioceses. Mostly, leaders on both sides maintained a good-humoured and generous respect for each other.

In Melbourne, opponents of women's ordination based their arguments on the two main strands of debate within the Church nationally. Some argued that Jesus had deliberately established a male-only priesthood by his selection of twelve male apostles. As the priest at the altar specifically represents Christ, and as the historical Jesus was male, so too must the priest who represents him be male, they claimed. The Church was not free to change this tradition, they said. Others argued certain texts in the New Testament forbade leadership roles to women, and confined 'headship', at least in the home and in the congregation, to men.

Those in favour of women's ordination argued principally from the Gospel accounts of Jesus' radical acceptance of women as disciples, apostles, and models of faith. They denied that 'the twelve' were set apart as priests, or as a model of priesthood, and argued that the priest at the altar did not symbolise the 'maleness' of Jesus anymore than the priest needed to model his Jewishness. Further, they claimed the tradition of a male priesthood was a tradition that the Church could change. They dismissed the New Testament texts about the role of women as either used out of context, or misinterpreted.

Giving lay women a voice

In taking this important initial step, Melbourne was building on earlier 'firsts' for women. In 1912, a prominent layman, Mr John Raw, had brought a Synod resolution to gain women the right to vote for members of Synod. Only lay men had had this right of suffrage since Melbourne's first Synod was inaugurated in 1854. Now that women had the right to vote in both state and federal elections, to refuse them the same right in elections for the Church's 'parliament' was manifestly silly. But though Mr Raw's resolution was supported, even obvious change seems always to be difficult in the Church.

The following year it had to be brought back in the form of an amendment to the Assemblies Act of 1878, to have the word 'male' omitted from the qualifications of the electors. Even so, it was not enough. In 1906, an earlier attempt had been withdrawn on advice from the then Chancellor of the Diocese that such a move was unconstitutional. So, not taking any chances, the Church tried the issue in a 'friendly suit' before the Supreme Court of Victoria.

The Court, however, readily ruled that the Church was free to alter the qualifications of its electors, and so in 1913 Melbourne diocese became one of the first – if not, indeed, *the* first – diocese in the Anglican Communion to grant women this simple but ground-breaking right.

Mr Raw gave notice the following year that he intended to pursue the cause of allowing women to be elected to Synod in future meetings, but the First World War intervened. So it was that in 1919 medical practitioner Dr James Booth took up the matter, the first attempt in his long and often lonely struggle to gain equal rights for women in the Church. In 1920, 1922 and 1923, Dr Booth's bills to allow women to be elected both to Synod and onto Vestry (parish council) were defeated. His leading opponent was the Diocesan Advocate, Mr E.C. Rigby, whose speeches ridiculed the notion of women sharing power with men. They were not 'physically, mentally or emotionally fitted to take the place of men in this world', he declared, pointing to the nonsensical notion of a mixed company of men and women actually taking up the collection!

In 1924, however, Dr Booth had a significant victory, when Synod allowed women to join its ranks. In the intervening years, Perth had already made this concession, so robbing Melbourne of the status of another 'first' in Australia. But while Melbourne was prepared to give leadership in this area, it persistently refused to allow women to serve on parish vestries, until finally capitulating as late as 1956, long after many other dioceses. At first sight, this seems an extraordinary anomaly – to allow women to be elected to the diocesan 'parliament', but not to the local parish's management board.

But the reason for the anomaly is not hard to find. The reports of the debates that persisted year in and year out through the 1920s reveal the fear that women's presence on Vestry would discourage male involvement, where it was so sorely needed. In the wider world of the Synod, presumably, the occasional woman member would scarely be noticed. But in the parishes, the women were already faithful and willing workers in church life; they did not need 'holding' by the carrot of Vestry membership. Men, on the other hand, did need every encouragement, and office-bearing was important to them. Vestries were presented as a form of 'male club', in which women would be little short of nuisances. In any case, as one Synod member said, men and women were complementary - which meant men 'directed what should be done and women carried out the directions given'.

From the 1930s to 1950s, the matter lapsed, except for one more crushing defeat in 1947. In 1953 - the year a woman was crowned Queen - a clergy wife and one of the still-few women members of Synod, Mrs E.M. Pethybridge, raised the issue again. The Church, she told Synod, was out of date and suffering without the advice of women on vestries. Significantly, she claimed that women were 'going

Canon Barbara Darling after her installation as the first woman elected Canon of St Paul's Cathedral, 1995.

elsewhere to serve, and thus being lost to the Church'. Even though the support was now much stronger, last-minute theological objections were raised - for the first time in that long debate - and the bill was once again defeated. But not for long. The matter was referred to a Select Committee, chaired by Bishop Donald Baker, who would eventually steer the necessary legislation through the Synod of 1956.

Contrary to the men's fears, women did not rush to join the Church's governing bodies. It took a couple of decades before women were elected to Vestries in significant numbers, and until the mid-1980s and beyond before the number of women on synod would be significant, and before women would, for the first time, be elected to membership of the Diocesan Council. Today, women number roughly one-third of the membership of Synod (now including women clergy, as well as lay representatives), and about a quarter of the membership of Diocesan Council.

The ordination debate

As with its record on the role of laywomen, Melbourne's response to the issue of women's ordination would vacillate between leadership and cautious reaction in the years ahead. From its strong 1976

stand, Melbourne had to watch the national church enter a period of unprecedented struggle, even while it continued its own high level of support. A second diocesan report in 1981, based on a wide parish-based survey, revealed strong support for women priests across the board.

But an attempt to recognise the priestly orders of a visiting woman priest in 1984 resulted in a shameful exercise in pettiness and ugly disputation. One of the first women priests in the Anglican Communion, the Reverend Joyce Bennett, an Englishwoman, had been a missionary in Hong Kong since 1949. Ordained priest in 1971, she was highly regarded in the colony, where she had been a member of the Legislative Council. On her way home to Britain on her retirement in 1983, she paid a brief visit to Australia to visit friends.

She was invited to celebrate the Eucharist at St Stephen's Church, Richmond, and Archbishop Robert Dann and his assistant bishops were initially happy to approve. The rest of Australia's bishops were not so sanguine, however, and believed offering the permission of 'hospitality' (such as any visiting male priest would have been offered as a routine matter) would endanger the unity of the Australian Church.

Sister Hilda CHN, Chaplain to people living with AIDS.

While Archbishop Dann told his Diocese that he believed he had to abide by the advice of the country's bishops, he did not expressly forbid the planned celebration until he phoned the Vicar of St Stephen's, Archdeacon David Chambers, the night before it was to be held. Chambers and his vestry believed that to stop Ms Bennett celebrating at such late notice would amount to an unacceptable denial of her priestly orders, so they agreed on a compromise: Ms Bennett and Archdeacon Chambers would concelebrate instead, a course of action Archdeacon Chambers has always insisted was not ruled out by the Archbishop.[12]

The storm that broke the next day was nevertheless as bitter and extreme as if Ms Bennett had celebrated alone. Petitions and letters denouncing Chambers flew thick and fast around the Diocese. Though the protest was noisy, on analysis it became clear that it was very much the work of the increasingly well-organised minority lobby opposed to women priests. But it signalled a new and initially surprising reaction in the Diocese that had been so solidly supportive of women's ministry for more than a decade. The Diocese, as a whole, was a sadder but wiser place. If those opposing women's ordination were marshalling their forces, so supporters would also need to join ranks. And they did, with the formation of the Melbourne branch of the newly-formed national Movement for the Ordination of Women in the following year.

Between 1983 and the first priestly ordinations in 1992, the struggle between the two groups was often as bitter as the Bennett affair had been. But the strength of the pro-women's forces did not at any stage diminish; in fact, they increased markedly, as events played out on the national stage caused increasing distress. The complex story of those tumultuous years has been told in detail elsewhere[13], though it would be ungracious not to record here the singular determination of the late Archbishop David Penman to see women ordained. He had persisted, in the face of last-minute legal moves and even a bomb threat, in ordaining Australia's first women deacons in Melbourne on 9 February 1986. Later, infuriated by the endless legalistic quibbles and other stalling tactics of those opposed to women priests, he had thrown down the gauntlet by announcing that he planned to ordain women priests in February 1990. But a massive heart attack in July, 1989 - just weeks before a crucial

General Synod meeting - put an end to that plan. His death in October left the women's movement shocked, bereft of its most high-profile and senior leader.

Because Melbourne did not have a new Archbishop until November 1990, much ground was lost, and the initiative moved away from Melbourne in that time. But it was a son of the Diocese, Bishop Owen Dowling of Canberra and Goulburn, who pioneered the costly 'go-it-alone' road that had become necessary to break the national deadlock, though it was the Archbishop of Perth, Peter Carnley, who actually stole the march in the end. While Bishop Dowling's intention to proceed with ordination without General Synod legislation was still before the Supreme Court of NSW in a highly-controversial action brought by forces from within the Diocese of Sydney, Archbishop Carnley ordained the first women in Perth Cathedral in March, 1992. The long-awaited General Synod legislation passed later that year, enabling Melbourne's first ordination on 13 December, was by then inevitable, even if extremely hard-fought.

In the Diocese's 150th year, women are Incumbents of major Melbourne parishes, area deans, canons of the cathedral, and exercising leadership roles that were

undreamt of just a few years ago. A 'Women in the Episcopacy' Commission is examining the inevitable next stage. Will Melbourne soon wrest back its pioneering role, and be the first Australian diocese to appoint a woman bishop? Or will its response once more be one of caution?

The end of the beginning - or the beginning of the end?

The Diocese of Melbourne - and the vast majority of Anglicans around Australia - had wanted women as priests for the best part of two decades by the time they were finally ordained. Only the severely restrictive provisions of the General Synod constitution, placing effective power in the hands of a tiny conservative minority which capitalised on the situation, had prevented the ordination years before.

It could be argued that those were the vital decades, the years between the early '70s and early '90s. In those years, women's lives changed beyond all recognition in the wider community. Given unprecedented personal freedom by reliable contraceptives, new divorce laws, and equal opportunity provisions, women began, in significant numbers, to have careers rather than jobs. Male/female relationships changed radically, if not always smoothly. In their inevitably changed environment, women's priorities were similarly open to change.

All the statistical evidence of recent years reveals that career women now attend church in the same proportion as men in the same age groups. This is significantly different from the situation of earlier generations, when women's attendance rates were markedly higher than those of men in each age-group. Since the 1980s, sociologists have sounded the warnings. Kenneth Dempsey, in a study published in 1983, argued that the absence of younger women not only from worship but also from the women's organisations that had been critical for the Church's local financial viability, was of serious concern. Younger women had different priorities to their mothers, he pointed out, and the fond expectation that they would return as they grew older was ill-founded. 'This development is likely to have a profound bearing on the future of the churches', he concluded.[14]

Various reasons have been given for this profound change in a pattern that had survived for centuries. The Church's persistent preoccupation with the home, family and personal morality issues that

Mrs Mary Britten, Diocesan Chairman then President of the Mothers' Union, 1964-73.

were once the entire scope of most women's lives, but are no longer, may be one reason. Career women, like their husbands, find this preoccupation no longer central. David De Vaus has argued that as women join the full-time workforce, they find it hard to maintain a religious commitment because the male-oriented and male-dominated work environment gives them a new framework. Like the males they share their work with, they move away from religious affiliation.[15]

Diesendorf, on the other hand, blames the Church's refusal to take women's changing needs seriously. Its long refusal

to grant them real participation and to persist in sex-role stereotyping, was increasingly alienating to younger women rapidly becoming used to partnership and leadership in the community. The bitter and prolonged ordination debate continually represented the Church as an anachronistic institution to women outside.

Perhaps the Church simply took women's commitment for granted for too long. By refusing, over most of this century, to honour that commitment in equitable power-sharing as the women's movement gave women different expectations, the Church itself set women adrift. In 1953, Mrs Pethybridge warned Melbourne Synod of the dangers the Church was already facing as it continued to lose the support of women.

Whatever the reasons, the loss of younger women is real and very serious, with long-term implications that cannot be ignored. More than church leaders realise, it is probably this change, rather than any other of the past two decades, that has altered the Church's situation radically. All other facets of modern life, from modern music to consumerism, pale into insignificance beside this one. Without women to do the fund-raising work they traditionally performed, parishes face a much tougher financial position. Sunday schools and youth groups miss the leadership women so often provided; the care of the church fabric and the social life that was once central to every parish, languish without them.

More seriously, without the attendance of the women, the men and children are even less likely to come. And the handing on of the faith to the next generation, within the simple rituals of childhood presided over by women, will not occur. Unless it can regain the support of younger women very soon, the Diocese of Melbourne, in its 150th year, might be facing a bleaker future than it is prepared to acknowledge.

1   This account of Melbourne's first clergy wives is drawn from Peter D. Sherlock, Well-known energetic and useful', Anglican Clergymen's Wives in Colonial Victoria, Honours Thesis, Department of History, University of Melbourne, 1995.

2   For this account of the work of Frances Perry, I am indebted to Patricia Grimshaw, Women, Christianity and the Australian Colonies, the 1988 Bishop Perry Memorial Lecture, the Anglican Evangelical Fellowship of Victoria with St James' Old Cathedral, West Melbourne, 1988.

3   See, for example, Grimshaw, op.cit., Sabine Willis, 'Homes are Divine Wokshops', in Elizabeth Windschuttle, ed., Women, Class and History,

Feminist Perspectives on Australia 1788-1988, and Patricia Grimshaw, 'In Pursuit of True Anglican Womanhood in Victoria, 1880-1914', Women's History Review, 12,3, 1993, pp.331-47.

4   See Muriel Porter, 'The Christian Origins of Feminism', Freedom and Entrapment, Women thinking theology, Maryanne Confoy, Dorothy A. Lee, Joan Nowotny, eds, Dove, Melbourne, 1995.

5   For this overview of the early history of the Mothers' Union, I am indebted to Ellen Warne, doctoral history student at the University of Melbourne, who is writing a thesis entitled: The Mothers' Union and Aspects of Social Anxiety in Melbourne 1895-1939. See also Sydney historian Dr Bill Lawton's astute summary of the reasons the Mothers' Union was formed: A Better Time to Be, Utopian Attitudes to Society among Sydney Anglicans 1885-1914, New South Wales University Press, 1990, pp.173ff.

6   Grimshaw, In pursuit of true Anglican womanhood..., passim.

7   This concern with building male numbers has not gone away, nor is it restricted to Victoria. The front page story of the Diocese of Sydney monthly magazine, Southern Cross for February 1996 was headlined 'Aussie men top church's wanted list'. The story promoted the launch of a 'Winning Men '96' program for the Diocese of Sydney, to counteract concern that only 39 per cent of church attenders were male.

8   For a full discussion of the beginnings of the deaconess movement in Victoria, see Morna Sturrock, The Anglican Deaconess Movement in Melbourne, an Office Coveted by Few, Melbourne College of Divinity B.Theol. research paper, 1989.

9   Conference of Bishops of the Anglican Communion, London, 1920.

10 For a fuller overview of the establishment of deaconess work in the diocese, see Sturrock, op.cit., and Muriel Porter, Women in the Church, the Great Ordination Debate in Australia, Penguin, 1989, pp.47ff.

11 For a full treatment of this debate, see Muriel Porter, The Great Ordination Debate, op.cit., and Muriel Porter, 'The End of the "Great Debate" - the 1992 General Synod Decision on women priests', in Mark Hutchinson and Edmund Campion (eds), Long Patient Struggle: Essays on Women and Gender in Australian Christianity, CSAC, Sydney, 1994, pp.161-85.

12 Joyce Bennett was not able to celebrate the Eucharist publicly in England until after the first women had been ordained priest there in March 1994, twenty-three years after her ordination. The Church of England refused to extend hospitality provisions to women priests until that point.

13 See Porter, Women in the Church, op.cit., and 'The End of the "Great Debate"', op.cit.

14 Reported in Eileen Diesendorf, 'Why Women Leave the Church I', Women-Church, 2, 1988, pp.25-30. This article, and its sequel, published in Women-Church, 3,1988, pp.30-35, provide an important overview of this development.

15 Quoted in Diesendorf, 'Why Women Leave the Church I', p.26.

CHAPTER EIGHT

PETER ADAM

Trinity College Chapel, University of Melbourne. Architects: North and Williams, 1915.

Theological Education
in the Diocese of Melbourne

The history of theological education provides a fascinating perspective on the Diocese of Melbourne, for it is a crucial test of the welfare of the Diocese, and the focus for many important questions: What is ordained ministry?

What model of education is appropriate? Who is responsible for training? What resources are available? This chapter will examine how the context of ministry has affected the Diocese, how changes and developments in theology have been

reflected in or achieved by theological education, how tensions within the Diocese have been expressed in it, and how priorities have varied over the years. To study the theological education provided by a diocese is a way of finding out the health of that diocese, and of studying its changing fortunes.

The evidence will be studied in three periods:

- Foundations 1847 – 1901
- Creativity and Conflict 1901 – 1956
- New Directions 1957 – 1995
  and then survey contemporary
- Challenges and Opportunities

Underlying this study are some questions which are relevant to each of these periods, and which will help provide some clarity of thought and reflection. The questions are:

For what ministry is education being provided? If we are concerned with education, we need to find out the nature of the ministry for which the education provides training. The obvious answer is ordained ministry, but as we shall see, there has been a variety of models of ordained ministry in mind. Theological education has also been provided for lay-readers, deaconesses, missionaries, and lay people: the provision has varied as the nature of the ministry in mind has changed.

What models of education? There have been a number of different models of academic and college training, as well as different ways of using supervised practical training. Of these, most models have been imported from England or the United States, while some have been developed in response to local needs.

Who is responsible? A variety of people have taken responsibility for theological education, including Bishops and Archbishops, General Synod, lay people and clergy, and local ecumenical bodies. However, government and universities have been reluctant to assume any responsibility for theological education.

What resources are available? A constant theme throughout 150 years has been the lack of resources available for theological education. Inadequately resourced colleges have collapsed, and while some good college buildings, staff and libraries have been built up, finding adequate ongoing resources continues to be a problem. Most resources have been built up by the generosity of the people of the Diocese: but while state or government aid has at different times been provided for the episcopate, parishes, schools, university colleges, and chaplaincy, theological education has not received any direct support, though in the 1990s indirect support has been provided as some theological students have been eligible for government grants.

Foundations 1847 – 1901

Bishop Charles Perry's view of the primary responsibility of the ordained ministry is clear:

Remember that the public preaching of the Word is the greatest means which God seems to employ for the extension of the Kingdom of his dear Son.

In his address at his first visitation for the Archdeaconry of Melbourne, Perry expanded on the nature of Christian ministry:

If you take your doctrine from the Bible, you cannot fail to be faithful stewards of the mysteries of God: and if you take your doctrine from the Prayer Book and formularies of our Church, you cannot fail to approve yourselves faithful ministers of her Communion.

And again:

The object of ministry is two-fold – to bring sinners to the Saviour and to perfect the saints of God. And the foremost means is the public preaching of the Word: This must be the Gospel, the love of God in the redemption of mankind by the gift of His Son, and in the sanctification of His elect people by the gift of His

Spirit. The offices of the Son and of the Spirit, with the doctrines and duties, the motives and encouragements, the hopes and fears, the promises and threatenings connected with and flowing from them, as all these are shadowed forth, proclaimed, illustrated, and enforced in the Scriptures, both of the Old and New Testament, furnish abundant topics for your sermons...If the Christian minister preach anything contrary to the Gospel, or if he do not preach the whole Gospel – the work of the Spirit as well as the work of the Son – faithfully and fully, he is unfaithful to his trust, and will bring upon himself the terrible wrath of God...if he preach anything else beside the Gospel, he exceeds his commission, and lays aside the character of an ambassador for Christ; the word spoken by him ceases to be the word of the Lord, and the work to which he has been ordained stands still.

These words pick up the text of his first sermon in St. James' Church which summarised his view of Christian ministry: 'Now then we are ambassadors for Christ, as though God did beseech you by us: we pray you, in Christ's stead, be ye reconciled to God' (2 Cor 5:20).[1]

This evangelical model of ministry became part of the Perry heritage of the Diocese of Melbourne, and was also represented in the first Bishops of Ballarat (Thornton, 1875) Bendigo (Langley, 1901), Gippsland (Pain, 1901) and Wangaratta (Armstrong, 1901).

One of the great problems for any colonial bishop was the provision of clergy; this was a particular problem for Perry who was so definite about the kind of clergy he wanted. An obvious method was to import clergy, as Perry did, from England and Ireland, and from elsewhere in Australia. He was, however, well aware that many English clergy

> ...do not possess the qualities essential for an efficient clergyman in this colony. In particular many of them do not possess the energy and intellectual power and talent of dealing with their fellow-men which are peculiarly required here.[2]

Another method was to provide theological education in Australia. What models were available to Perry and his contemporaries? Four different models can be identified.

(i) General liberal education.

The most common model in England was that of providing a general liberal education such as that found at Cambridge or Oxford, with no particular vocational training in theology, the Bible, or ministry. This was the education that Perry himself had received, in his case in mathematics and classics.

The assumption was that this general education would be sufficient: Perry's biographer quotes the Bishop of Ely's comment as he prepared to ordain him: 'It would be quite superfluous, Mr Perry, to examine a gentleman of your well-known aquirements.'[3] This was in fact the kind of training that Bishop Broughton had begun to provide at the first short-lived training institution in Australia, St James' College in Sydney (1846-48).[4]

But it was the kind of training that Perry knew to be inadequate. In 1841, when he was still in England, he had written a pamphlet on theological education, entitled *Remarks on Clerical Education*, pointing out the deficiencies of the general liberal training, and making various recommendations which will be outlined below. While Perry encouraged those who could gain general education (a University degree) to do so, he recognised that this training by itself was inadequate. According to Hastings Rashdall, this kind of training produced people of liberal culture, social influence but with a low standard of theological attainment.[5]

(ii) University Theology

Perry's pamphlet of 1841 had recommended that training for ministry should be provided at a university by the appointment of a Professor of Pastoral Theology, who would provide the necessary training in the preaching of sermons, reading of lessons and the liturgy, the interpretation of rubrics and canons, ecclesiastical law, pastoral visiting, and the supervision of parochial schools. He criticised the isolated diocesan colleges such as Chichester (1839) and Wells (1840) because of their remoteness from the university and their tendency to a dangerous narrowness of outlook.[6]

Perry's pamphlet resulted in the provision of the Cambridge Voluntary Examination (1843), and later both Cambridge (1871) and Oxford (1870) began teaching for a degree in theology, following the example of Durham, which began doing so in 1833. But Perry's preferred option was not possible in Melbourne, for the University, founded in 1853 had statutes which prohibited the teaching of religion.

The only way forward was to take up the Government's offer of land on which to build a University College, which Perry did in founding Trinity College in 1872. Perry's plan was to include a Theological School within Trinity, but he was unwilling to do this until Trinity was firmly established. The Theological School at Trinity was founded by Bishop Moorhouse, Perry's successor, in 1878. Because it was part of a University College, it could admit only matriculants, when many of those wishing to be ordained did not have that academic status. But despite its small numbers, Trinity provided many leaders for the Australian church until the disruption of 1904 when Warden Leeper fell out with Archbishop Clarke.

(iii) Vocational training colleges

Another model available college, often rural, such as the recent foundations in England: St Bees (1816), the Church Missionary Society training College in London (1825), Chichester (1839), Wells (1840), and St Augustine's Canterbury (1848), founded to train men for overseas work. This model was available to Perry in Moore College, at Liverpool near Sydney, founded in 1856. Perry recognised that there were not sufficient resources in Melbourne to found a theological college, and his policy was to send his ordinands to Moore College, which provided training in the evangelical tradition.

In refusing to open his own college, Perry was swimming against the tide, for one of the features of Australia was that Bishops of most dioceses opened their own colleges (St James Sydney, 1846; Moore College Sydney, 1856; Trinity Theological School Melbourne, 1878; St Barnabas Adelaide, 1880; Brisbane Theological College, 1897 renamed St Francis College, 1910; St John's Armidale, 1898 which moved to Morpeth near Newcastle in 1926; St Wilfred's Tasmania, 1904; St John's Melbourne, 1906; and within Victoria, St Aidan's Ballarat, 1903 and St. Columb's Wangaratta, 1903.

In addition, Perry Hall and Langley Hall Bendigo, and the Divinity Hostel at Sale, provided training for readers preparing for theological college (Later foundations included Ridley in Melbourne, Wollaston in Perth, St Mark's in Canberra, Perry Hall in Melbourne, and St Michael's House Crafers in Adelaide).

The promiscuous opening of under-resourced colleges was of course a mistake. It represented a widespread case of excessive diocesanism, and produced what was described by an official of the SPCK in 1899 as 'one horse Colleges'.[7] In the light of this widespread episcopal

Archbishop Frank Wood's first ordination, 9 March, 1958.

activity, Perry displayed admirable strength of character in refusing to open a college without adequate resources. His policy of sending ordinands to train at Moore College was criticised by some clergy and laity in Melbourne: students at Moore did not learn enough Latin, and were subject to monastic seclusion at rural Liverpool. And inter-colonial rivalry also played its part, as did denominational rivalry in Melbourne: the Congregationalist College was opened in 1866.

But Moore College trained thirty-two ordinands for Melbourne and nineteen for Sydney between 1868 and 1878, a significant contribution to the life and ministry of the Diocese.[8] Candidates for Ballarat were also sent to Moore until St Aidan's was opened in 1903.

Bishop Tyrrell in Newcastle also decided not to open a College, but to send his candidates to Moore; he too was aware of the lack of adequate resources to found a College.[9]

(iv) Lay reader training for ordination

Another model which was developed in Australia by Perry, and by Tyrrell, Bishop of Newcastle, was that of training lay readers who were engaged in parish ministry. This ideal of supervised on-the-job training was perhaps ahead of its time, but it was difficult to learn academic theology in such a context. For Perry, it had two advantages: one was that candidates' abilities in ministry were tested before they were ordained, and secondly, that it provided an economical method of training for people spread throughout Victoria. Perry's ideal was that potential candidates should serve as lay readers for a few years, and then spend two years at Moore College before ordination.

This model continued after Perry's departure: in 1887, Melbourne had 131 clergy and 45 lay readers. It was criticised as a 'miserable makeshift' but it certainly provided ministry where it could not otherwise have been found. It worked well when well resourced, as for example when Perry Hall Bendigo, still of course in the Diocese of Melbourne, was opened as a Readers' Training College in 1893 under Nathaniel Jones, later Principal of Moore College.[10]

In these circumstances, Perry did the best he could but also planned for the creation of the Theological School at Trinity College which Bishop Moorhouse opened in 1878. Moorhouse wrote that

It is to be our school of the prophets, an institution wanted here more urgently than any other. Our younger clergy are ignorant and uncultured, and have had only one year's training at a theological college - in Sydney - in connection with no university'.[11]

Moorhouse's aim was that

'our candidates for orders would obtain the advantage not only of theological teaching, but of a large and liberal education, and would further gain the inestimable privilege of daily association with their peers in age and knowledge'.[12]

Theological education was thus provided in a university setting, with candidates gaining the benefits of general education by being themselves graduates, and by a kind of osmosis from their fellow students. Moorhouse recognised the importance of good training. He wrote of '...the grand future before the Church of England if only I can succeed in importing and training the right kind of clergy'.[13]

Initially it was diocesan bishops such as Broughton, Perry and Moorhouse who had to take responsibility for the selection and training of clergy and readers and the provision of training institutions. As we have seen, this led to a large number of diocesan colleges. A venture of the newly formed General Synod was the creation of the Australian College of Theology in 1891. This was to be an examining, not a teaching body: its aim was 'to foster and direct the systematic study of Divinity, especially among the clergy'. It at least provided a recognised standard of theological examination across Australia.

While its first Licentiate Theology graduates were of course men, the first Associate in Theology graduates were women. Colleges in Australia also continued to use overseas examining and degree-granting Universities, such as London, Durham, and Toronto. An advantage of London and Durham degrees undertaken in Australia was that they were recognised in England, if clergy wanted to serve there.

* * * * * * *

The new ministry that developed in Melbourne in the 1890s was that of deaconesses. The first record of a women worker was a Mrs Davies, a 'Bible-woman' of St Paul's parish in 1887. As Morna Sturrock has shown, a number of the deaconesses, licensed by Bishop Goe in the 1890s, were also nuns and followed the example of Emma Silcock, who as Mother Esther was a 'reluctant pioneer' of women's ministry, especially to the needy. Insofar as they were deaconesses, they were licensed by the Bishop: as nuns, they were responsible to their Superior.[14]

A further impetus for the ministry of women was found with the promotion of the ministry of the Church Missionary Association in Victoria. Of the first missionaries sent out by the Association, two were Nellie and Topsy Saunders, who left for China in 1893. There was obviously a need for a training college for women who would serve either as deaconesses in Australia or missionaries overseas. The

Reverend C.H. Nash opened a college in Hawthorn in 1901, called St. Hilda's, and this was later combined with a home opened by Mr and Mrs James Griffiths in Fitzroy, then in East Melbourne, to train women missionary candidates for the China Inland Mission and for the Church Missionary Association. So the development in the 1890s of women's work, serving both at home and overseas, becomes apparent.

Creativity and Conflict 1901-1956

This second period was initiated by the arrival of Bishop, later Archbishop Lowther Clarke who had a considerable commitment to education, including theological education. His contributions were both positive and negative, in their intentions and effects. From one perspective his motives were admirable, but in this area he gave that kind of leadership which was as effective in galvanising his opponents into action as it was in producing his desired results. In the words of Dr A.E. Floyd, the Cathedral Organist, 'the Archbishop came from that part of Yorkshire where it was not so much that people had bad manners as that they had no manners at all'!

Clarke's conviction was that 'the best clergy are those who have enjoyed the advantages of a liberal education,' and

his hope was that a faculty of Theology could be created at the University of Melbourne, to be used by his ordinands. This hope was frustrated, so Clarke led a coalition of Protestant denominations to petition Parliament for permission to found the Melbourne College of Divinity. This ecumenical venture was established in 1911 as a creative response to the exclusion of theology from the University, and reflected the new world-wide ecumenical enthusiasm of the early years of this century.

It was of course a prophetic act: ecumenical coalitions, now of course including Roman Catholics, are to be found around Australia; they are enjoying increasingly close connections with universities, and are a common context for the training of Anglican ordinands. Clarke presided over the Melbourne College of Divinity, held its meetings in his room at St Paul's Cathedral, and its graduations in the Chapter House. It was set up as an examining body, and was thus in effect in competition with the Australian College of Theology, the creation of General Synod.

Clarke faced the dilemma of the diocesan Bishop, whether to support the local ecumenical coalition or his national denominational institution, a dilemma that would continue to be faced in later years. His founding of the Melbourne

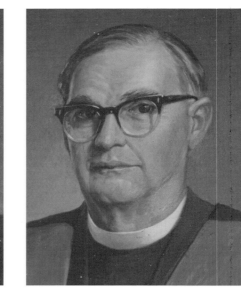

*below: Ridley College,
University of Melbourne.*

above, from left to right:

*The Rt Reverend Donald
Baker, Principal of Ridley
College, 1938-52*

*The Reverend Canon Leon
Morris, Principal of
Ridley College, 1964-79*

*The Reverend Dr Stuart
Barton Babbage,
Principal of Ridley
College and Dean of
Melbourne, 1953-62.*

College of Divinity was his major contribution to theological education in Melbourne.

A less successful venture of Clarke's was his founding of St John's College in St. Kilda in 1906. The theological faculty at Trinity College had been operative since 1878; the Archbishop first of all removed lectures for ordinands to the Cathedral, and then diverted diocesan grants from Trinity to found St John's. His aim was to provide one diocesan college for graduates and non-graduates, and training which reflected liberal Catholicism of the *Lux Mundi* school in England, and the liberal and social theology of F.D. Maurice. His hope was to provide a college for the national church. Of course if he had succeeded

making St John's the permanent College for Melbourne he would have removed theological education from its university context.

This move was of course a devastating blow to Trinity College. The Warden, Dr Leeper, wrote to the Archbishop that 'Your Grace's act was a violent undoing of the best and most important work that Bishop Moorhouse did for the church...It has gone far to ruin my own life's work'. Robin Sharwood suggests that the Archbishop was motivated by the desire for economy, and refers to a pencil note by Dr Leeper, 'No butter at lunch at St John's'. L.L. Nash, in his history of Ridley College, points out the unsatisfactory

financial arrangements made for St John's.

In due course the theological school returned to Trinity in 1912, and St John's was closed in 1919. It was yet another inadequately resourced Australian theological college, and it failed to gain the support of the people of the Diocese. It was divisive in its effect, if not in its purpose. It also suffered from the effects of the First World War.

Meanwhile evangelicals in Victoria, who still treasured the heritage of Bishops Perry and Goe, felt increasingly marginalised by Archbishop Clarke, and offended by his policies and practice, not least in his treatment of Canon C.H.Nash, an able evangelical leader. They objected to the theology being taught at St John's College, and to the High Church practices being introduced into the Diocese. Their response was the founding of Ridley College in Parkville in 1910 'to provide theological training in accordance with the Constructive and Evangelical Principles of the Reformation Settlement of the Church of England for students who are seeking for Holy Orders or preparing for Mission Work'. Ridley was founded by a coalition of evangelical clergy and laity, led by the Bishops of Bendigo and Gippsland.

As it prepared people for the examinations of the Australia College of Theology, it was able to accept non-graduates as well as

graduates. Clarke accepted it only grudgingly. Relations were rather better with Trinity College, as the first two Principals of Ridley lectured at Trinity, and served as Chaplains. The attempt to provide buildings for Ridley in the grounds of Trinity was frustrated by the Archbishop.[15]

From the Archbishop's point of view, Ridley was 'born in conflict and nurtured in distrust', though he was soon in 1913 to accept its graduates for ordination. Ridley prospered, despite the antiquity of its episcopal midwives, for five reasons. It represented a grass-roots determination among clergy and laity to preserve the Evangelical heritage of Bishop Perry. It captured a ready market in ordinands who were not graduates, and who could not attend Trinity, of whom a notable example was Joseph Booth, student at Ridley in 1913, and the first Archbishop of Melbourne trained for the ministry in Australia. It gained the approval of Archbishop Lees, Clarke's more benevolent and evangelical successor. It attracted men preparing for missionary work under the renewed missionary commitment of the Church Missionary Society.[16] It could provide training for women and did so from 1920 onwards.

As we have seen, there had been a renewed interest in missionary work in the

Diocese since the delegation from CMS in England in 1892. The first two missionaries from the newly-formed Church Missionary Association left for China in 1893. There was now a need to begin providing specialised vocational training in Melbourne for missionaries. St Hilda's training home moved to East Melbourne in 1907. St Hilda's provided training for women for both home and overseas service, and provided deaconess training for many years. A training home for men was opened in North Melbourne in 1906, but closed in 1908. From 1910, this training was provided at Ridley College.

Missionary training was also provided by the Melbourne Bible Institute, part of the world wide Bible Institute movement, opened in 1920 by C.H. Nash. In his twenty-two years as Principal, one thousand missionaries were trained.[17] MBI was of course interdenominational, but it represented a considerable output of Anglican energy.

Meanwhile the deaconess movement was given new leadership with the appointment of deaconess Minna Johnson, and deaconess training was then provided by St Hilda's in East Melbourne. Here of course the training provided was evangelical in character, appreciated by some but not all of those in training. A diocesan institution, Deaconess House was opened in 1940 in Fitzroy, and moved to Fairfield in 1947. Meanwhile Ridley College continued to provide training for women, especially for deaconesses.[18] Early training for women was provided by 'independent' institutions, St Hilda's and Ridley. Trinity College was a male preserve, and the Diocese did not open its own Deaconess House until 1940.

To return to ordination training: after the closure of St John's College in 1919, the Diocese made no official provision for the training of non-graduates, despite the fact that in the days when university attendance was only possible for the wealthy, the majority of those offering needed non-graduate training. Ridley College filled the gap, and was soon training the majority of ordinands. There was some attempt to coordinate the training being offered and from 1922 there were some joint lectures between Trinity and Ridley. This arrangement was formalised in 1932 with the creation of the Joint Board of Theological Studies by the Bishops of the Province of Victoria. The bishops authorised lecturers, and this system was in place until 1955. It ceased to work when Dr Barton Babbage, the Principal of Ridley and church historian, wanted to be allowed to lecture his own students in church history; legal opinion indicated that the Ridley Council was *ultra vires* in becoming a partner in the Joint Board, and the Bishops of the Province began to lose interest in the scheme.

Another problem was that students found the arrangement unsatisfactory: high church candidates objected to being sent to Ridley; while Ridley had always welcomed students from any background, the students themselves objected to this arrangement; and evangelical students at Ridley found some of the lectures at Trinity less than inspiring.[19] Ordinands who could not go to Trinity and did not want to attend Ridley were usually sent to St Columb's Hall Wangaratta or St John's College, Morpeth.

Meanwhile Trinity College had recovered from the St John's College debacle, and its Theological School had been re-formed, and, as we have seen, it was able to join with Ridley College in some lectures. However, as Robin Sharwood has pointed out, the Theological School was weakened in 1918 by the College's new Constitution. Until then, the lecturers had formed the faculty, and had made their own decisions on the training to be provided. After 1918, the Bishops of the Province became the Theological Faculty, and appointed lecturers to teach on their behalf. Sharwood comments that as a result, the period from 1918 to the late 1960s was 'largely one of stagnation', with little or no consultation or strategic planning.[20] The School was also weakened by low numbers of students.

There is of course a certain irony in the fact that the official Provincial Theological School, governed by the bishops, had small numbers of students while the unofficial College, Ridley, continued to grow and develop, not least with the impetus of ever increasing numbers and because of the sterling leadership of Bishop Donald Baker, 1938-53. The balance of responsibility for theological education had shifted to the voluntary societies, such as Ridley College and the Church Missionary Society. The question of the attitude of a bishop to voluntary societies within the Diocese is a continuing theme within Anglicanism. Bishops of dioceses in England had no choice but to accept voluntary societies and lay patronage of various kinds, and in fact had right of appointment to only a minority of parishes or positions within their diocese, with the right of appointment to a majority of positions lying with the Crown, University Colleges, trusts, or clerical or lay patrons.

In most colonial dioceses the situation was very different: a bishop often held right of appointment to every position, and might well resent the emergence or intrusion of a voluntary society. Archbishop

Clarke was a centralist in policy, and resisted the initiatives of others: as he opposed the founding of Ridley, so he refused entrance to the Diocese to G.K.Tucker and his Brotherhood of St Laurence despite the fact that Tucker was a graduate of St John's College.

But voluntary societies have been a feature of Anglican life for many centuries, and are evidence of that 'dispersed authority' which is characteristic of Anglicanism. Certainly the Diocese of Melbourne would be less interesting without its band of voluntary societies, including the Community of the Holy Name, The Brotherhood of St. Laurence, many of the church schools, Ridley College, and the Church Missionary Society. Once again, it was the determination of clergy and laity to preserve and promote Bishop Perry's evangelical heritage that led to the foundation of the missionary colleges, Ridley College, and the Melbourne Bible Institute, now the Bible College of Victoria.

Another venture of CMS at this time was the League of Youth, begun in 1929, a weekly meeting for young people which attracted over one hundred to the Chapter House basement on Friday nights from the 1930s to the 1960s. It provided solid training in Bible study and evangelism, and produced generations of trained lay

people, clergy and missionaries. G.K. Tucker opened Keble House in East Melbourne, providing training for ordination in 1933, which aimed to provide the most economical training package for ordinands. But it was another ill-resourced experiment, and soon ceased to function.[21]

The other development during this period which would later have a great effect on theological education was the provision of chaplains to schools and hospitals. If Archbishop Clarke's vigorous educational policies led to a rapid increase in the number of church schools which needed chaplains, Archbishop Booth's contribution was the establishment of hospital chaplaincy in 1953.[22] The Diocese of Melbourne would later develop a large number of chaplains, and the specialist training they required would later have a profound impact on theological education.

It is understandable to dismiss the disputes of the early years of the century as merely conflict over churchmanship, matters of aesthetic taste in furnishings or *haute couture* in dress. To do so is to miss the point: for churchmanship's importance is that it reflects and expresses deeper matters of theology, including matters of crucial importance such as the doctrines of Christ and salvation.

The Reverend Dr John Gaden, Lecturer at Trinity College, 1977-84 and Archbishop's Consultant Theologian, 1976-85.

Churchmanship is 'sacramental'; the outward and visible sign of inner meaning. Disagreement over churchmanship was disagreement over theology.

New directions 1957 - 1995

The basic structures of theological education were established between 1847 and 1920, and between 1920 and 1945 there were few significant developments. With the arrival of Archbishop Woods came a period of change and development which has created the present shape of theological education. Some of these changes Woods initiated; others occurred independently of him. It was an exciting time, not least because of the leadership given to the Trinity School by Barry Marshall (1961-69), and to Ridley by Leon Morris (1964-79).

With respect to missionary training, the significant development was the provision of St Andrew's Hall as the Church Missionary Society Federal Training College in 1964, providing quality training for both men and women. St Andrew's has been a strategic centre for theological and practical training in missiology, and has sent a regular supply of ordained and lay missionaries to countries around the world. It has also made good use of its proximity to Ridley College, and the availability there of theological training for men and women.[23]

The rapid growth in lay ministry and lay training has opened up new possibilities in theological education: the hope of enabling 'God's Frozen People' to engage in significant Christian ministry has now reached all areas of the Church: its origins may be identified in the ministry of women and men on the mission field. Woods caught the mood of the moment in his inauguration of the *Forward in Depth* movement. He was perhaps aware that the Diocese of Melbourne had not engaged in rigorous training of its lay people for Christian ministry. If there was to be significant spiritual growth and useful ministry, then a plan of education would need to be implemented:

> people are frightened of the word 'theology' but...let us all become theologians. Let the clergy get down to some pretty stiff theology and confer together on how to teach it. Let the readers get out a scheme of doctrinal preaching. Let every organiser of youth or adult groups in the diocese submit a scheme for the teaching of doctrine to those in his or her charge...Let our faith be based on the Scriptures.[24]

The general desire for lay-training increased in the 60s, and by the mid 70s lay people began attending courses in theology run by Ridley and Trinity, and the General Board of Religious Education established its *Education for Ministry* program in 1978. However it seems a pity that Melbourne parishes have not seized the opportunity of provided challenging theological and practical training in ministry themselves. Perhaps the clergy have been trained to teach, but not to teach others how to teach.[25]

The Reverend Dr Barry Marshall, OGS,
Chaplain of Trinity College, 1961-69.

The Reverend Dr Evan Burge, Warden of Trinity College, 1974-97, with the
Reverend Dr Richard McKinney, Director, Trinity Theological School, 1986-96.

In regard to theological education for ordinands, we can see a number of significant developments:

The selection of ordinands was regularised and made more effective by Woods' institution of Selection Conferences in 1958. Post Ordination Training was established in 1963 and provided ongoing practical training for four years after Ordination, to complement the training provided by colleges and vicars.

The training of married ordinands began in the 60s and represented a big change in theological education. Formerly, ordinands had been single and young, and this had enabled residential communities to be formed in colleges, with a regular round of chapel, lecturing and meals. The grown number of married ordinands meant that the residential community became no longer possible. The nature of a non-residential College

community of ordinands became even more problematic when the number of non-ordinands came to exceed the number of ordinands.

There were two attempts to meet the challenge of married ordinands. Ridley College built flats for married ordinands in 1968; but as more married ordinands came to College with already established families and as the number of married ordinands increased, this accommodation quickly became inadequate. Woods opened Perry Hall in 1962, especially for older ordinands, many of whom were married with children. Perry Hall migrated from North Melbourne to East St. Kilda to East Melbourne, and was seriously under-resourced. Woods claimed that it would not be in competition with Trinity or Ridley – though of course it was – and liked to think of it as a kind of 'finishing school' for clergy: candidates were 'required to shave before chapel'. Perry Hall was not well resourced, and it is fascinating that at the same time as Woods opened the short-lived Perry Hall, he was urging the closure of St Columb's Hall Wangaratta, because of its inadequate size and resources. Woods at one stage decided to send all his candidates to Ridley, until dissuaded by his close advisers.[26]

This period also saw an increase in the number of women engaging in theological education, culminating in the ordination of women to the diaconate in 1986, and the priesthood in 1993. The deaconess movement in Melbourne had virtually collapsed, but after long debate, women were ordained. Their participation in theological education had its own effect, not least in questioning many of the assumptions of the style of academic theology.[27]

The growth in the number of people studying theology, men and women, ordination candidates and others can be seen in the following chart:

Theological students
full-time and part-time[28]

	1967	1977	1987
Trinity			
- total	6	17	61
- female	-	1	36
Ridley			
- total	46	156	302
- female	-	48	134
Perry Hall			
	4	-	-

Another change which was to have a profound effect on theological education for all was the continued development of chaplaincy, especially hospital chaplaincy. Those who worked as hospital chaplains realised their need of specialised training for their particular ministry. Clinical Pastoral Education was introduced and began to be used for all ordinands, not just for those preparing for hospital chaplaincy. The priorities of CPE include personal integration, healing through self-expression and self-awareness, the use of personal inner resources and non-judgemental counselling.

This method and approach has been added to the traditional academic theological diet, without serious attempt at theoretical integration. As a parallel to the practical training in counselling provided by CPE, there has also been a growth in the teaching of skills of ministry within the colleges, including preaching, evangelism, communication, leadership, education, and pastoral care.

The formation of the United Faculty of Theology in 1969 was a further development of Clarke's creation of the ecumenical Melbourne College of Divinity in 1911. But whereas the MCD had been a Protestant examining body, the UFT was an ecumenical teaching consortium, including Roman Catholics, based in Parkville, and for those studying for MCD qualifications. This meant big changes for Trinity College: its theological students were now taught by an ecumenical team, and non-graduates were now able to be accepted as students. Some form of ecumenical theological body is now found in most capital cities around Australia.

This positive step forward was, however, marred by an unfortunate move in which Archbishop Woods, supporting the Melbourne College of Divinity, lobbied against the application by the Australian College of Theology to the Victorian Government for accreditation to grant degrees. This happened despite the fact that Woods, as Primate, was President of the Australian College of Theology. It was an interesting example of the triumph of local ecumenical interests over the welfare of the national church, and was deeply resented by many. However Ridley College, still making use of the Australian College of Theology, continued to grow, and the ACT gained accreditation in NSW, and developed its own B.Th. degree.[29]

The period also saw the development of what was then called the distinctive diaconate. The distinctive diaconate was an attempt to express the church's responsibility to serve the world, and attracted interest among those already serving in a lay capacity. However, it was difficult to develop a specialised training program, perhaps because the most relevant training had already been undertaken in secular agencies, and it

became difficult to distinguish how the distinctive diaconate differed from the responsibility of every Christian lay person to serve God and their community in daily life and work.[30]

Changes in Australian society which affected the context and content of theological training included a general rise in the standard and availability of tertiary education, following the Martin Report of 1964. These changes resulted in a growing interest in theological education among lay people. This increase in the level of theological education among the laity has also put pressure on the clergy to be better educated.

This period also saw the creation of more voluntary societies, parish-based training institutes, including Spiritual Studies at St Peter's, Eastern Hill, Contemporary Christian Leadership at St Hilary's, Kew, the Discipleship School and Timothy Institute at St Jude's, Carlton and the Carringbush Centre at St Stephen's, Richmond.

Challenges and opportunities

What, then, of the challenges and opportunities of the present day?

Trinity and Ridley are the two colleges which currently provide ordination training

as well as a wider Christian education programme. They experience similar pressures. Both have experienced the radical changes brought about by the increasing age and maturity of ordinands, and by the fact that so many are married and may have children. Colleges are no longer residential communities, and this has meant that the old model of community has collapsed. The old pattern of meals, chapel, lectures and community life has gone, and both colleges, in common with other seminaries around the world, are trying to find new models of community.[31]

This problem is further increased because both colleges conform to the Perry-Moorehouse ideal of providing theological training in the context of a university college. While this has undoubted advantages, both theological communities meet in colleges where they are now no longer resident, and where the university students have taken over the vacated rooms, and have their own rather stronger residential community. As a result, the theological communities of both colleges feel today more fragile in comparison with the past.

Both colleges now provide general theological training. Some of this is vocational training, as with the Ridley

College Youth ministry course, but in most cases it has meant opening *all* courses to any who want to enrol. Colleges need to do this to stay financially operative, and no doubt it has other advantages. Negatively both lectures and college life become more and more generalist in flavour, and the cutting edge of ordination training is easily lost.

Both colleges now exist in an ecumenical context, Trinity as part of the United Faculty of Theology, and Ridley participating in the Australian College of Theology, set up and controlled by General Synod, but now including a variety of denominational and ecumenical colleges. These ecumenical commitments reflect good theological priorities as well as good pragmatics: the Anglican church does not have the resources to go it alone.

Yet as a result of these ecumenical contexts, both colleges are criticised for not providing a sufficiently Anglican context for theological study. It must be of some

comfort to learn that at a recent meeting of Heads of Theological colleges from around Australia, it was discovered that all colleges face the same criticism. This suggests that the problem of Anglican identity is a problem of the Australian church, and not one for which our theological colleges can be held solely responsible.

Both colleges must face the fact that none of their present full-time staff are products of Melbourne parishes, served for so long by graduates of the two colleges; and that only one out of nine diocesan or

regional Bishops in Victoria is the product of a Melbourne parish. This suggests a sterility which must be of concern to the colleges, as well as to others.

In addition to these comments which apply to both colleges, here are some further comments on each college.

Trinity college (14 ordinands in 1995):

The problem of the difficulty of building a theological community is increased because most lectures are taken with other UFT students, and are given by people

Ridley College Chapel, 1989.

who are not on the staff of Trinity. The system of control of the Theological School by the provincial bishops has continued to be unsatisfactory. The move to have a local committee to manage the School may well help.

The theological flavour of Trinity is an important issue. It describes itself as Liberal Catholic in tradition and yet underneath this self description lie some major theological and practical differences of opinion. The clearest way to put the issue is to say that Trinity faces the question of whether its tradition is Liberal *Catholic* or Catholic *Liberal*. (The noun is the key.) To be Liberal *Catholic* means that one's basic tradition is Catholic, that one holds the Catholic faith represented in the Creeds, the Councils, and the long standing traditions of the content of Anglican Theology, and approaches these in a liberal spirit, studying them in the light of current issues and ideas. Whereas to be a Catholic *Liberal* means that one's basic theological stance is liberal, determined by the ideas, priorities and assumptions of one's age and time, and that these convictions are accompanied by an appreciation of Catholic liturgical style. The Liberal *Catholic* is convinced about the heart of the Catholic faith, and

Liberal about its application. The Catholic *Liberal* regards the centre of the Christianity as unknowable mystery, though is happy to be dogmatic about the less central issues - pensively agnostic about the Trinity, but emphatic about priesthood. Those bishops of the Australian church who would regard themselves as Liberal *Catholic* rather than Catholic *Liberal* have lost confidence in Trinity College, and Trinity itself is currently facing the tensions of trying to hold together these two different theological strands.

The effects of the review of Trinity carried out in 1995 have yet to be seen.

Ridley College (21 ordinands in 1995):

In addition to the issues raised above in connection with both colleges, Ridley is facing the problems associated with growth and diversification of ministry, and especially the difficulty of paying sufficient attention to the discipleship and formation of candidates for ordination. It is not a large institution, but tries to fulfil many different aims. It is always attractive to add more activities, but not always easy to work out the consequences for existing programmes.

While Ridley welcomes and attracts theological students from a variety of

traditions, it is clearly within the tradition of Reformed Evangelical Anglicanism. However, Evangelical Anglicanism is now pluriform, especially in England. Ridley, like other institutions, has to work out how to respond to this situation, and how to deal with the different traditions of Evangelical Anglicanism, including charismatic, liberal, reformed, post-evangelical and the rest. Ridley faces a crisis of theological identity similar to that faced by Trinity.

Ridley continues to serve the national church, accepting ordination candidates from Melbourne, Bendigo, Ballarat, Gippsland, Armidale, Grafton, Riverina, North Queensland, Perth and Tasmania. It also provides a national evangelical alternative to Moore College.

Ridley also provides an integrated training and formation program, with a cohesive pattern of lectures, chapel, ministry formation and practical training and supervision undertaken within the one community of students and staff. This provides a great opportunity for the integration of learning, worship, living, and ministry, and is a distinctive model of theological education that Ridley contributes to Melbourne.

Melbourne diversity

There are two aspects of diversity in theological education in Melbourne, diversity in responsibility and diversity in theology, both of which are characteristic of Melbourne Anglicanism in general. Theological education is a microcosm of wider church life.

Diversity in responsibility

Of course all church activities that are 'Anglican' find their cohesion within ministry that is licensed by the Archbishop. But under this episcopal umbrella there are a number of different agents and agencies making a substantial contribution to theological education.

Within the training of ordinands, for example, we have Examining Chaplains and the Director of Field Education appointed directly by the Archbishop, the Director of the Theological School at Trinity appointed by the provincial bishops, and Ridley college as a voluntary society. The colleges are intimately involved with the United Faculty of Theology and the Australian College of Theology. And once we move beyond ordination training, we must include the GBRE *Education for Ministry* program, and other voluntary societies such as the CMS St Andrew's

Hall, and the parish-based agencies such as the Institute for Contemporary Leadership at Kew, the Institute for Spiritual Studies at East Melbourne, the Timothy Institute at Carlton, and the Carringbush Centre at Richmond.

This represents a wide range of people taking some sort of responsibility for the provision of theological education, and it must be agreed that this diversity is a great source of strength and richness. We should also note that many lay people and clergy make use of many resources beyond those which can be described as Anglican. This is also a great source of enrichment.

Diversity in Theology

The theological diversity of Melbourne is reflected in its theological training institutions, and it is in training for ministry that we ought to see a positive model of theological diversity, debate and discussion which is illuminating and positive. Unfortunately this is not the case; often theology is dismissed and replaced by sociology, slogans are repeated without reflection, or an arbitrary statement of 'the Anglican view' is given in order to end discussion rather than promote it. If theological debate does not occur in

the context of theological education, then it is unlikely to happen within the wider life of the Diocese. We have still to find a healthy model of theological diversity.

The theological diversity of the Diocese began with the arrival of Archbishop Lowther Clarke and the founding of St. John's College. He intended the college to be a means of promoting the *Lux Mundi* school of theology. With the disappearance of St John's, the Diocese was left with a more uniform theological stance. There was cooperation between Trinity and Ridley and their theological stance was reasonably compatible: Evangelical matriculant ordinands studied at Trinity from its foundation until the 1940s.

This cohesion was furthered by the liturgical agreement brokered by Archbishop Head (coloured stoles and eastward position in celebrating communion) The significant moves have been made by Trinity, first in the direction of more catholic worship (the chasuble was first worn in the 1960s), and then towards more Liberal theology in the 1970s.

The main debate at present is not about churchmanship, but about the definitive source of theology. On the one hand are those who regard the locus of revelation as being in the past, tied to the 'scandal of particularity' of the Incarnation, and found in the 'first text' in verbal form in scripture, and expounded in the statements of the early church. On the other hand are those who look mainly to the 'second text', that of daily life and experience, for whom revelation is primarily a contemporary experience. This 'second text' of contemporary experience was written on reams of butchers paper in the 60s and 70s, and is now verbally expressed in terms of 'personal journey'. The distinction between 'first text' (scripture, and, for many, tradition) and the 'second text' (contemporary experience) becomes increasingly conspicuous in a 'post-Christian' age.

Thus it results in the much acclaimed 'three-fold cord' of scripture, tradition and reason looking a little frayed. At present, for example, ordination training includes two of these elements, the first in the 'theological' subjects of Bible, doctrine, and church history; and the second in Clinical Pastoral Education, field placements, and theological reflection. Relating these two different theological systems requires considerable dexterity, and these serious issues remain unresolved within the Diocese.

It might also be noted that the charismatic movement has not yet found a place within the public theological scene in Melbourne, though it is certainly having powerful and widespread effect at the grass-roots level. We will all suffer if this situation is not remedied.

The great danger in our age is that 'theological education' will include less and less of traditional theology, and more and more sociology, pragmatics, skill-learning, and reflection on personal experience and progress. A church without theology is a church without direction, and training which does not find time or room to grapple with the deep theological substance of the faith is one that will most rapidly be obsolete in a time of rapid social change. James Moorhouse *prepared* himself for his formal theological education by learning Greek well enough to read his New Testament as quickly in Greek as in English! Theological education which loses a firm grasp on its foundations is ultimately sterile.

Conclusion

Alister McGrath, in his book *The Renewal of Anglicanism* claims that the way forward for a deeply fruitful Anglicanism will by

a renewal resourced by our seminaries and colleges, leading the way in teaching and forming clergy and laity in theologically responsible and vibrant faith. Leaders of this kind of renewal that he identifies are not in fact connected with theological colleges![32] Nevertheless, the point that he makes is a good one. It has been a characteristic of Melbourne to provide inadequate resources for theological education, and then blame its theological institutions for their failures, which are so often in fact the failures of the wider church. Colleges are limited by the quality of the students sent to them by the Diocese.

We should be thankful for those who have left us good resources, and determine that theological education needs to happen in our parishes, and that our colleges need better resources for their important ministry, so that God's people may be equipped for every ministry, that Christ's body may be built up, so that we may all come to the unity of the faith, to the maturity of the fullness of Christ.[33]

1   George Goodman, *The Church in Victoria during the Episcopate of the Reverend Charles Perry*, Melville, Muller and Slade, Melbourne, 1892, pp.68, 180-3, 45.

2   *Ibid.*, p.459.

3   *Ibid.*, p.33; but see also A.de Q Robin, Charles Perry Bishop of Melbourne, University of Western Australia Press, Nedlands, 1967, p.17.

4   Stephen Judd and Kenneth Cable, *Sydney Anglicans*, A.I.O, Sydney, 1987, p.58.

5   (Bernard) Rex Davis, *An Account of Theology in Training Colleges*, A.C.C. paper, Sydney, 1966, p.61.

6   Rex Davis, The Beginning and Development of Training Men for the Ministry, with special reference to the Diocese of Newcastle 1825 - 1925, M.A.Thesis, University of Newcastle, 1966.

7   Rex Davis, *An Account*, p.64.

8   Marcus L. Loane, *A Centenary History of Moore Theological College*, Angus and Robertson, Sydney, 1955.

9   A. P. Elkin, *The Diocese of Newcastle*, Australian Medical Publishing, Glebe, 1955, p.376

10 L.L. Nash, 'A short enquiry into the development of the 'reader' system of training for Holy Orders' in *Forward Flows the Time*, G.B. Publications, Melbourne, 1960, pp.115-184; Keith Cole, *A History of the Diocese of Bendigo*, Keith Cole Publications, Bendigo, 1991.

11 Edith. C. Rickard, *Bishop Moorhouse of Melbourne and Manchester*, John Murray, London, 1920, p.80.

12 James Grant, *Perspective of a Century*, Trinity College, Melbourne, 1972, p.104.

13 Rickard, *op.cit.* p.73.

14 Morna Sturrock, The Anglican Deaconess Movement in Melbourne, a U.F.T. B.Th. Research Paper, 1989.

15 S.E.Blackler, *Henry Lowther Clarke and Educational Policy in the Anglican Diocese of Melbourne 1903 - 20*, Melbourne University Ph.D., 1990; Robin Sharwood, Some aspects of the history of the Faculty of Theology at Trinity College, Sydney Smith Memorial Lecture, 1985; R.H.B.Williams, St. John's College Melbourne, lecture, 1960.

L.L.Nash, *op. cit*, pp 203-205; James Grant, op.cit.

16 Darrell Neil Paproth, C.H.Nash and his influence, Deakin University Ph.D., 1993.

David Chambers, *Tempest Tost*, Church Press Publications, Melbourne, 1959. L.L.Nash, *op. cit.*,

Barbara Brinsley Darling, Ridley College 1910 - 1930, University of Melbourne, M.A. Thesis, 1979; A.de Q Robin, *Making Many Rich, a Memoir of the Fourth Archbishop of Melbourne*, Wilke, Clayton, 1978.

17 L.L.Nash, *op.cit.*, and Darrel Neil Paproth, op.cit.; Keith Cole, *A History of The Church Missionary Society of Australia*, Church Missionary Historical Publications, Melbourne, 1971

18 Morna Sturrock, *op.cit.* Ridley Council Minutes.

19 L.L.Nash, *op.cit.* Ridley Council Minutes, Diocesan Archives, and a memorandum from Dr. Barton Babbage.

20 Robin Sharwood, *op.cit.*

21 John Handfield, *Friends and Brothers*, Hyland House, South Yarra, 1980, pp. 80ff.

22 A. de Q Robin, *Making Many Rich*, and J.B. Moroney, 'Joseph John Booth' in Brian Dickey (ed.) *The Australian Dictionary of Evangelical Biography*, Evangelical History Association, Sydney, 1994.

23 Cole, *op.cit.*

24 F.Woods, Synod Sermon 1960', in Brian Porter (ed.) *Frank Woods. Forward in Depth*, JBCE Melbourne, 1987, pp. 39-44.

25 2 Timothy 2:2.

26 Melbourne Diocesan Archives.

27 Muriel Porter, *Women in the Church*, Penguin Books, Ringwood, 1989.

28 Anglican Theological Year Books.

29 Memorandum from Dr. Barton Babbage, August 1994.

30 *The Distinctive Diaconate: Selection and Training*, and *The Diaconate: Its relation to other Ministries*, Policy Papers of the Board for the Diaconate, 1990.

31 ACCM Occasional Paper No. 38, R*esidence, an Education*, 1990, London.

32 Alister McGrath, *The Renewal of Anglicanism*, SPCK, London, 1993.

33 from Ephesians 4:12, 13.

The Anglican-Oriental Orthodox Dialogue, St Paul's Cathedral, September 1991.

Ecumenical Life
in the Diocese of Melbourne

Happily through the wise conduct of the Bishops of Adelaide and Melbourne in meeting ministers of other denominations on a common platform, whenever the cause of Christianity or of good and right in any way can be served thereby, and in showing sympathy with them in a multitude of ways, this unreasonable jealousy is losing ground and a better feeling springing up; but there are too many colonists that have felt the disabilities of Dissent in the old country who are unable to put on the armour of forgiveness, or rather forgetfulness in the new. The enemy has lost his sting, but they will not allow him to live on the remembrance of his past greatness without a reminder of his present impotence.   Richard Twopeny, *Town Life in Australia.*[1]

* * * * * * *

In what way has Anglican encounter with Christians of other churches in Melbourne shaped its identity over the past 150 years?

The Diocese of Melbourne has passed through periods that have at different times posed threat or offered promise to the enhancement of identity. Encounters with other Christians have played an important part in that pilgrimage. The reminders of 'present impotence' of the Anglican Church in the Victorian scene were sometimes welcomed, sometimes rejected. The ability to encourage and embrace the opinions of others has not always been easy, but has, in the long run, enabled it to find a greater understanding of itself, and of its place in the Body of Christ.

The Euphoria of 1910

Events in and around Melbourne in the year 1910 express something of the response of the churches at a time of openness and hope. Churches in the state of Victoria displayed a remarkable willingness to sit lightly on their traditions for the sake of wider unity. That year the Australian Student Christian Union met at Daylesford for its January summer conference. Frank Engel describes the Conference photograph:

It shows 116 made up of 61 women
in long skirts and enormous hats,
except two daring hatless ones in
the front row, and 55 overdressed
men of whom several sport straw-

deckers with university colours. A number of tennis racquets, a couple of furled umbrellas, the long galvanised roof of a hall, some trees and a white church complete the picture. In that beautifully rural holiday resort of a former gold-mining town, something profound happened in the lives of those lively students. [2]

The conference was prepared in a spirit of prayer, and participants bore witness to the way a 'new experience of the presence and power of the Holy Spirit had come into their lives'. The event was seen as a key moment in the life of the Australian Student Christian Movement, and of the ecumenical and missionary history of the Victorian churches. The meeting saw forty-one students committed to missionary service through the Student Volunteer Movement. This missionary policy was conveyed in a 'Manifesto from the Australian Student Volunteer Movement for Foreign Missions to the Churches of Australasia', and led to discussions with official church leaders and missionary organisations. The Report of the Australian Student Christian union described the gathering as 'having an extraordinary sense of unity and spiritual power.'

In August of that year an ecumenical university service was held in St Paul's Cathedral, attended by the Vice-Chancellor of Melbourne University and staff in academic dress, and students. The procession included among the church dignitaries, a Greek priest. The music was, to quote the main organiser, 'as good as the Abbey', and concluded with the 'Halleluia Chorus'. [3]

The service was arranged by the Student Christian Union, but mainly at the instigation of visiting lecturer, the Reverend William Temple. Temple (the future Archbishop of Canterbury) had recently been ordained, and had been gaining ecumenical experience as a steward at the Edinburgh World Missionary Conference earlier in that year. John Mott, the main organiser at Edinburgh, was too involved in its work to accept an invitation to visit Australia, and saw it important to send a deputy. Having experienced the hostility of Australian universities to Christianity in previous visits, Mott was anxious to find a deputy who could counter sectarian and agnostic tendencies.

He was not disappointed. Temple saw his university services in Australia as exhibitions of universities at prayer, and they marked a turning point in student Christian confidence. His address at Melbourne was entitled 'The Edinburgh

Conference and the Unity of the Church'. In it he pointed to the growing significance of the movement for Christian unity. The other notes that Temple continued to strike in his Australian addresses were the Christian challenge to materialism and agnosticism, the 'new sense of responsibility for foreign field', and responsibility in the social challenges of the time. In these he saw the new sense of unity undergirding the work in universities, and in the missionary and social task.

In December of the same year, the Victorian Parliament passed an act to provide for the incorporation of a college of divinity under the name 'the Melbourne College of Divinity'. Inter-denominational meetings in 1906 to 1909 had prepared the way for cooperation in the field of theological education. A resolution had been agreed to, describing in some detail a scheme for conferring degrees by an interdenominational board. At the same time, steps for the establishment of a faculty of theology at Melbourne University had fallen through, despite the combined efforts of the Anglican, Congregational, Methodist and Presbyterian Churches, who had submitted a long memorial to the University Council. Opposition had come from Roman Catholic Archbishop Carr, and

from a counter-memorial submitted by a large number of graduates, who asserted that the establishment of such a faculty would be divisive, to the point of doing lasting injury to the university. [4] The alternative strategy of establishing a degree-conferring body outside the University was put in place in 1910. Once the enabling legislation was passed, the co-operating churches moved quickly to establish the body, and the Melbourne College of Divinity, also including the Baptist Church, first met on 23 March 1911.

Anglicans took an important part in these 1910 activities. The work of William Temple was backed by a Student Christian Union in which Anglicans were significantly represented. Its membership included in its earlier years, E. Selwyn Hughes, who later as Vicar of St Peter's Eastern Hill took an active part in the major Australian ecumenical missionary conference of 1903. Percy Wisewould, an Anglican priest of fundamentalist and evangelical background, discovered in the Student Movement a 'larger freedom'. He became a travelling Secretary, and later Acting General Secretary of the Student Movement during the war years. In the post-war years he took a leading role in facilitating inter-church and inter-faith cooperation

in providing funds for European relief. The Student Christian Union also influenced the first Bishop of Gippsland, Dr A.W. Pain, who went to the Edinburgh Conference in 1910, and was a member of the Continuation Committee of that body. Dr Alexander Leeper, Warden of Trinity College, played an important part in arranging the ecumenical university jubilee service of 1906 in St Paul's Cathedral. He saw the John Mott visit of 1903 and the foundation of the Student Christian Movement as 'events second to none in importance in their bearing upon the life of our students.'[5]

Early Lay initiatives
The Australian churches found early in the colony's history an encouragement to act ecumenically in the ministry to a thinly scattered population in the interior. In 1870 a number of laymen in the Anglican and PresbyterianChurches in Melbourne proposed to their respective assemblies 'that joint action should be taken by the two churches for supplying divine ordinances in the thinly populated districts'.[6] The two assemblies agreed to confer on the issue, and a body for that purpose was convened in 1870. Anglican representatives included Bishop Perry,

Dean Macartney, and Archdeacon Stretch. The Conference agreed to the setting up of a joint Pastoral Aid Society, to 'collect and distribute funds with a view of securing more adequate provision for the religious instruction to the people resident in thinly-populated districts of the colony, and for the better maintenance of the ministers of the district.'[7]

A committee was appointed which worked actively for a decade, gathering and distributing substantial amounts of money. Its work was aided by modification of Anglican regulations that allowed the use of Anglican buildings for other purposes than divine service according to Church of England usage. The cooperation cooled, mainly over the controversy surrounding the exchange of pulpits between St Paul's and Scots Church in 1883, when Canon Bromby and Dr Strong changed places on 25 February. While funds continued to be channelled to the two churches, their two assemblies found it progressively difficult to give it formal support. Bishop Perry, while approving of the fund, had regarded it as 'not, however strictly a fund of the church.'[8] By 1884 the committee appears to have become an association of Anglican and Presbyterian laymen.

'Union in the air, and in the heart of every church'

It is probable that the post-Federation climate in Australia contributed to its acceptance of the ecumenical movement in a significant way. Federation was accompanied by a corresponding movement towards organic union by Protestant churches. The first General Assembly of the newly united Presbyterian Church in Australia occurred in 1901. The four separate Methodist churches united in 1902 and the Congregational Union of Australasia was established in 1892. Wider union was seen as a natural outcome of these moves, and the first national Presbyterian Moderator, John Meiklejohn, addressed himself to the matter at length at the second Assembly in 1902. The meeting was practically unanimous in the recognition of the desirability of wider union, and made their submission to the Anglican and Protestant churches in Australia.

The response by Anglicans was surprisingly warm. The Bishop of Gippsland, Dr Pain, dwelt on the submission at some length in his address to his 1903 Church Assembly, describing it as 'the first official overture to any part of the Anglican Communion made by any other church'. He was applauded by his following statement that 'the efforts to provide for the spiritual needs of our scattered population are considerably weakened by much wasteful overlapping and much unseemly competition' and 'the religious rivalry which exists is a scandal and the effect produced upon our people is oftentimes disastrous in the extreme'.[9] Melbourne Anglican Church Assembly of the same year was equally warm to the Presbyterian overture. The references to the proposal by Archbishop Lowther Clarke received great approbation, and a motion was adopted expressing 'concurrence with the objects sought to be obtained'. In moving the resolution, Archdeacon Hindley noted that 'in old days emphasis was wont to be laid on the points in which they (the denominations) differed. Now it was rather upon what they agreed'.[10] The Australian General Synod of 1905 appointed Anglican representatives to discuss 'the possibility of closer union' with the Presbyterian Church.[11]

Part of the background to the move was the scarcity of resources within the churches to meet the needs of a dispersed population, and for the training of the clergy. But union was also, as John Meiklejohn put it, 'not only in the air, but in the heart of every church that has any claim to be a

Members of Victorian Council of Churches with the Dalai Lama, September 1982.

church of Christ.' The federation of the Australian states carried with it a growing feeling of fellowship which transcended previous community and church antagonisms. There was a hope that something greater would arise out of the fellowship and cooperation. Engel describes this pre-world war period, with its optimism, and enjoyment of the apparent limitless possibilities for the future, as pervading every aspect of culture and society. The ecumenical committee which was formed as a result of the responses to the Presbyterian submission found itself in St Paul's Cathedral vestry in 1911, listening for the large part of the afternoon to the Archbishop, speaking of his great desire for union.

It was always expected that the Anglican Church would take a leading part in any new venture. From the early beginnings of English settlement establishment was ruled out, yet the Anglican Church, and the bishops and archbishops in particular, continued to be looked to for leadership in new activities. The churches were not unaware of the costs of reunion. Meiklejohn, in bringing the Presbyterian overture forward, noted that church union might involve 'some sacrifice of sentiment, though not of principle'.[12] He expressed the hope that there might be a closer union of churches in Australia, 'even at the expense of some measure of separation from those churches in the Old World'.

Anglicans also recognised that their future identity included both links with the historic episcopate, and new-found links with the fellow-Christians and friends in the new country. The legal status of the Church of England in Australia and its freedom to operate independently of its mother church were under question at the time when the ecumenical committee exploring reunion was meeting in Melbourne. While much creative work was done by the committee, including a fairly detailed agreement on the nature and method of ordination, a 1910 legal decision blocked progress. It stated that 'the Anglican Churches in Australia and Tasmania are all organised upon the basis that they are not merely Churches "in communion with" or "in connection with" the Church of England, but are actually parts of that Church.' When this judgement became public knowledge, enthusiasm for church unity cooled for both Anglicans and their negotiating partners.[13]

Engel describes how in the first two decades the pendulum swung rather unevenly and unsteadily from church federation to full union, and back to a measure of cooperation, and then to rest in denominationalism.[14]

'A bigoted howl against Rome'

From the early days of colonial settlement the notion of Anglican supremacy, based on its role as the established church in the mother country, was challenged, both by the religious plurality of the new community, and by the greater separation of church and state. In the 19th century the matter was focused on the issue of state aid to religion in general, and education in particular. A growing secularism in the 1860s led to the abolition of state aid to religion in 1870, and in the process of arguing a case for continued aid, the Anglican Church found itself in conflict with other Christians. There is plenty of evidence to indicate that Anglicans continued to assume the role of ascendancy. In analysing the Irish-English conflict in Australia, Niall Brennan maintains that the most jagged class distinction this country has ever known was drawn along a line that clearly contained religions. Although the Church of England was never established as the official church of the colony, he notes that it rarely occurred to anyone to think of it in any other way. Brennan affirms that the Anglican Church of 19th century Australia was 'subservient, disinterested, inclined to snobbery, detached at most points from true Christian practices, employed only to maintain Christian observance, and the status quo'.[15] He concludes that in many ways this image trailed by the Anglican Church coloured its ability to enable and its ability to hinder ecumenical activity in the new colony.

Anglicans and other Protestants did work together against perceived common enemies, including the growing secularism, but also against the Roman Catholic Church. Their attitude did little to endear them to the local population or advance the cause of ecumenism. With Roman Catholic relations, a pattern of antagonism was established, with few opportunities of reconciliation. The growing strength of the Anglo-Catholic Oxford Movement in the 19th century, and the gradual emergence of a Roman Catholic hierarchy in England were seen as threats to the authority of the Protestant supremacy. This was transferred strongly to the Australian colonies. Bishop Perry, on his arrival in Melbourne in 1848, refused to receive or return the call of Father Geoghegan. This act was viewed in the local scene as extremely uncharitable towards a priest noted for his toleration. Before Perry's arrival Protestants had shared in fund-raising for Melbourne's first Roman Catholic chapel. Although Bishop Perry endeavoured to be courteous in his opposition, his opinions overrode his charity. As a firm Evangelical, he led a strong campaign against the Roman Catholic Church, describing it in the first issue of the *Church of England Messenger* as 'an apostate and idolatrous Church, the subject of the prophetical denunciations of Daniel, St Paul and St John'.[16] Alongside these controversies, anti-catholic feeling was fuelled by English-Irish tensions. In the 1840s and 1890s the annual parades in celebration of the Battle of the Boyne were scenes of violent confrontations.

Bishop Moorhouse, who followed Perry, adopted a more eirenic approach, seeking cooperation between all churches in the 1880s to have included a schedule of Bible lessons in state schools. He writes, 'All the Nonconformists went with me, till it came to the question of giving a separate grant to the Roman Catholics, and then the Wesleyans in a body left us, "not", they protested, "because they loved Christ less, but because they hated Rome more." Nothing will induce me to join in a bigoted howl against Rome.' He adds, 'the hatred of Rome here is incredible'.[17]

In the years of the First World War, Catholics and Protestants were aligned on opposite sides on the question of conscription. In September 1916, the Melbourne Diocesan Synod voted unanimously, and without discussion, in favour of 'the conscription of men and income', because it was 'convinced that the forces of the Allies are being used of God to vindicate the rights of the weak.'[18] The motion was moved by Dr Leeper, seconded by Archdeacon Hindley, and was followed by the singing of the National Anthem. Anglicans and Protestants at that time made charges of Roman Catholic disloyalty, focused particularly on Archbishop Daniel Mannix. The formation of the Victorian Protestant Federation in 1919-20 with a constitution that was quite specifically anti-Roman, widened the gap between the two groups. Roman Catholic policies, in particular with reference to rules on mixed marriages, had the effect of cementing these differences. It was not until after the Second Vatican Council and the local leadership of Archbishop Frank Woods, that there was any real and meaningful contact made that drew Roman Catholics into the ecumenical movement.

Contemplations of reunion

The exploration of reunion continued after negotiations arising from the Presbyterian overture concluded. Congregational layman, Horace Wooton, convened one hundred Anglican and Protestant leaders at a dinner in the Grand Hotel in Melbourne at the beginning of 1913, for the purpose of obtaining 'diversity in co-operation'. Those present formed themselves into a Council, which grew in number to 169 clergy and laity and prepared for a congress later in the year. Anglicans occupied twenty-nine places on the Council, and Canon Hart, later

Bishop of Wangaratta, was a vice-president. It was expected that the conclusions of such a congress would not be binding on any church, but that participants would be expected to introduce them into their church courts for consideration. Three commissions were appointed, on home missions, on standardisation of theological curricula, and on mutual eligibility of ministers. The emphasis was on practical cooperation to avoid denominational competition in the developing towns of the state, and in theological education.

While these cooperative ventures were the stated basis of the Congress, the Commission on Ministry considered matters of reunion. It examined the way in which Anglican episcopacy placed a stumbling block on the mutual recognition of ministries. While recognising the difficulties, it concluded that it had found 'sufficient reasons for hopefulness'. The work of the commissions led to responses in the daily press.

The Congress itself began on 31 August, with the preachers giving special Sunday sermons in city and suburban churches. These included Canon Hughes at St Peter's Eastern Hill, on 'Church Union and the Historic Episcopate', and Dean Stephen at St Paul's Cathedral, on 'That they all may be one'. The Congress assembled the following afternoon in the Melbourne Town Hall for four days of deliberations, and the three commission reports were debated and 'adopted unanimously', with some criticism by Canon Hart over theological education. In concluding, the Congress expressed 'its deep thankfulness to God for the manifest presence and guidance of the Holy Spirit in its deliberations'.[19]

Further conferences were held on a national basis in the 1920s of a 'Joint Australian Council of Churches Contemplating Reunion'. These were at the initiative of Anglicans, particularly Archbishop Wright of Sydney, following the issue of the Lambeth 'Appeal' in 1920. Progress was halted when the concurrent negotiations between Presbyterian, Methodist and Congregational Churches ran into trouble. The conferring of the 1910s and 1920s had an important result in educating the churches about their separate viewpoints, and in particular, the problem of Anglicans over a non-episcopally ordained ministry.

A council of churches

The Edinburgh Conference gave encouragement to initiatives of practical cooperation. Meanwhile the international faith and order discussions, commencing with the first World Conference at Lausanne in 1927, moved the churches towards the formation of more permanent conciliar instruments. Bishop George Cranswick of Gippsland took the initiative in setting up the 'Victorian Regional Committee of the Faith and Order Movement' in 1934. Archbishop Head chaired the first meetings of this body, which comprised four member churches, Anglican, Congregational, Methodist, and Presbyterian. He was ably supported by a Methodist, the Reverend L.M. Thomson, who became secretary of the body in 1939. By that time nine other churches had joined (Baptist, Churches of Christ, Salvation Army, Society of Friends, Welsh Church, together with two Orthodox churches, Greek and Syrian, and two Lutheran churches, German and Swedish).

The body was thus substantially representative of non-Roman Catholic churches in Victoria. It became the formal means of cooperation between the member churches, eventually becoming the Victorian Council of Churches in 1960. Anglicans have continued to play leading roles in the fifty-two years of this body's existence, chairing this body for a considerable portion of its life. Substantial contributions were made by Archbishops Booth and Woods, who occupied the chair from 1949-54 and 1958-64 respectively. The only Anglican to hold secretaryship is the writer of this essay (1966-82).

The late sixties and early seventies saw a high point in the activities of the Council, in the lead up to the inauguration of the Uniting Church in 1977, and the Roman Catholic entry into membership of the Council in 1979. Three ecumenically based lay study programmes were held in 1966, 1971, and 1972.[20] The widening of cooperation on an ecumenical basis took place in a number of fields, including industrial, welfare, and hospital chaplaincy, work on Christian education in schools, in theological education, and in television.

The Vatican II floodgates

The Decree on Ecumenism (1964) of the Second Vatican Council of the Roman Catholic Church provided new openings in a developing relationship between that church and others in Victoria. This was made more possible by a growing trust through contacts developed in the 1950s. The Week of Prayer for Christian Unity began to be observed each year after Fr Gabriel Hebert, SSM, visited Melbourne in 1954 and initiated a committee which included an Anglican priest, the Reverend Godfrey Kircher, and Roman Catholic priests,

Pope John Paul II being introduced to Archbishop Sir Frank Woods, 1986.

Pope John Paul II lights the unity candle in St Paul's Cathedral, 1986.

Antony Cleary and Percy Jones. The Vatican Council Decree opened a floodgate of activity, enabling the ecumenical movement to find a new lease of life. Roman Catholics began participating in local ecumenical councils, as well as engaging in wider expressions of Christian Unity.

This author remembers how steep the learning curve was for clergy and laity in the Catholic Archdiocese. It was particularly seen when they opened the 1973 International Eucharistic Congress to ecumenical participation. It was the first time since its inception in the 19th century that such a major Roman Catholic event had included a significant ecumenical dimension. As the ecumenical representative on the planning committee, one noted with pleasure the way in which the more strident expressions of eucharistic triumphalism gave way to more considered, educational programs, including international speakers from different traditions, and an Ecumenical Night at the Melbourne Cricket Ground, attracting 60 000 participants. A highlight was the meeting in the Melbourne Town Hall on 16 February, when after a lengthy treatise on the eucharist by Cardinal Willebrands, Archbishop Woods received an ovation for his call for a greater and richer ecumenism.

Organic unity: 'Facing one another'

The hopes held out for organic unity in the early years of the century persisted through the decades. Anglicans drew to the periphery of these discussions, but in the 1940s did engage in 'The Bishopscourt Conferences on Church Union' with the Methodist Conference. Archbishop Head, who was the initiator of these discussions in 1932, had returned from Lambeth with an ecumenical vision for the church. In the Report of the discussions it is noted that the Archbishop's conviction was 'that we should discuss our differences more wisely if we knew one another more familiarly. Souls that have toiled, and wrought, and thought together would better appreciate the sunshine and the shadow which fell across their journey, and in such an atmosphere moods would be less likely to petrify into principles'. [21]

The conversations took place on a regular basis, with the representatives meeting for a full day every three months. Dr Calvert Barber, a Methodist representative, tells of the way the group began by each group preparing statements, which were filed in a growing book on pages facing each other. He notes 'that after some years this seemed to some of us to be a symbol of "facing one another". It was then decided to make a fresh beginning and aim at making a united statement' [22]. This was produced at the conclusion of the conferences in 1947, and sent to the Lambeth Conference for consideration. It included agreed statements on the Church, the Gospel, the Sacraments, the Ministry, and Episcopacy.

While the Report contained a basis for any future negotiations between the two churches, it was laid aside as the Methodist Church moved towards more serious discussions with the Presbyterian and Congregational Churches, leading to the formation of the Uniting Church in Australia in June 1977.

The arrival in Melbourne of the Reverend Dr Davis McCaughey brought a persuasive ecumenist whose contribution to the whole movement cannot be underestimated. His friendship with Archbishop Frank Woods was of long standing.

On a national level, Anglican General Synod in 1966 resolved to approach the uniting churches to ask whether it might become a participant in the negotiations. At the same time, it requested the Anglican Church to make a thorough study of the relevant documents. In Melbourne, the Archbishop's Ecumenical Affairs Committee prepared a study booklet for that purpose.

At that stage, the proposed basis of union included provision for a threefold order of ministry, including episcopal functions. It thus excited Anglicans and Roman Catholics, and interesting responses were made at an ecumenical conference convened by Archbishop Woods' Ecumenical Affairs Commission. The Uniting Church's response to General Synod was that the Anglican Church should not become a full participant in the Joint Commission on Church Union, but that it should engage in consultations with the federal commissions of the three bodies. Two useful consultations were held, and the Anglican Church continued to have an observing role on the Joint Commission. The subsequent removal of the episcopate from the Basis at the request of the Presbyterian Church meant that Anglicans could no longer see themselves as serious negotiators. Nevertheless they welcomed the Uniting Church, and its inauguration was marked in Melbourne with an ecumenical service of thanksgiving in St Paul's Cathedral on 22 June 1977.

Practical cooperation

In the lead-up to the formation of the Uniting Church, much was done by its constituents in ventures of cooperation at state and local level. There was a stimulation for other churches to participate in these ventures, and Anglicans were included. Two Australian surveys of Anglican involvement in ecumenical activities appeared in the 1970s. The Missionary and Ecumenical Council in 1971 commissioned a survey of inter-church activities in which Anglicans shared.[23] The 1975 Standing Committee of General Synod arranged for the documentation of general Anglican progress in ecumenical matters, both related to the forthcoming church union, and alongside it.[24]

Both reports are interesting, in that they enable ecumenical progress in the Diocese of Melbourne to be compared with that in the rest of the Australian Anglican Church. Bishop Garnsey, who edited both the 1971 and 1975 national reports cited above, drew attention to the strong development of chaplaincy work on an inter-church basis in schools, universities, hospitals and in industry. Anglicans had played a leading part in that work. At that time, Bishop Dann was instrumental in encouraging Anglican involvement in the Inter Church New Areas Commission, which sought to coordinate strategy between the churches, and to encourage new cooperative ventures. While this work was not as spectacular as the well-known projects of Canberra and East Gippsland, it continued to foster a number projects with the shared use of buildings and ministry in the metropolitan area.

The Melbourne Diocesan Ecumenical Affairs Committee in this period served as an Anglican focus for ventures in ecumenical cooperation, including the sponsorship of annual clergy schools. It arranged ecumenical study conferences on the *Basis of Union of the Uniting Church*, and on the Vatican II *Decree on Ecumenism*, and in doing so created opportunities of 'theological cross-fertilisation' for these churches. It made a special study on the sharing of the Eucharist, and by encouraging the Melbourne Synod, finally obtained a General Synod canon on inter-communion in 1973.

The bonds of friendship

The deepest contributions to Christian unity by Anglicans in Victoria appear to have been made, not by resolutions and committees, but by personal relationships. Attention has already been drawn to the role of personal relationships between lay people in the early history of the colony in establishing goodwill, through working ecumenically to assist the churches. At times they appeared to do so in opposition to their member churches. John Pascoe

Fawkner took issue with Bishop Perry over his attack on the Roman Catholic Church. Mr Justice Higinbotham, who was an Anglican layman, believed that it was only the action of the laity which would overcome the opposition of the clergy to the challenges of modern science. In this matter he was supported by mutual friends, Dr Charles Strong and Canon Bromby, both of whom were present when Higinbotham delivered a lecture to the Scots Church Literary Association in 1883. In it he stated that 'the salvation of the mind of Christendom appears to depend, so far as we can venture to hazard an opinion, upon union amongst laymen of all churches who still retain an intelligent hold upon the ultimate object of faith.'[25]

Higinbotham's lecture attracted much attention in the press, and provoked angry responses. Bishop James Moorhouse encouraged a more eirenical attitude. It was at a time when Melbourne was sharing with the rest of the Christian world the upheavals caused by new discoveries of science, and of their application to the study of the scriptures. Moorhouse had supported the Church Pastoral Aid Society, and had encouraged the exchange of pulpits between Dr Strong and Canon Bromby. He had done this as a practical demonstration of his own conviction, expressed at the inter-colonial Church Congress of the Anglican Church, held in Melbourne in 1882. He had asserted there that the reason why the community did not take the Church seriously was its preoccupation with sectarian differences. Moorhouse told his own Church Assembly in the following year that he was deeply disturbed by the bickering and standing apart of Christians in the face of the serious challenge of those who assert that the sole reality is 'matter without mind, laws without a purpose, man without a future, the unwise without God'.[26]

A succession of Victoria's Anglican bishops followed Moorhouse's lead in taking prominent roles in developing friendships across denominational boundaries. Engel[27] notes the particular contribution of Bishop George Cranswick of Gippsland – a 'sombre, serious, almost "heavy" person'. From the time of the 1920 Lambeth Conference, which framed 'the Appeal to all Christian People', Cranswick took an active part in linking Christians in Victoria with the wider ecumenical movement. He was involved in the 1926 Australian Missionary Conference, which led to the formation of the National Missionary Council of Australia. He initiated

above: Archbishop Frank Woods with Cardinal Knox, Catholic Archbishop of Melbourne, 1973.

right: Ecumencial occasion in St Paul's Cathedral, 26 June, 1977.

PHOTO: THE AGE, MELBOURNE. USED WITH PERMISSION.

the discussions which led to the Victorian Regional Committee of the Faith and Order Movement, and went on to assist in the setting up of the Australian Council of Churches in 1945, of which he was the first Commissioner. In his retirement he took

Council for its 1964 session. During his time in Rome he provided first hand impressions to the Australian churches, who in turn conveyed their good wishes to the Council. He took a leading part in the formation of the national Joint Working Group of the Anglican and Roman Catholic Churches, and was a member of the World Council of Churches' Faith and Order Commission from 1968 to 1975. After returning to Melbourne in 1975, Frank Cuttriss took a leading part in the work of the Melbourne Diocesan Ecumenical Affairs Commission, and especially in the post-Vatican II conferences.

Archbishop Frank Woods

It is hard to overestimate the contribution to ecumenism of Archbishop Frank Woods. Like others mentioned in this essay, his burning concern for Christian unity began in his student days through work with the Student Christian Movement. As President of the Cambridge SCM, he was following in the footsteps of his father, the Bishop of Lichfield, who was a long time member and leader of the British SCM.

The twenty years in which he was Archbishop of Melbourne occurred at a time when new ventures in ecumenism were becoming possible, with the entry

steps to assist in the care of Asian students coming to Melbourne.

Relations with the Roman Catholic Church began to develop after the Second Vatican Council (1962–5). Archdeacon Frank Cuttriss played an important role in fostering relationships. He recalls that while Rector of St James' King St, Sydney, he was 'deeply stirred' by the announcement of the Second Vatican Council in 1959, and prayed daily for it.[28] He was appointed as Australian Council of Churches' observer to the Vatican of the Roman Catholic Church into the ecumenical movement, and the formation of the Uniting Church in Australia. The Archbishop drew attention to these matters, and stimulated Anglicans to become involved, and also to consider wider organic unity. In his presidential address to the Anglican General Synod in 1973 he expressed his hope 'that our church may be ever ready to respond fully to the call of God to move more deeply into unity, not just within itself, but with other Christian traditions which share with us Bible, Creed and Sacraments.' In the same address he pointed to 'the wealth of ecumenical adventure, even of ecumenical risk, going on in the local scene.'[29]

Archbishop Woods relished that adventure, and pursued it in a way that enabled others to take similar risks. His ability to make close friendships outside his Anglican circle was an important aspect of his success. During his episcopate, Melbourne Anglicans took a much greater role in the wider ecumenical movement. The Archbishop attended three World Council of Churches assemblies, and served on the Central Committee of that body from 1961 to 1975, and was for a time Vice President. He was also a member of its Faith and Order Commission and presided at the Australian Council of Churches in 1965 and 1966.

He felt deeply the divisions between Christians, and was dismayed by what he perceived to be a hesitancy, and in some cases a reversal of Roman Catholic commitment to ecumenism. He expressed it in particular as a response to a lecture by Cardinal Hume at the 1988 Summer School on Ecumenism. His disappointment did not deter his continuing friendship with Roman Catholics, especially with Archbishop Sir Frank Little, who in introducing him to Pope John Paul II in a welcome in St Paul's Cathedral in 1986, described him as 'Our Abraham'.

Towards a wider ecumenism

Other Anglicans of the Melbourne Diocese have contributed in a notable way to work on the international ecumenical scene. These include Dr Harry Smythe (Anglican Centre at Rome), Bishop Max Thomas and Dr John Gaden (International Anglican-Orthodox Dialogue), Dr Charles Sherlock (Anglican-Roman Catholic International Commission) and the present Archbishop, Keith Rayner, who is a past President of Christian Conference of Asia. The recognition of Australia's part in the Asian scene, and the emerging multi-cultural nature of our own country, have given rise to exploration of wider concepts of ecumenism. Archbishop David Penman introduced Melbourne Anglicans to the importance of dialogue with people of other living faiths, and was elected President of the World Conference on Religion and Peace in 1989, a work cut short by his untimely death in October of that year. These latter moves point towards the ecumenical challenges for the future, which Melbourne Diocese is well positioned to take up. Challenges ahead include relationships with the Orthodox churches. The Anglican-Oriental Orthodox dialogue arranged in Melbourne in 1994 at the request of General Synod has indicated that there is a long way to go in achieving mutual understanding.

A jubilee year

The year 1998 will mark both the 150th anniversary of Bishop Perry's arrival in Melbourne, and the 50th anniversary of the World Council of Churches. The eighth General Assembly of the latter body will be held in Harare, Zimbabwe, in that year. Preparations for the event have stressed the biblical roots of the 'jubilee', and called the member churches to a new step in the ecumenical pilgrimage.

The 20th century has been entitled 'The Ecumenical Century', marked, as this essay notes, with the amazing enthusiasm flowing from the Edinburgh 1910 World Mission Conference. Bill Lazareth, a Lutheran theologian, has pointed out that over this century the doctrinal convergence has been so great that there is no excuse for remaining apart. He notes that there is a hesitation from moving forward, because of 'neo-confessionalism', as churches search more consciously to discover their own identities.[30] The experience of the Uniting Church since 1977 has borne this out.

The identity problem faced by Anglicans in the early years of the Diocese thus still lives with it in today's ecumenical scene. The hostile environment of the early colonial period has given way to new secular challenges. The question remains – how can a church discover its identity while maintaining fellowship with the other Victorian churches? Bruce Kaye states his belief that Anglican diversity in the Australian Anglican church places it strategically to develop an identity as a 'church in society'.[31] But in developing his thesis he does not envisage a closer relationship between the churches, but rather the acceptance of denominational plurality as a 'gift rather than a judgement'.[32] Such a conclusion leaves out the essential dynamic of ecumenical encounter, which leads a church on a pilgrimage, where identity is discovered through engagement. However, he recognises that fidelity to historical positions in matters of doctrine must also be respected.

The Groupe des Dombes stresses that Christian identity is always a 'Christian becoming'. It is 'an opening up to an eschatological beyond, which ceaselessly draws it forward and prevents itself from shutting up in itself. Thus it is a radical opening up to others beyond all walls of separation.'[33]

'Are Anglicans serious about the ecumenical movement?'

The question was asked of me in particular by a Greek Orthodox bishop. He was meeting in the 1970s, as a vice-chairman of the Victorian Council of Churches with senior Anglican clergy of the Melbourne Diocese, to encourage their involvement in the Council. He faced a critical comment by one bishop, who felt that the Council would be supported by the Anglican Church only when it had earned that support. It is a question not unlike those asked by other churches in the earlier phases of ecumenical encounter. It was raised by Presbyterian Moderator, the Very Reverend John Walker, in Melbourne in 1918. Speaking out of the recent experience of friendships developed across denominational boundaries by army chaplains in Gallipoli and France, he asked Anglicans whether 'adhesion to...the historic episcopate must be a *sine qua non* in all discussions on church union.'[34] The question was reiterated by the past secretary of Anglican General Synod, John Denton, in reflecting on Anglican involvement in the national 'Living Under the Southern Cross' ecumenical conference in 1991. He wondered whether Anglicans were content to let bishops represent them in ecumenical activities, without themselves being committed.

The danger of Anglicans falling back on their 'past greatness' still remains. But the record of 150 years of encounter points to a 'future greatness', discovered in its continuing willingness to be open to others, and to respond in the search for greater unity.

1   Richard Twopenny, *Town Life in Australia*, Elliot Stock, London, 1883, pp. 113-4.

2   F.G. Engel, *Christians in Australia. Volume 1: Conflict and Unity 1788-1926*, Joint Board of Christian Education, Melbourne, 1984, p. 142.

3   F.A. Iremonger, *William Temple, Archbishop of Canterbury: His Life and Letters*, Oxford University Press, London, 1948, p. 130.

4   R.L. Sharwood, 'Theology and Tertiary Education in Australia', in Rex Davis (ed), *The Morpeth Papers, being papers read at the Bishop of Newcastle's Conference on Theological Education*, Morpeth, Sydney, 1966, pp.5-6.

5   *Australasian Intercollegian IX*, June 1906, p. 5.

6   Presbyterian Church of Victoria, *Proceedings*, Vol II, minute 9, Commission of Assembly, 9 May 1872, p.14.

7   Presbyterian Church of Victoria, *Proceedings*, App. II, General Assembly, November 1872, pp.117-118.

8   *Church of England Messenger*, 8 November 1873, p.9.

9   *Church of England Messenger*, 2 November 1903, p. 135.

10 *Ibid.*, Supplement, p.7.

11 *General Assembly of Australia Minutes*, 1906, p. 122.

12 *General Assembly of Australia Minutes*, 1901, pp. 21-2.

13 R. Border, *Church and State in Australia 1788-1872*, SPCK, London, 1962, pp. 275-80.

14 F.G. Engel, *Op. cit.*, p. 168.

15 Niall Brennan, *Dr. Mannix*, Rigby Ltd, Adelaide, 1964, p. 220.

16 *Church of England Messenger*, Vol I., 1850, p.3.

17 E. Rickards, *Bishop Moorhouse of Melbourne and Manchester*, London, 1920, p. 90.

18 M. Clark (ed), *Sources of Australian History*, World Classics, London, 1957, p. 545.

19 *The Official Report of the Congress on the Union of the Churches*, Melbourne, 31 August to 3 September, 1913.

20 1966, 'The Church and Life Movement; 1971, 'Action for World Development'; 1972, 'The Year of Renewal' (preceding the International Eucharistic Congress).

21 *Report of the Melbourne Anglican-Methodist Conferences on Re-union*, Diocesan Book Society & Methodist Book Depot, Melbourne, 1947, p.1.

22 G.C. Barbe (n.d.), *Specific Approaches to Church Union in Australia*, Victorian Council of Churches, Melbourne, p. 3.

23 D.A. Garnsey, *Survey of Inter-church activities in which Anglicans share*, Missionary and Ecumenical Council of the Church of England in Australia, Melbourne, 1972.

24 D.A. Garnsey, *Anglicans, Unity and the Uniting Church*, General Board of Religious Education, Melbourne, 1976.

25 *Argus*, 2 August, 1883, p. 9.

26 J. Moorhouse, 'Address to Church Assembly', in *Theology Pamphlets*, vol 57, September 1883, State Library of Victoria , pp 3-8.

27 F.G. Engel, *Christians in Australia, Volume 2, Times of Change 1918-1978*, Joint Board of Christian Education, Melbourne, 1984, p.79.

28 M.L. Moorhead, *Journey Begun, Destination Unsighted: The Ecumenical Movement in the Roman Catholic Archdiocese of Melbourne 1960 - 1990*, David Lovell Publishing, Melbourne, 1991, p. 3.

29 *Proceedings of the Fourth General Synod*, the Church of England in Australia, May 1973, p. 19.

30 W. Lazareth, *Lecture at the Ecumenical Institute*, Bossey, June, 1981

31 B. Kaye, *A Church without Walls: Being Anglican in Australia*, Dove, Melbourne, 1995, p.188.

32 *Ibid.*, p. 196.

33 Groupe des Dombes, *For the Conversion of the Churches*, WCC publications, Geneva, 1993, p. 20.

34 *Presbyterian Messenger*, 18 October 1918; and *Presbyterian*, vol. 1, no. 51, 3 October, 1918, p. 897.

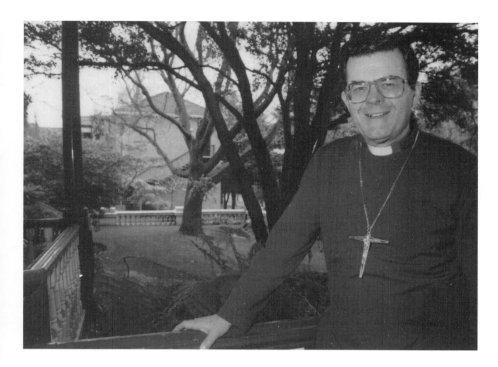

10

*Archbishop Keith Rayner, elected
Primate of the Anglican Church of
Australia in 1991.*

Yesterday and Today: What of Tomorrow?
Melbourne Anglicans 1847-1997

Meanwhile the disciples were urging [Jesus], "Rabbi, eat something" But he said to them, "I have food to eat that you do not know about." So the disciples said to one another, "Surely no one has brought him something to eat?" Jesus said to them, "My food is to do the will of him who sent me and to complete his work. Do you not say, 'Four months more, then comes the harvest'? But I tell you, look around you, and see how the fields are ripe for harvesting. The *reaper is already receiving wages and is gathering fruit for eternal life, so that sower and reaper may rejoice together. For here the saying holds true, 'One sows and another reaps.' I sent you to reap that for which you did not labour. Others have laboured, and you have entered into their labour."*[1]

Church history goes beyond recording the formative events and personnel of those communities that intentionally associate themselves with Jesus of Nazareth. At the end of the day, their collective memory and experience must also be studied and assessed. Jesus was not just another charismatic figure creating his own sect. As the above passage from John's Gospel asserts, he saw his endeavours bringing to fruition a long and continuing process of obeying God. Much of his public ministry crossed social boundaries and opened up unexpected lines of communication and changes of attitude. He set out neither to abolish nor entrench the Jewish verities, institutions and factions of his day. Instead, he himself became the overarching source of identity and energy for those who followed him. They believed that through him the God of the Old Covenant was doing a radical new thing for the benefit of all human beings, which would nevertheless incorporate the particular gains and promises of Judaism. The traditions of the past would condition but not prescribe the future of the Christian mission.

Written with such a perspective in mind, this chapter seeks to accomplish four tasks. Drawing on the previous essays and adding material of its own, it lays out some of the main themes that are discernible in Melbourne Anglicanism. It canvasses the endeavours, pressures and perceptions that have shaped the past 150 years. It suggests features of church and society that would give the diocesan project a broader explanatory context. Finally, it ponders the way forward if God's will is to be done more effectively.

It makes no pretence of being objective, disinterested or comprehensive. While sharing the same intent as the previous essays, to record and celebrate the past, it also aims to stimulate the reader to consider whether or not the Diocese is entitled to embrace the future.

1. One sows and another reaps

The Diocese of Melbourne is quintessentially Anglican in character.[2] To some observers, therefore, and indeed to some members, it looks suspiciously like a Clayton's Church. But others have found it a spacious environment within which they might gather to receive God's blessings in Christ and be apprenticed to him for life. Or, to change the image, the Diocese has been like an amateur dramatic company with one great play in its repertoire. Although the lead character and significant aspects of the script are fixed, each performance is of a work in progress. The current cast and crew are called on to give of their creative and interpretive best; but they have some leeway to revert to rehearsal mode if conviction or passion should flag for a time.

This unit of the Australian Church and the worldwide Anglican Communion is as replete as they are with paradox and irony.[3] It believes its mandate comes from God, who sent the Church with the good news of Jesus Christ from England to the people of Victoria and Melbourne; yet it has exercised that mandate, as its forebears did, with a proper local discretion over second-order matters, such as allowed the English Reformers to re-introduce a vernacular liturgy and a married clergy.

It is Catholic in creed and polity, anchored to the finality of God's revelation in the canon of Scripture; and yet is pledged to remain responsive to the winds of reform and change, not just to those.

that blew in the sixteenth century. Created from Jewish and apostolic stock, it has been modified by its own 'tribal' — European and Western Christian — and now supranational heritage, yet must make its way in today's Australian world.

Proud of its English Established Church provenance, the Diocese has moved, if slowly and unevenly, to embrace pluralist, polyethnic Australia. Geared to a well-educated and genteel membership, it has tried fitfully to heed and to touch a much broader swathe of the community, including fringe minorities: one thinks in 1997 of the Aboriginal Working Group or the AIDS Education and Ministry Committee.

Nominal membership has always been a feature of Anglicanism, and Melbourne is no exception. Over the period of white settlement, only about five to fifteen per cent of those Australians identified as Anglican have attended church at all regularly or practised their faith in concert with other church members. From a situation where over half the population called itself Church of England, Anglicans in the 1990s comprise less than a quarter. Melbourne, being the city that after the Second World War received the largest numbers of immigrants from southern Europe, has seen its Anglican proportion drop to about

one-sixth. Strict Roman Catholic policy on 'mixed marriages' and the education of children born to them was another factor that accelerated the dramatic shift away from Anglican ascendancy.[4]

Ironically, the last time a fulsome if somewhat defensive yearning was voiced to enhance Melbourne's links to the mother Church of England - the mid 1950s - the prayer was answered to unanticipated effect. The Anglophile orientation of the Diocese issued in the appointment of an unknown English bishop to succeed Joseph Booth. Yet Frank Woods, from the day of his enthronement in December 1957 and with increased conviction as he grew into the task, craved an authentic and contemporary Christian witness for Melbourne. He endorsed existing local mission ventures and evoked new ones, to which he gave wholehearted backing. Thus did any diocesan cultural cringe begin to seem *passé*!

A central problem of the last 150 years revolves around leadership and clericalism: the lopsided relationships between bishop and clergy, and between parish priest and people.

Episcopate is pivotal to the character and profile of the Diocese. Yet it is mostly conferred by serendipity and has only

the authority of suasion over lay Anglicans' daily lives. The bishops preside at all major diocesan or regional occasions; but much of their time is spent behind the scenes — in staff meetings, on committee work, and responding to crises and unusual pastoral demands.

Where there is little comradeship, encouragement or edification exchanged with their priests, the bishops' role in clergy appointment and patronage sets them very much apart as a managerial elite. Their special status is emphasised by the distinctive dress and jewellery they wear and by other marks of office (intriguing in Australia's or Christianity's supposedly egalitarian society). In turn, when *esprit de corps* is poor, a show of deference to the diocesan leadership may mask a lack of enthusiasm for regular contact and a diffidence about the personal wisdom, strategic competence or communication skills on offer[5].

Moreover, rather than affirming the need for enrichment of the mainstream, the diocesan structures and ethos have developed an uncanny knack of absorbing, bypassing or marginalising unusual clergy, including some of the most creative figures of our history.

Clericalism is as much a reality in parishes. The phenomenon is endemic to

Anglicanism. The *Book of Common Prayer* Ordinal sets out a doctrine of ordained ministry more demanding than any other which exists in Christian tradition. The priest becomes the symbolic, representative person ('parson'), sent in from outside by the diocese to act on behalf or even instead of the laity, thereby relieving them of full responsibility for their own fidelity to God. This may create a peculiar sort of compact.

Where such a compact works in practice — and it often has, among all types of churchmanship — it nevertheless damages both the well-being of clergy and their households and the capacity of the laity to reach the full maturity which is the prerogative of all those baptised into Christ. Where it fails, and there are clashes over churchmanship, organisational or aesthetic details, clergy work ethics or domestic situations, a grim stand-off may occur between priest and people, engendering survivalism, paralysis or withdrawal.

Generally speaking, parish clericalism seems to be on the wane: clerical stipends and conditions have improved, and lay leadership is better equipped and authorised by diocesan law to press for mutually satisfactory decision-making and division of labour.

Melbourne has been blessed with some remarkable Anglican laypeople whose total contribution to Church and society manifestly flows from their Christian stance — for example, former Geelong Grammar School headmaster, the late Sir James Darling, and former Deputy Premier of Victoria, Robert Fordham.[6] But lay ministry has tended to be under-valued and kept at arm's length, or recognised and developed for internal and liturgical use rather than to spearhead the Church's mission wherever in the surrounding world there is opportunity.[7]

'In my Father's house there are many dwelling-places.'[8] Against the backdrop of Australian Anglicanism, Australian Christianity and Australian society at large, the Diocese of Melbourne can claim to have occupied and sometimes shared a good number of such dwelling-places.

Preaching at a liturgical welcome in St Patrick's Cathedral, Melbourne in 1985, the Archbishop of Canterbury Robert Runcie said that the Australian churches formed a 'unique ecumenical laboratory'. For no other metropolitical diocese has this statement been truer than Melbourne. To be sure, much of the potential for ecumenism has been driven by demographic changes which not all Anglicans have welcomed.

Nevertheless, the Diocese has prided itself on being a leader in inter-denominational relations, from the anti-papist pan-Protestantism of Perry to the full-blown ecumenism of Woods. Currently, despite local activity being at a low ebb,[9] the bilateral and multilateral lines of communication still manage to function at official levels. Heads of churches meet among themselves and with the Premier and other leaders. The National Council of Churches in Australia and its Victorian counterpart receive — somewhat token — support from the Diocese of Melbourne both for their core work and for their various agencies and commissions. The Christmas Bowl competes for Anglican favour with AngliCORD,[10] Anglican Board of Mission (formerly Australian Board of Missions) and Church Missionary Society overseas work, and a multiplicity of explicitly or tacitly Christian agencies like TEAR (The Evangelical Alliance Relief) Fund or World Vision.

In terms of mass outreach, the Awakening campaigns of the 1990s, sparked by the youth-oriented organisation Fusion and prepared by inter-church committees, have given a distinctively Australian flavour to the public presentation of the Gospel each Easter but have so far persuaded very few Anglican parishes to participate.

The diocesan household of faith encompasses people of widely differing viewpoints, each one claiming residential rights. Four tendencies have been prominent in Melbourne Anglicanism over the years.

The dominant one started its Melbourne career as a diffuse version of Erastianism, juggling church and faith loyalties with patriotism and the requirements of morally correct citizenship. It has taken its ecclesiastical colouring chameleon-like from low or high church surroundings. As fealty to the monarch has weakened and former slogans of Anglicanism appear less supportable or relevant, a broad and pragmatic liberalism has supplanted it, reflecting both a dislike of extremes and a willingness to intersperse contemporary wisdom somewhat haphazardly with Christian rhetoric. Synod debates of recent years have given ample evidence that an instinctive Erastianism is alive and well.

Secondly, there has been from the beginning a significant presence of conservative evangelicals in the Diocese. Informed by not only the Reformation's perspectives but the English and American revivalist movements since the eighteenth century, they set great store on the Bible's inspired authority, the centrality of the Cross, and the call to conversion and active evangelism. Always protective of Anglicanism's Protestant character (which they consider more important than denominational loyalty), today's evangelicals feel that their movement has lost ground as a result of Frank Woods' alleged bias against them,[11] with only a brief and ambiguous reprieve afforded by David Penman's surprising election and tenure of the See. They are horrified by the slackness, complacency and degeneracy of attitude and behaviour,[12] they detect among today's 'liberal Catholic' Anglicans, clergy particularly.

At the time of Melbourne's sesquicentenary Evangelicals are re-grouping around their own networks and leadership, and are enjoying a surge both of keen, theologically thirsty laypeople and of ordination candidates. The Evangelical Fellowship of the Anglican Communion (EFAC) has proffered a new strategy to revitalise and uplift the church scene in Victoria[13] while relying on its tactical arm, the New Cranmer Society, to mobilise evangelicals into standing for election to diocesan bodies and pressing for greater representation in leadership personnel, agenda and decisions.

Thirdly, as previous essays have made clear, the Anglo-Catholic cause appeared early in the life of the Diocese. Bishop Broughton was aligned to its English High Church antecedents, and Tractarianism was in full flower in the mid-1800s. Its emphasis was and is on the God-given and intimate connection between the Church's life, especially the sacraments and liturgy, and the divine plan of salvation. Stress is laid on a high ecclesiology which relies on tradition, the religious life, and excellence in the arts. Although embraced by many lay supporters who have associated themselves with suitable parishes, its leadership has inevitably been clerical. Resort to priestly guilds like Friends in Council or to confessors and spiritual direction from clergy of the right stripe has reinforced its power.

Reacting against the hostility of bishops like Perry to Catholic beliefs, ceremonial and music, or the incomprehension as to their approach of many of Perry's successors, Melbourne's Anglo-Catholics have, ironically, verged on the congregationalist and sectarian.

Divisions over the ordination of women have split the Catholic cause in Melbourne. The opposing minority feel embattled and deprived of genuine episcopal care. Despite having a few parishes as beacons (e.g. St Peter's, Eastern Hill, and Christ Church, Brunswick), they have no seminary available, and some covet greener pastures and pastors, say in Ballarat or Wangaratta. A few have left, preferring Rome, Orthodoxy or schism to the apostasy they consider rife in Melbourne.

The majority of Melbourne's Catholic-minded Anglicans have welcomed the ordination of women, but other tensions have arisen — how far biblical criticism can be pressed, what sexual behaviours might be acceptable, whether catholics can or must be universalists, how important clinical pastoral education is, and so on. The result is a blend of 'liberal Catholicism' with 'catholic Liberalism (Erastianism)', in which Trinity College and certain inter-state seminaries have been formative influences.[14]

Fourthly, from the late 1960s and early 1970s charismatic religion began to grip parishes and clergy with an exciting sense of the Holy Spirit in the midst. Staid representatives of the other three well-established tendencies suddenly found themselves on fire with enthusiasm for the living, healing God. There was and is a delight to worship God through the repeated singing of Bible choruses; and a confidence that God will inspire believers directly and that the scriptures, even chosen apparently at random, will impart direction and wisdom. Boundaries formerly hard and fast between the other three tendencies were crossed as people entered, and sometimes passed through, charismatic renewal.

Sydney hardline evangelicals' rejection of the charismatic emphasis on signs and wonders, deliverance, speaking in tongues, and the like, is much less evident in Melbourne. More to the fore in the southern city is a shared espousal of personal holiness and a common animosity towards those catholics and liberals who appear to flout or disregard the plain meaning of God's Word. The Cursillo Movement[15] and other training courses have infused a more articulate and ardent faith into the hearts of many Anglican laypeople and their clergy.

These tendencies have sometimes been contagious as to fundamentals, eliciting a total conversion to their spirituality.[16] More often they have gained currency from influential individuals. Their staying-power has been unpredictable.

In 1997, talk of factions is commonplace. The election of a new archbishop in 1990, for the first time by Synod, expressed graphically how volatile was Melbourne's diversity of hopes and dreams, fears and anxieties, about the future. Despite official disapproval, how-to-vote tickets — however uneven their success — continue to appear each year, moves are still made to dominate Synod and other diocesan bodies, and one major group or another aspires to control key factors, from clergy numbers to financial and property management.[17]

Yet any faction's capacity to capture the Diocese is, in this writer's opinion, overstated. The only relatively homogeneous group with a hope of achieving critical mass comprises evangelicals. Their strength is growing, but, even when united and able to draw on the support of charismatics, they can still only count on about a third of the clergy and a slightly smaller proportion of the laity in Synod.[18] The much larger broad-based 'liberal Catholic' or 'catholic Liberal'[19] group is really an anti-faction. It has no substantial agenda of its own, apart from fighting hardline conservatives from right or left who try to make the running as the force of the future or the voice of undivided Christendom recalling the Diocese to the straight and narrow.

Inadvertently the Diocese has become more conscious of its need for coherent organisation, and more deliberately committed to underwrite strategic mission, than ever before: some 56 percent of its total income in 1996, for expenditure on episcopal-related ministry, administration and diocesan services, was derived from parish assessments — double the figure of ten years earlier.[20]

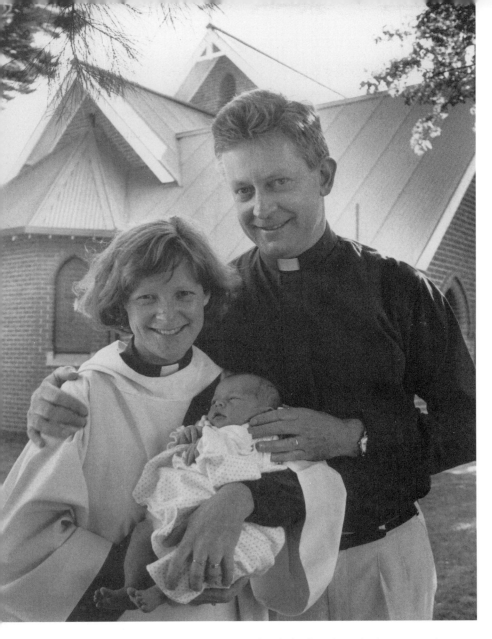

A new church phenomenon: husband and wife both ordained. The Reverend Roger Prowd, the Reverend Kate Prowd and Phoebe Prowd, 1988.

PHOTO: THE HERALD AND WEEKLY TIMES.

One of the most significant changes of the past 150 years — the ordination of women to the priesthood — received cross-factional support. Admittedly it came about only after many decades of meagre gains for women's involvement in church leadership,[21] twenty years of widespread debate and scrupulous if frustrating observance of due process at every level of church life.[22] Nor was it a unanimous move: charges were levelled by opponents that heresy and schism were being spawned.

But the experience of many Melbourne Anglicans has been that, apart from the sheer refreshment of having new streams of energy flow into the ordained ministry[23] and the corporate mission of the Diocese, the profoundly orthodox basis of the church — trinitarian and incarnational — has been burnished. Anglican priesthood is no longer quarantined from fleshing out the image of God within and beyond its own ranks, as the rest of the baptised people of God can do by definition, through women and men interacting and co-operating in the Body of Christ.

The Australian Church Constitution was not produced as the Anglican Communion's most conservative document of its kind in order to appease the Melbourne Diocese.[24] Melbourne has never been affected as much as (say) Sydney by any of the extremes of churchmanship that had to be contained if Australian Anglicans were to stay together, albeit in a rather loose federation of dioceses. It is intriguing to speculate that this characteristic of Melbourne might relate to the fact that only two archbishops of Melbourne have been primates of the national Church.[25]

Of greater consequence is a political by-product of opening priestly ordination to women candidates. The longstanding ability of certain hardline Protestant forces in Sydney to maintain disproportionate sway over the General Synod process and voting, its national office and its principal elected bodies – and so to hold the rest of the Church in check – has had its bluff called. For good or ill, the national Church is currently much more in harmony with Melbourne than with any other metropolitical see.[26]

In almost every way, Melbourne is a curious mixture of the radical and the conservative. It is prevented by its inner tensions and factions from being overly libertarian in its formulation of doctrinal and ethical stances, yet the logic of these same factors leads it, almost despite itself, to espouse a non-sectarian and open style. Melbourne, by contrast with Sydney Diocese since the 1920s, has been able to weigh into all the great debates over public values, equity and truth with a widely perceived right to do so.

There has been direct intervention or support channelled into coalitions with other Christian, civic or professional groups. The bishops, notably Moorhouse and Penman, have spoken out publicly or negotiated discreetly with people of influence, many of them having come up through church schools or Trinity College. Church-based initiatives have been instrumental in achieving beneficial change to welfare policy and implementation, and notable contributions have come from charismatic individuals and from church agencies and their leaders.[27]

What has been characteristic of recent decades, particularly since the Vietnam War, is the co-existence in the Diocese of divergent, even opposing viewpoints on almost every matter of public concern. From a modest unanimity in the first half of the century, in which moderately liberal theology went along with conservative ethics and loyalist politics,[28] the collective mind of Anglicans has become harder to read. Arguments have arisen across the board over specific issues in personal morality, social and economic policy, bio-ethics, the peace movement, or the immigration and population debate. Many of the disagreements are tinged as much by the surrounding society's values as by churchmanship. In fact, there are currently Anglicans from both Catholic and Evangelical wings willing to line up against big government and substantial welfare spending.[29]

Melbourne has also striven to give sensitive and inclusive liturgical shape to those great global, national or local occasions when the whole community has instinctively rejoiced or mourned, commemorated the past or anticipated the future. A memorable instance was in January 1991: with the Gulf War looming a great Prayer Service was held in a packed St Paul's Cathedral to petition God for peace. What was revealed and fostered there was a readiness among Christian, Jew and Muslim — not forgetting people of other faiths — to express goodwill and spiritual commonality even if only fleetingly, and in the face of many contrary currents.[30]

There remains a 'gloom' of doomsayers convinced that the Diocese of Melbourne — along with other traditional 'worthy' causes — is in terminal decline. Vigorous faith reaching out to unbelievers is in short supply. Income from parishes may well have peaked; the See's endowment is relatively small and so far has been hard to capitalise. With ageing congregations and low rates of return on investments, expenditure will probably have to be cut further.

Ostensibly, there is too high a proportion of the elderly, women in particular, in congregations. The Diocese lacks sufficient young members — children, teenagers, young adults — to guarantee replacement stock, let alone vitality or growth. It is accused of having little to offer certain age groups, ethnicities or socio-economic classes. It appears ill at ease with people who think or feel themselves to be proudly modern - let alone post-modern! Its customs, its language, its preoccupations are quaint or irrelevant in the eyes of a fast-changing, media-dominated world.

Even if each of these 'prophecies' could be countered or shown to be baseless, in some respects blasphemous, their dispiriting effect on diocesan morale should not be underestimated.

2. Entered into their labour

Earlier chapters have documented the enriching or constraining effect the labours of previous generations have had. Many and varied are the ways Melbourne Anglicans have engaged with their context. Occasionally one can detect a self-consciously Christian, even sectarian, stance of hostility and suspicion towards community and government. More often the rhetoric has come from the high ground of duty to monarch and nation or to Judaeo-Christian moral teaching in matters great and small.

Not surprisingly, the practice of dual loyalties - simultaneously seeking to serve Gospel and Mammon, or State, or private venture, or artistic excellence - is rarely perceived as a problem by those who are busy doing it. Those who quote Scripture or tradition to forbid a certain practice or point to its non-viability can often be disregarded for reasons that have little to do with faith in Jesus Christ. For a comfortably liberal diocese, Melbourne has had at best a slim record of giving the time of day to socialists, for instance, let alone to Marxists of any stripe, or to others who claim dominical precept and early Church precedent as inspiration for their communised worldview.[31]

But of course the Diocese developed within particular horizons where the Luddite nightmares of a William Blake or the protests of a Charles Kingsley at English industrialists' callousness were robbed of their force by the sheer energy of a new and prospering colony.

From the outset, shortly after Batman and Fawkner founded the settlement, the Anglican Church began with small congregations of free men and women cared for by itinerant clergy. Good land and rich resources indicated a bright future, soon to be compounded by the discovery of gold. Ports in Geelong and Melbourne were focal points for these burgeoning trade centres and their populations. The dislocation or buying-off of the original inhabitants was a minor obstacle en route to a Protestant empire of expansionist, civilising, commercialising men and their ladies.

Theologically speaking, the Melbourne ethos was more compatible with the confident *soi-disant* elect of Presbyterianism. The low-church monarchist Protestantism of the Empire was almost equally accessible to those of Scottish origins. The Presbyterian version probably comported better with Melbourne's non-aristocratic, non-hereditary, yet socially non-inclusive capitalism. Anglicanism in its more churchy or trans-Protestant modes could never capture the essence of Victoria; nor was there any serious likelihood of it being established. Rather, it had, for the first century of its history, to be content with guarding an outpost of English metropolitan Christianity, or sharing its soul with the powerful if secret guild of

Freemasonry, whose ethos of mutual advancement and fraternal spirituality drew on its own independent sources.[32]

Perry felt the force of Melbourne's incipient political culture yet unwittingly made his contribution to it: because and in spite of being a committed Evangelical in a less than zealous context, he failed signally to advance the more explicitly Christian and doctrinaire dimension of his bifocal Anglicanism (true Gospel and godly crown). His need to rely on laypeople for temporal support - to mobilise resources and money so that Anglican structures and ministry could flourish - proved ambiguous.

On the one hand, his authority over his Bishop-in-Council was great. Each subsequent diocesan has received the legacy intact, even if its obverse is that he bears ultimate responsibility. Perry and his successors have also had less of the English dilemma of clergy benefice and patronage being out of their control and in the hands of opinionated laymen and organisations. On the other hand, he ventured out into new territory with his establishment of a Church Assembly, precursor of Synod.[33] Its legislative and deliberative powers were to be real enough, but its strategic partnership with the bishop would be frustrated because, unlike

Sydney Diocese, it lacked a standing committee to set its own agenda and take virtual charge of its own business.

But on the face of it, the sharpest blow to the Anglican Church's *modus operandi* was the determination of Victorians and all Australians to have a state-based universal education system that was thoroughly secular. Even though not totally so in practice — and the Council for Christian Education in Schools and the Church-related schools have done much to keep the rumour of God alive, as have local communities and individual mentors or teachers whose faith has rippled out into the lives of countless citizens — the net result has been reductionist. How can any human being reach adulthood unstunted if there is no sustained attention in his or her educational mainstream to the fundamental questions 'Who made me? the world? and why?'.

The perception of high-fee-charging church schools has, moreover, presumed that their real purpose is not encouragement of faith but trade in privilege and valuable social connections.[34]

Yet the Anglican Church in Melbourne, as elsewhere, has proved resilient to such blows. More broadly than other denominations, although less intensely than Roman Catholic, Orthodox and Baptist

communities in their spheres, the Diocese has retained reasonable access to the majority of people within its boundaries. Churchgoing Anglicans belong to multiple networks through work, family, commerce, voluntary or professional organisations, recreation, and neighbourhood. Anglican communities provide rites of passage, pastoral care and almsgiving, via parishes or institutional chaplaincies. Anglican schools are in fact, along with welfare agencies, key contact points. Some access also comes through all levels of church media, and even chancy appearances in the mass media can attract appreciation rather than mockery or criticism.[35]

As of 1847, the Australian Church was a colonial outpost of congregations and clergy loosely linked to one another and tightly dependent on the Churches of England (including Ireland). That year saw five dioceses come into being, and suddenly the ancient role of diocese and bishop, to oversee organisational liaison and exchange within and beyond their jurisdiction, came back into relief. On 29 June, the Diocese of Melbourne was created to be a new and autonomous unit of church life, with the consecration of its first bishop.

As we saw above, Charles Perry would have a far more constitutive role than any bishop in England. At the same time, he would be utterly dependent on the free consent and participation of his laity and the canonical obedience of his clergy.

Bishop and diocese ever since have been intrinsically more important and more vulnerable in Australia than in England. This is different from a noisy centralism: indeed, Melbourne's leadership has sometimes kept quite a low profile, for instance, in Joseph Booth's time, when forward planning and church extension happened without fanfare.

In 1997 much more has come to be expected of the Archbishop and the Diocese. The old distinction between temporal and spiritual has been blurred, so that economic rationalists can depict what they want to do as God's demand for efficiency. People at every level of the Diocese can call on their leaders to do forward planning. Besides, the structures themselves are far more complex, and have become so in inverse ratio to the trends in numbers and assets.

However, the real 'culprit' in the upgrading of expectations was Frank Woods, the Englishman eventually captured by Australia, the liberal evangelical become high churchman, the inter-church activist become attuned to God's plan for all humanity. He presided over a host of initiatives, as James Grant and others have documented in this book. Some were oriented to the ecumenical scene, some to the community at large; others were designed to strengthen episcopal care for the parishes and sector ministries across a sprawling diocese. All statutory units and voluntary organisations were drafted into a diocesan framework in which 'life-and-mission' policy could be developed, resourced, co-ordinated and implemented, and major questions of faith (such as the individual's prayer life) or of ethics (such as remarriage of divorced persons) or of ecclesiology (such as the ordination of women) be addressed at every level of diocesan life. The pragmatism of his predecessors and of his own key assistants was caught up in a vision born of deep faith.

One of Frank Woods' most endearing characteristics was his implicit trust in those with whom he worked most closely. He increased the number of Melbourne's assistant (formerly known as 'coadjutor') bishops.[36] Their role in the Diocese has been hard to define but very important. Keith Rayner, then Archbishop of Adelaide, preaching at the consecration in 1989 of John Bayton, drew attention to the anomalous character of assistant bishops. They could exercise certain distinctively episcopal ministries, yet had no final authority.

The pattern of assistant bishops deputising for the diocesan or holding down specific portfolios was modified in 1971 in favour of their being assigned regions of episcopal care. This conferred a measure of territorial jurisdiction but only within the college of bishops under the archbishop of the day.

David Penman overtly institutionalised a balancing of churchmanship in his selection of assistant bishop,[s3] something that had been taken into account *sotto voce* when he himself had been called back by Robert Dann from New Zealand to oversee the Western region.

By most classical and modern criteria, the regions do not lend themselves to becoming separate dioceses. Apart from Geelong, currently the centre of half a region, the choice of other sites for a cathedral would be quite arbitrary. The fact of working to a diocesan budget allows appropriate cross-subsidy and resources to be targetted where needed rather than demanded. Yet the principle of subsidiarity would seem to endorse the present devolution to the regions themselves of strategic planning functions directly relating to their own territory.

An unintended consequence[38] of

enlarging the episcopal team has been the loss of clarity — but not workload — attaching to the ministry of archdeacons. In general, Anglicanism has restored to them the vital office their forebears occupied in the urban churches as mediatory figures with administrative, pastoral and communicative functions. The history of the Diocese of Melbourne would be unrecognisable without the steady work of its Archdeacons. But over recent decades there has been a failure to affirm or re-define their position. To cap things off, there are no full-time Archdeacons at present, and most Archdeacons have charge of very busy parishes.

Space restraints do not permit adequate record either of the contribution St Paul's Cathedral and its Deans have made, or of Melbourne's part in the Province of Victoria. These are matters which must await a more comprehensive history. A few remarks must suffice.

Being the mother church of a large diocese and housing the Bishop's throne is already basis enough for its centrality. But the cathedral is also blessed with a wonderful location. It has been a daily focus of prayer and worship and pastoral care. It is a gathering place for ecclesiastical and civic occasions, for concerts and exhibitions. It is called to set standards in liturgy, teaching, preaching and the relevant performing arts, and to be a powerhouse of mission and outreach. Most of its Deans have been very active in the City of Melbourne. From time to time the dean of the day has also provided an alternative point of reference or model of leadership for both clergy and laity *vis-à-vis* the archbishop.[39]

The Province of Victoria, comprising five dioceses, barely registers in most Melbourne Anglicans' minds. But the provincial bishops are bound to their metropolitan, the Archbishop of Melbourne. They meet and discuss the health of their dioceses and other common concerns, such as Trinity College and its theological school. They must ratify each diocese's episcopal elections or appointments. Archdeacons from all the dioceses gather when they can, as does once a year Provincial Council, which is a representative body made up of of bishops, other clergy and laity. Various provincial committees and task forces, for example on stipends, rural ministry or church law, add value to the Province.

The quiet strength of provincial connections was underlined when financial and other crises came to a head and devastated the Diocese of Bendigo early in 1993. With Melbourne taking the lead in arranging appropriate assistance, Bendigo was able to make a fresh start, signalled by the consecration of its new bishop in December 1995.

The unpredictability of farm income and the leaching of lifeblood and resources from the rural areas into the major towns and cities are factors that have led to desperate questioning about the future of at least three of Victoria's country dioceses and their staffing. To the extent that a continuing Anglican identity is pursued rather than closure or ecumenism born of either necessity or principle, a process is beginning to occur of formulating new boundaries, possibly involving Melbourne and its regions, and of co-ordinating administration more productively.

For good or ill, the Diocese figures much more prominently in Melbourne Anglicans' self-definition than ever before. It is not to be equated with its headquarters, or its Bishops, or the Melbourne Anglican tradition. The arguments over its status in God's eyes - whether or not it is more than the sum of its parts, even has some mystical soul of its own or is a proper manifestation of the Body of Christ - are unlikely to be settled conclusively. But in day-to-day terms it covers the gamut of being 'umbrella', command structure, coordinator, enabler, irrelevance, and so on, to its constituents. The worry would be if there arose — in some eyes it has already happened — a widespread and abiding perception that the Diocese had lapsed into a 'them-and-us' mentality or a stifling mediocrity, and had therefore become a serious impediment to the Gospel's progress.

3. Look around you

It is time now to look at the wider social context of Melbourne Diocese. This will also bring into sharper relief those features of Christianity and Anglicanism that have been in play and might help explain the emergence of the themes already outlined above.

The leading energy of Melbourne, reflected in the city being for many decades Australia's political and financial hub, may once have flourished in vigorous debate over the exercise and balancing of authority, in behind-the-scenes deals over lunch at the Melbourne Club, or in arrangements between governments and citizens of 'substance'.

But the consensual democracy that went hand-in-glove with a free settlement like Victoria also required governments to guarantee a more or less workable mixed economy. To that end, not only the federation

but also the individual states, not only the city but the suburbs, the provincial centres and the rural areas, not only the capital owners, investors and speculators but also the professional classes and the whole gamut of working people and their families, had to be central considerations. It has not been the private sector alone, or even primarily, but rather the whole electorate[40] that has demanded a substantial infrastructure of decent housing, transport and communications, education, health, police and welfare services.

For the first twenty-five years of Federation, the Diocese was potentially in a commanding position to deal with all three levels of government in Australia. But inevitably the Great War and the debate over conscription kept a patriotic and sectarian bias to Anglican energy, well away from the long-term business of nation-building or the immediate tasks of consolidating Australia's very real social and political gains.

Once the federal parliament moved to Canberra, Anglicans were under less pressure to deal with broader perspectives. Thereafter, single issues tended to tumble over each other into the spotlight without an agreed diocesan method of handling or even ranking them: urban social and ethical concerns,

protection of ecclesiastical privileges, or international crises of the moment.

As it happens, the sesquicenenary of the Diocese coincides with a dramatic shift in the governance of the State, for which few citizens could have been prepared. So a brief survey would be timely.

The bipartisan standards of policy and performance to which most past governments aspired, such as those of Sir Rupert Hamer and Mr John Cain, have given way since 1992 to the neo-corporatist program for which the current Premier, Jeffrey Kennett, and Treasurer, Alan Stockdale, are the front men. Inheriting a messy budgetary situation from their Labor predecessors and strapped for revenue by a nine-year squeeze on the states by federal Labor leaders determined to expose Australia to international market forces (and indebtedness), Messrs Kennett and Stockdale have presided over the privatisation of public assets, the rapid down-sizing of services and the bureaucracies who provide them, the erosion of judicial and statutory review, and the tight control of planning and delivery processes. The parliamentary opposition, severely weakened internally and reduced to a small minority in both State houses of parliament, has had difficulties in securing accountability.

The Liberal-National Coalition Government has promoted major events and facilities, and within four years made Victoria the nation's gaming centre. All agencies and spokespeople, including those of the churches, that have questioned or criticised this turn of events have been either reminded of their dependence on the public purse to carry out the welfare tasks government has now abrogated; or else dismissed as 'yesterday's people'. [41]

With such a shift in full swing, no one can be sure of what lies ahead. The people of Melbourne and Victoria are more than their government would have them be. The shibboleths emanating from the entrepreneurs of Spring Street, the wizards of technology, or the high priests of the commercial media may seem perpetuate the uniquely twentieth century method of handling unbridled change by discarding the past and making a totally arbitrary selection of strategies to greet the future.

But, although this approach has taken the populace, as in most other parts of the Western world, on a roller-coaster ride, turbulence has not yet become chaos. The assault on natural and artificial environments is partly compensated for by the quality and standard of living in and around most parts of Melbourne and Geelong, and the riches of a multicultural, sports-mad society.

The facts of birth, life, relationships, disease and death are powerful and mysterious enough to assert their primacy from time to time over the self-delusions of unbridled human cleverness. Spiritualities also evoke the transcendent out of wellsprings that owe little or nothing to the mainstream religions or the prevailing political and economic wisdom. Citizens' groups continue to arise and seek redress for burgeoning poverty and injustice. Another antidote comes from the passionate and faith-informed humour of cartoonists like Michael Leunig [42] or the satirical comedians for which Melbourne has become famous.

In this climate, most Anglican institutions are bound to feel out of their depth or lost on foreign soil, although there are some areas in which church schools have some chance of gaining *entrée*. How can churchgoers relate, for example, to those young people who experiment freely with the identities and experiences the modern world offers but have confidence in neither the past nor the future? to non-Anglo-Saxon communities seeking to preserve their spiritual heritage? How can they relate to the struggles the union movement is undergoing, or to conservationists' passion for the environment? To understand these groups and individuals, and learn their idiom, let alone share the Gospel with them, requires humility and commitment. [43]

The Christian Church exists to do God's will as revealed in Jesus of Nazareth. Its members' energy is to be spent not only gathering each week for worship, fellowship and instruction but dispersed for the rest of the time as salt or yeast to take the love of Jesus into the workaday suffering world for which he died. Of its very nature the Church must depend on local communities and individual believers to find their own way of engaging with each new context, offering reconciliation, healing and fulfilment in Jesus' name.

Reliance on their divine mandate and inspiration does not protect Christians from having to discern what mixture of things old and things new they must bring out of the treasury of faith. In some situations their inheritance may become burdensome or moribund; in others their quest for relevance facile or compromising.

The emergence in many places of an Anglican Church without juridical ties to the Church of England, the British monarchy, or the English language is testimony to the ultimately contingent character of the English connection. [44] The fundamental principles of Anglicanism were not invented at the Reformation but reformed and re-stated: Holy Scripture as the rule of faith, the centrality of the creeds, the dominical sacraments and the historic episcopate.[45] Once these principles are accepted, there is freedom to develop in a way that at least begins to be attentive to contemporary context.

To be sure, Anglicanism is intrinsically cautious, and has always retained traces of its earlier incarnations. Its approach to mission has tended to be curiously active and passive all at once. Sometimes it has presumed, as the *Book of Common Prayer* does, that the whole nation is already God's flock. Sometimes it has made tentative forays into new fields on the back of trade, warfare or expatriate chaplaincies. Often there has been a zeal among missionaries and adherents in far-flung outposts quite unlike anything to be found countenanced back home!

Anglicanism has also fought losing battles with the distinctive British heresy, Pelagianism. Late in the fourth century Pelagius, a British monk, put forward the view that human beings could by good works contribute to their salvation and help earn it. The persistence of this view is evident among those who equate faith with correct doctrine, making it a human work rather than a gift of grace; or among those who consider that correct liturgy, practice, and prayer will satisfy God and perhaps conceal the mess beneath: and it dogs those Anglicans who want a formal, if somewhat loose-fitting, faith to co-exist with their own civic and economic circumstances and privately construed conscience.

The truth is that no church can guarantee freedom from cant or decay, certainly not if that church seeks to respect God's active presence in both the Christian tradition and the contemporary milieu. Confessional or sectarian purity is not an option. Jesus' own teaching anticipated the reality of the Church being a *corpus permixtum,* a thoroughly mixed body, where wheat and weeds must be left growing side by side until the final, critical harvest.[46]

The worst charges levelled against Anglicanism — snobbishness, humbug, lordly ennui, 'the Tory party at prayer', worldliness, repetitive worship and lukewarm fellowship punctuated by the odd patronising gesture of charity — may well be provable. The miracle is that other, more generous and God-centred models of church life have asserted themselves from time to time.

For those who are profoundly troubled by the ambiguous or muddled signals about belief and behaviour given out by the Diocese of Melbourne, its bishops and other clergy, and its representative membership gathered in public, any such analysis is cold comfort. Likewise, judged by human standards, many of the former glories of the Diocese are irretrievably on the way out — numerical superiority, ubiquity and size of church buildings, reliance on the *Book of Common Prayer* and predictability in formal liturgy or church music. Nor can Anglicans expect to recover the high degree of opportunity for ministry they used to have — and tended to exploit, more or less altruistically — among the otherwise unchurched masses from cradle to grave.

4. Ripe for harvesting?

Is the future bleak or will there still be paddocks ripe for harvesting?

Those who long to win souls for Christ are bound to be impatient with the Diocese of Melbourne. Where are the Anglicans who are serious about any aspect of discipleship or evangelism, who are willing to go outside the old familiar terrain from which a modest supply of church membership used to come? They are there, but only in a minority of parishes. Otherwise, the critics see just business as usual: dwindling numbers of ageing people trapped in the rut of empty formulas and exhausted patterns of church life.

For reasons amply documented in these essays, a grand revolution is unlikely, humanly speaking, to overtake a diocese which has been evolutionary at best — or static at worst, and therefore timid. Evangelicals and other ardent Anglicans may propose and pray for revival; God alone can dispose it, and on terms that may owe nothing to church growth manuals, may come from unexpected quarters, and may turn denominational projections inside out.

In the absence of persecution, with half-heartedness or possessiveness at work within the Church, and indifference outside it, fervent prayer for the Day of the Lord might well be dismissed as neurotically wishful.

Yet there are signs to be seen and heard that there is still a place for the Diocese of Melbourne in the divine scheme of things.

The Gospel is being preached, wrestled with, celebrated and embraced by Anglicans from many backgrounds, if the quiet fruitfulness of their lives and communities is anything to go by. The experience of people who have little in common being reconciled in one fellowship is itself a powerful testimony. Here is a social laboratory where horizons can be pushed back and conflict handled creatively at the foot of the Cross.

Anglican polity, which authorises its bishops, priests and deacons principally (but not solely) to build up the church and its laity principally (but not alone) to be the Body of Christ in the world, continues somehow to outgrow its self-caricature. It works best when there is creative tension between the local church and other Anglican communities, or where there is both deliberate cooperation with other denominations and spontaneous absorption of their gifts and energy in areas such as catechetics or church music.

There is a growing call in Melbourne for the ministry of women bishops. Currently the Registrar and the Director of Diocesan Services, occupying two of the three positions in the diocesan management group, are women, and exercise substantial executive and pastoral oversight. Visitors of the calibre of Dr Penny Jamieson, Bishop of Dunedin, have also been paving the way, along with many of Melbourne's own women priests.

Synod, which now can number up to eleven hundred members and is more representative than ever, has shown that it is able to deal well with business before it if adequately briefed and chaired. Here again, the Church has something to offer: a model of assembly for participative democracy in action, albeit under controlled conditions, at a time when most public discourse is fragmented and privatised or reduced by the mass media to cliché and prejudice.

Melbourne Anglicans continue to probe the frontiers between traditional faith and contemporary experience. How should they treat scripture intelligently and responsively, with neither literalism or Gnosticism nor evasion of the questions of truth posed by textual exegesis? What sort of ethic can be charted for Christians who nowadays can express their sexuality without fear of legal or technical restraints on contraception or divorce or relationships between consenting adults?

Over matters of contention such as an Australian republic or native title to land, a contribution is increasingly expected from church leaders. Other Anglicans, clergy and laity, are engaging with the prevailing philosophies, religious systems, and cultures of our time. Through connections with the international Christian community, not least in the Asia-Pacific region, and local counterparts, a veritable cornucopia of resource and witness is coming to light. [47]

There have been modest attempts to stimulate and commission creativity in every aspect of the arts, from music to architecture. The results have benefitted Anglican liturgy and the equally sacred context of a modern society choosing what remains of heaven from the ashes of rational thought and abstract calculation run riot[48]

Friction in the Diocese over these and other tasks or questions of mission has grown; but apart from touches of spite or pettiness it has its positive side. Firstly, the developments and exigencies of recent decades have compelled interaction where for so long it was avoidable, and parishes and sectors were laws to themselves; secondly, Melbourne Anglicans' transparency to their society makes their internal arguments much more visible.

Another recent harbinger of angst turned out to bear unwitting promise. In 1995 a document called 'Parish Viability and Restructuring' was launched by the then Strategy Committee of the Diocese.[49] At first glance, it looked like an unsubtle blueprint for closing down struggling parishes and reducing the number of stipendiary ministers. There followed some

dismay at its inadequate treatment of viability and some irritation that diocesan leaders had not indicated their own resolve to undertake a comparable exercise. Nonetheless, the thought and energy needed to address or re-shape its terms of reference have borne fruit. A cautionary note has also been sounded: promoting change in a diocese or parish means more than tinkering with a mechanism or structure; it requires fidelity to the organic character and interdependence of what St Paul was inspired to call the Body of Christ.

What then lies ahead?

If even prosperous parishes have been feeling the pinch, how much more is this the case with struggling areas of the northern and western suburbs, let alone rural communities with shrinking population and income? Bucking the trend, some parts of inner-suburban Melbourne may be poised for renewal through gentrification or the opportunities which diverse housing stock near the city creates for bridge-building churches. Where is the overall stocktaking and planning - diocesan, provincial, ecumenical - which would enable cross-subsidy and intentional re-location of parishioners or ministries for as long as needed to seed and grow new ventures?[50]

A development of note, long germinating

in the Diocese through significant changes to the *Trustees and Vestries Act*, and now coming to flower, is the upgrading of vestries to be *de facto* councils of elders.

Circumstances are pushing all parishes to assess their mission capabilities. How suitable and sustainable is their plant and facilities? What kind of ordained ministry do they need — stipendiary or not, part- or full-time? Is theirs a one-priest or multiple-staff parish? Should clergy continue to live on site or away from the church buildings? If the latter is the case, what will happen to existing parish housing and property? Will there be room for small parishes to continue, provided they can sustain their own operations while tithing to the Diocese and the wider Church? Will there be coalitions of formerly separate parishes or will some willingly disappear into mega-churches? Will team ministry be constructed collegially or hierarchically? Where the Diocese has put effort into reaching genuine consensus with a parish, modification, rationalisation or even painful closure has been carried out harmoniously: forcing the pace or result is not the way forward.

With the gradual demystifying of Anglican sacerdotalism[51] and the constraints of projected further decline in numbers and finances, the time is ripe for a systematic reconstruction by the Diocese — with the whole Province — of ordained ministry, including the diaconate.[52] Theological education should be better juxtaposed with clerical formation, having due regard for the respective roles of the Colleges and the Diocese. The training of curates is in need of a thorough overhaul, so that the timing of ordination and the allocation of resources or subsidies is determined in accordance with the choice of suitable clergy mentors and placements.

Already numbers, age and profile of candidates for ordination are being monitored carefully, and outplacement training is being offered for those who cannot obtain another position or have gone through some kind of breakdown or loss of vocation.

Professional training, comprising since the 1960s a compulsory quota of clinical pastoral education, has refigured the balancing of priestly responsibility and availability over against the personal needs of the cleric and household. As in all matters of ministry, new directions and outcomes have to be checked against the template of the Gospel.

James Grant noted in his overview that the diocesan structures have been reorganised from the unwieldy five divisions set up in 1987 to a system better suited to an episcopal church. There are now three divisions: the Archbishop's office, which is responsible for management of the episcopate, clergy training pre- and post-ordination, and certain other prerogatives of the archbishop; Diocesan Services, to help equip parishes for their outreach to the community and provide health and welfare chaplaincy; and the Registry, which administers and implements policy.

While not derogating from the present work of these divisions, there would be great benefit in strengthening them. The Archbishop's Office might regain a full-time Archdeacon of Melbourne and become a co-ordination centre and clearing-house for strategic thinking and practical ecumenism[53] It might also assume greater responsibility for social justice advocacy and the media. The Division of Diocesan Services might improve its integration of voluntary (specially retired or under-employed) and stipendiary labour, parish, sector and agency resources.

The Registry might extend existing data-banks of information about facilities and expert personnel available to the work of the regions, Diocese or Province.

This writer has pressed in other places[54] for two measures to enable diocesan relationships to be more democratic, task-oriented and outgoing. The first is a liturgical protocol which would set ground rules for experimentation. General Synod enacted the 1995 *Prayer Book for Australia* as a normative collection of resources and texts that offers frameworks, variations and options rather than a definitive set of texts and rubrics to be followed scrupulously from A to Z. The bishops and their clergy should negotiate a protocol adjusted to each parish or sector ministry.

The blossoming of liturgical idiosyncrasy is at odds with Anglicanism and engenders anarchy quickly in the Diocese and sooner or later, in congregations. The protocol would establish heads of agreement over such matters as the frequency of eucharistic celebration,[55] the evangelistic dimension of all worship including the eucharist, the reception of existing texts and the method of preparing local liturgies, the types of music and their match with liturgy.

The other innovation would be some procedure to identify controversial matters that are or should be before the Church. Anglicans everywhere are used to internal factions and arguments. Many of them also wear the badge of civic or political involvement with pride. From their ranks have come remarkable ministries of prophetic reconciliation, extending well outside the church's domain, in South Africa, Northern Ireland and the Middle East, and — less visibly — in various other parts of the world.

The temptation in the calmer environs of Melbourne has been for Anglicans to become reactive to agenda set by the media or other purveyors of influence, or to give up. But it need not be so.

Even though the Anglican form of Christianity is decidedly Western and Protestant, it has some striking resemblances to Eastern Orthodoxy. Both traditions treat liturgy as the normative bearer of true doctrine; both practise autocephaly while claiming to belong to the universal Church; and both espouse fidelity to the Vincentian canon.[56] But there is one other fascinating similarity, admittedly not tested by fire among Anglicans to anything like the same extent as among the Orthodox: a determination to persevere under God in periods of chaos or persecution or cultural imperialism.

The present moment calls for just such determination. Discernment of the signs of the times is bound to mean resisting some aspects of the spirit of the age, be it in parliamentary politics or media standards or the integrity of family and community or the insatiable lust of technology and money to override ethical restraint. This firm sensitivity to context will be negated if the Diocese is convinced that even its meagre assets are liabilities.

Take the doomsday caricature with which the first section closed. Why should disproportionately high numbers of elderly women presage a moribund future? It is not impossible that as in the early Church many of them are people of mature and substantial faith. From their kind did not God in the past bring great benefit for the chosen people and the world? Is it not true that many are, or are well-placed and could be better equipped to be, missionaries in all their circles of contact?

Is not the Gospel itself counter-cultural and transcultural, freely penetrating, challenging, affirming or transcending as necessary any group's way of thinking or behaving - which will otherwise be determined by age, class, gender, race, ideology?

It would be a true irony (of the sort that has happened sometimes in the last three decades when liturgical revision has been in full flight) if the very ones who bear the brunt of parochial change are told that their alienation is a necessary sacrifice in reversing the Church's decline. How long must they wait for the upturn to occur?

There can be no guarantees that the Anglican Church will exist in another fifty or one hundred and fifty years' time. Jesus promised that all communities belonging to him would be pruned by his Father.[57] This might entail the Diocese of Melbourne being cut right back, or even uprooted. It also entails vigilance lest other less divine gardeners be allowed to do damage.

Whatever the future holds, fidelity to the high priestly prayer of Jesus demands a more wholehearted quest for unity in Melbourne. Why should not this Diocese and Province — and national Church — become a modern Antioch, set beside the sea of the Asia-Pacific region, blessed with a culturally rich hinterland of indigenous and transplanted cultures, and bearing fruit for an apostolic faith which has come from Palestine, via Celtic, Roman, European and English messengers, to these shores?

The chapter opened with some verses from the fourth chapter of John's Gospel. Jesus, having encountered the woman at the well and then her fellow villagers, interprets the mission prospects in terms that offer a suggestive parallel with the Diocese of Melbourne today. Here also is a setting that can only be assayed by being responsive to a mixture of secular, interreligious and multicultural cues. Out of the 'accidental', unthreatening, teasing dialogue between a confident Jewish rabbi, his bemused disciples in tow, and a vulnerable if unconventional and independent-minded Samaritan woman, there transpired for her a contagious personal faith and for the men a new sense of wonder at the scope of God's inbreaking blessing.

Or, to view the situation from a rather different angle, Mao Zedong's dictum might be applied: 'Let a hundred flowers bloom, a hundred ideas contend'. Many diverse ways of doing mission and evangelism are needed because there are so many fronts on which to push forward, so many sub-cultures to reach, and so many battles to be fought against principalities and powers. As with the past, so with the future, there can be no substitute for doing God's will and completing his work solely through faith in the living Christ. There can be no panacea from liturgy, doctrine, spirituality, structure, program, or technique.

Nor can there be a wholesale rejection of the Church's heritage. 'Others have laboured, and you have entered into their labour.'

1 John 4:31-38 (NRSV).

2 as judged from the perspective of the evolving Anglican Communion, cf below in this essay.

3 unlike monochrome dioceses where church or gospel purity seeks to eliminate paradox and irony.

4 By the 1990s Roman Catholics comprised three in ten of the Melbourne population, although nominalism was fast increasing in their ranks too – one in four of them practising their faith regularly as against two in five only a decade earlier.

5 In 1986 this writer conducted a series of deanery forums throughout the Diocese to ascertain parish attitudes to evangelism and church growth. There was spontaneous endorsement of the role of the bishops (not an agenda item) but there were also heartfelt pleas from all quarters (equally unsolicited) for better two-way communication. In the event, the Archbishop refused to show his bishops the detailed report prepared confidentially for them, on the grounds that they needed no further demoralisation!

6 Darling's interests before and after 'retirement' were legion: *inter alia* he chaired the Australian Broadcasting Commission, the national Road Safety Council; he pioneered the Australian College of Education and the Christian think-tank, Frontier; he regularly wrote a much-appreciated Saturday leader for the *Age* (see *Reflections for the Age*, Joint Board of Christian Education, Melbourne, 1993); and he was named in 1988 as one of the 200 most eminent citizens of Australia since European settlement; he preached and broadcast widely on matters of Christian faith, and Archbishop Woods relied on him as one of his principal advisers.

Robert Fordham worked tirelessly (and still does) in educational reform. He launched the unfairly maligned Victorian Economic Development Commission, some of whose sunrise industry projects are now paying dividends. Within the Church, he chaired Melbourne's Board of Nominators for the Archbishopric election of 1989-90, the Retreat House board, and he has served in several other provincial or national capacities.

7 Bruce Kaye's stricture is salient, against the equation of lay ministry with quasi-clerical roles in liturgy, church housekeeping or intra-church affairs.

cf his *A Church without walls*, Harper Collins, Melbourne, 1995.

8 John 14:2a (NRSV).

9 cf Douglas Dargaville's essay above, on ecumenism.

10 formerly known as the Archbishop of Melbourne's International Relief and Development Fund, and established during David Penman's episcopate cf James Grant's essay above.

11 and in the mistaken view that Melbourne Diocese was (ever) an Evangelical stronghold before Frank Woods' time.

12 particularly homosexuality among the clergy.

13 Evangelicals play a significant role in two of the four dioceses outside Melbourne – Bendigo and Gippsland – but, especially over recent years, have made little impact on Wangaratta and none on Ballarat.

14 cf Peter Adam's essay above.

15 an adult faith-renewal movement originating in southern European Catholic circles but successfully adapted, with a charismatic flavour, for Australian Anglican use.

16 No one is likely to be convicted and strangely warmed by the appeal of Erastianism, *pace* Richard Hooker and any Australian disciples of his!, or of liberalism; but, not only have many found new life from Evangelicalism or the charismatic movement, others have embraced Anglo-Catholicism with an almost mystical joy in 'discovering' the Body of Christ: e.g. Charles Perry (not the bishop), who was one of this writer's predecessors (1908-12) at Holy Advent, Malvern (latterly Armadale), and was converted to a Catholic vision of priesthood during his curacy under E. S. Hughes at Eastern Hill; his testimony is recorded for his son in an untitled memoir held in the State Library of Victoria.

17 Almost every item of recent Council or Synod business has had a churchmanship spin; the differences have multiplied, or at least shifted in character, to the extent that only strong and subtle diocesan leadership could hope to draw from them a unified mission strategy. In fact, the co-existence of these groups and tendencies has become chronically fragile and unproductive: if left to themselves, as is the case, they are often more at ease with their non-Anglican or even secular counterparts than with each other.

18 These percentages have been calculated from voting at the 1990 electoral meeting of Synod members and updated from time to time in the light of additions to clergy and of Synod trends.

19 cf Peter Adam's essay above for his reading of the nuances differentiating the two labels.

20 preliminary figures from the Diocese's 1996 Financial Statements. The fact of dwindling interest returns on investment should not be forgotten in cataloguing the changing nature of diocesan income but is outweighed by the gradual increase in the overall quantum.

21 documented by Muriel Porter in her essay above.

22 The vote was facilitated both by informal contact among General Synod members from around the country before the two sessions of 1992 and then, on the floor of the decisive November 1992 Synod, by the brilliant thinking on his feet of Robert Fordham (see above) who used parliamentary procedures to stave off demands from hostile and canny Sydney quarters for an open ballot – which would very likely have denied the two-thirds majority vote from the House of Clergy needed to enact the national Canon clarifying the right to proceed of dioceses that wished to ordain women priests!

23 including diaconal ministry – from early 1986 onwards women were ordained to the diaconate, and although many of them went on to priestly ordination at the end of 1992 because that was their calling tested and recognised by the Diocese, the delay enabled much creative reflection about the distinctive diaconate – as well as creating a backlog of women to be given outlet for their ordained leadership.

24 cf John Davis, *Australian Anglicans and their Constitution*, Acorn Press, Canberra, 1993.

25 Some years ago, this writer's researches into Archbishop Woods' role in the national Church unearthed the hesitancy of the (clerical and lay) Board of Electors to choose Sir Frank as Primate, a hesitancy which emanated from two Melbourne electors and was only rendered superfluous when the other candidate withdrew.

26 The holding in Melbourne of the first General Synod outside Sydney (July 1995) and the first National Anglican Conference (Canberra, February 1997) bespeak this changing reality.

27 NB the public profile of the Brotherhood of St Laurence in particular, with Canon Peter Hollingworth (now Archbishop of Brisbane) and Bishop Michael Challen as executive directors.

28 For example, 'The people of Britain in every quarter of her world-girdling empire are girding themselves for a mighty conflict and a glorious victory' *Church of England Messenger*, November 6 1914, p. 1421.

29 Professor Ian Harper, an evangelical Anglican, is a leading economist who has serve on the Wallis Inquiry and advised the State Government on privatisation policy and on health cutbacks and hospital amalgamations; Mr Brian Parry, a catholic Anglican and Chairman of the Metropolitan Fire Brigade, who has a similar outlook, has sought to apply a modified form of market principles to management of the Diocese.

30 The first two Secretaries-General of the Australian branch of the World Conference on Religion and Peace – an inter-faith movement that gathered momentum from the mid-1980s onwards – were Melbourne priests, Philip Huggins and John Baldock respectively.

31 The saga of Canon Farnham Maynard, Vicar of St Peter's, Eastern Hill, is alluded to in David Hilliard's essay above, and told in great detail by Colin Holden *From Tories at Prayer to Socialists at Mass*, Melbourne University Press, Melbourne 1996; the story of such as the late Fr Leo Ball, a paid-up Communist, is yet to be told.

32 Freemasonry enabled the one persistent inroad into Melbourne's clerical dominance to be made by diocesan laity: notwithstanding that many senior clergy, including bishops and deans, have been Masons, their lay counterparts, such as Dr George Bearham, wielded real power in the councils and electoral boards of cathedral and Diocese.

33 cf the first essay by James Grant above.

34 cf Stuart Blackler's essay above.

35 Archbishop Rayner's 1995 prayer over Melbourne with its burgeoning casino complex was a powerful and timely gesture, widely appreciated within and beyond Christian circles.

36 Joseph Booth was Melbourne's first coadjutor bishop.

37 During his time, Bishop James Grant moved from being Bishop of the Eastern Region to become the first episcopal Dean of Melbourne; he has maintained full participation in the bishops' meetings and decision-making; with his encyclopaedic knowledge of the Diocese past and present, he continues to wield great influence in Melbourne and beyond.

38 cf James Grant's essay above.

39 Dean Tom Thomas was a notable case in point during Frank Woods' time.

40 for as long as compulsory voting remains.

41 whereupon the Archbishop of Melbourne, Dr Keith Rayner, accepted the slur as a badge of honour.

42 still with Anglican connections, and having been a Footscray churchgoer in his boyhood.

43 There are good straws in the wind: e.g., Melbourne's cross-cultural ministry; and the growth of youth outreach at national, diocesan and local levels, based on listening and vulnerable engagement, pastoral care, camping programs, and varied and freer forms of worship from Taizé to rock services.

44 as Austin Farrer remarked in a sermon on Anglicanism reproduced in the posthumous collection *The End of Man*, SPCK, London, 1973.

45 These four principles underlie the Lambeth Quadrilateral first stated in Chicago in 1886 and used subsequently as the irreducible minimum Anglicans bring to re-union negotiations (needless to say, it has been modified, particularly in achieving intercommunion with the Scandinavian churches).

46 Matthew 13:24-30.

47 Ecumenically this is happening via the National Council of Churches in Australia and its Christian World Service Commission, the Victorian Council of Churches and various commissions such as Gospel and Cultures and the Christian Conference of Asia this writer is text editor of its all-Asian hymnal *Sound the Bamboo*, CCA/AILM, Manila, 1990. For Anglicans it is emerging via the local 'ethnic' congregations and the diocesan Department of Cross-Cultural Ministry; and via the Council of the Church of East Asia, or the missionary bodies ABM, SAMS, CMS, or AngliCORD.

48 The Institute of Spiritual Studies, based at St Peter's, Eastern Hill, offers a wide range of programs along these lines.

49 cf James Grant's essay above.

50 In the 1980s, St Hilary's Kew assisted the Port Melbourne parish to survive, giving its blessing to several families who pledged to move and take up residence there.

51 The use of inappropriate clerical titles is a particular concern of the writer, and must be a matter for further work.

52 Melbourne, with its six-and-a-half year gap between the first ordinations of women to the diaconate and their priesting, and with the appointment of the first honourary archdeacon in Australia for deacons, Marjorie McGregor, was able to explore distinctive diaconate and the inwardness of having deacons as leaders, if not the leaders, in parishes.

53 The Province of Victoria is investigating recognition of non-episcopal ministries; but co-operation in joint-venture parishes or itinerant ministries or even substantively united parishes lies much further down the track. Brisbane with its more open Roman Catholic leadership offers wider horizons.

54 (i) re a liturgical protocol: in his chapter 'The Bishop's Liturgy' in Alan Cadwallader (ed.), *Episcopacy: a view from the Antipodes*, Adelaide Board of Christian Education, Adelaide, 1994; (ii) re identifying and handling any significant controversy proactively: in General Synod Resolution 62 of 1992 which was passed at the end of the meeting by dint of being referred to Standing Committee where it was subsequently adopted and re-worked into a regular agenda item for the General Secretary to raise.

55 This writer is convinced that the question of lay presidency cannot be dealt with satisfactorily until there is agreement that the regular celebration of the eucharist (however it is done) is absolutely central to life in Christ. In most parts of Victoria pastoral necessity and the absence of ecumenical goodwill will not be factors of enough weight to make casual lay presidency something that anyone would contemplate – and doctrinaire lay presidency would despise the ethos of Anglicanism or else be authorised with a ceremony so similar to ordination that it would beg the question.

56 The Vincentian canon: the rule of St Vincent de Lerins that the boundaries of Christian truth are defined by what has been believed by Christians: 'semper, ubique et ab omnibus' – always, everywhere and by all.

57 cf John 15:1-6